Ambidextrous

The Secret Lives of Children

Also by Felice Picano

from Beautiful Dreamer Press

Justify My Sins:
A Hollywood Novel in Three Acts

Ambidextrous

The Secret Lives of Children

Felice Picano

Beautiful Dreamer Press

Ambidextrous: The Secret Lives of Children
Copyright 1985 by Felice Picano
Author's Foreword to the 2024 Edition Copyright 2024 by Felice Picano

ALL RIGHTS RESERVED. No part of this book may be reproduced or utilized in any form by any means, electronic or mechanical, or by any information storage and retrieval system, or conveyed via the Internet or a website, without written permission from the publisher, except in the case of brief quotations embedded in critical articles or reviews. Please address inquiries to the publisher:

Beautiful Dreamer Press
309 Cross St.
Nevada City, CA 95959
U.S.A.
www.BeautifulDreamerPress.com
info@BeautifulDreamerPress.com

Revised Paperback Edition, 2024
Issued by Beautiful Dreamer Press
10 9 8 7 6 5 4 3 2 1
Printed in the United States of America

ISBN: 979-8-9895595-0-3
Library of Congress Control Number: 2023952187

Cover design by Tom Schmidt
Front and back photography by Dot

*for Robert Ferro and Michael Grumley
playmates of a later childhood*

Foreword

p. i

One: Basement Games

p. 3

Two: A Valentine

p. 75

Three: The Effect of "Mirrors"

p. 179

Ambidextrous

The Secret Lives of Children

Foreword to the 2024 Edition

THE ENVELOPE WAS FROM Her Majesty's Inland Revenue and Customs Service, located at a dock outside London, England, addressed to the publisher of Gay Presses of New York. I was one of the three owners of GPNY, so I opened the envelope and read the letter. In the politest possible language, I was informed that the twenty copies of my memoir, *Ambidextrous: The Secret Lives of Children*, intended for Gay is the Word Bookstore at Russell Square, had been "seized by the signatory, declared obscene, and destroyed by immolation."

Since my early twenties, I had done as much as possible to protest and rebel against a society I had hopes for but wanted to reform. More than one person had told me in no uncertain terms, "Someday you will go too far!"

That day had arrived: it was March 17, 1989.

I was astounded, and at the same time I was very pleased. I'd never been censored before. Having a book censored means something. It means you have deeply offended one or more people who felt they needed to protect unsuspecting readers from your inflammatory words, thoughts, and images. I'd been nominated for important literary awards. I'd had a few best sellers, my books had been translated into many languages, but *nothing* before this had ever truly satisfied me that I was having any real effect as a writer.

Oddly, the book was already selling in the U.K. Earlier shipments had sailed past customs and it was even reviewed in *The Guardian*, not a minor journal. True, the review was deeply unintelligent. "Mr. Picano," the reviewer instructed, "children do not have sex." I, of course, wrote back suggesting the reviewer check his hefty Oxford

English Dictionary for the definition of the word "memoir." I had written a memoir showing middle class children on Long Island having sex—hetero, homo, with dripping chocolate, and with airplane glue as stimulants. Ergo, children *did* have sex.

I photocopied the Queen's letter and sent it to my business partners and then to almost everyone I knew. I had it framed and for years displayed it. In the dozen or so residential moves I made since it has become hopelessly lost, alas. No worries, because apparently my ability to offend was only just beginning. Both *The New Joy of Gay Sex* (1992) and its revision for the age of the internet, *The Joy of Gay Sex, Third Edition* (2002), were censored, banned, and protested against.

Given the U.S.'s strong Puritan bias, those reactions to *Gay Sex* were expected from the beginning. But what exactly was it that got people so riled up about *Ambidextrous*? The five publishers my literary agent sent it to refused it, despite my record: finalist for the PEN/Hemingway Award, other award nominations, four best sellers. The answer is probably what that conformist *Guardian* reviewer hit on the head when he wrote that children don't have sex.

At least not with each other. Or so the public was supposed to believe: children only have sex when assaulted by perverted adults. I'd already published a story in which a ten-year-old boy, who didn't even know what sex was, had a sensual relationship with a young man, a relationship in which the boy was not only the initiator, but also the person in full control. Like *Ambdextrous*, that was based on my own reality. It was only when the young man involved realized how he was being used and that it could lead to something criminal that he ended the friendship, as well as the job that brought him in contact with the boy.

All of that goes against the general hypocritical adult

view that children are completely innocent—whatever that word really means. Contrariwise, there is a reason why books like *Lord of the Flies, A High Wind in Jamaica,* and a batch of YA novels are so popular among young readers. They show not only how not innocent children are, but exactly how far children will go.

One rejecting editor was so incensed he added that the book was unpatriotic. We're talking about 1983, not that long after the ignominious U.S. pullout of Vietnam. Another offered me ten grand to not publish it.

Despite that, *Ambidextrous* was published. My partners in Gay Presses of New York signed it up as a Spring 1985 title. Terry Helbing and I had previously okayed promoting the publication of our partner Larry Mitchell's *The Faggot and Their Friends Between Revolutions* in GPNY's Calamus Books line. This was Larry's third book, and it had also failed to be taken by any mainstream publishers. *The Faggot and Their Friends Between Revolution* quickly became one of GPNY's successes, remaining in print through Larry's life. Recently, a decade after Larry died, it was republished in the same format and with the same artwork as the original.

Meanwhile, in 1983, I had published through SeaHorse Press my collection of stories, *Slashed to Ribbons in Defense of Love.* That, too, had been successful and was already in its second printing in 1984. So it was a wise commercial decision by my business partners to put out *Ambidextrous* in hardcover.

True to expectations the book was barely reviewed in the mainstream press. I already mentioned the British review. *The Publisher's Weekly* reviewer gave it two sentences, showing he had read the first twenty pages and no further. Or that he'd read it all and was too horrified to write more. Reviews from LGBT reviewers more or less repeated the front cover copy. But *Ambidextrous* sold well through word of mouth. It was on the *Christopher Street*

Magazine best seller list for eighteen weeks in a row. Then an editor at New American Library, a mass paperback line which had begun putting out trade paperbacks, bought the paperback rights to *Ambidextrous* and its follow up of a few years later, *Men Who Loved Me*. Both books fell out of print when that editorial line ended, but were picked up quickly by Harrington Park Press, and republished along with a third memoir, *A House on the Ocean a House on the Bay*, with gorgeous cover paintings by Deni Ponty.

When reading my Wikipedia entry a few years ago I was surprised to see that, of all my books, *Ambidextrous* had its own small "wiki-page." When people ask me what is my favorite among the books I've written, I always say the one I'm working on. But *Ambidextrous* has a special place in my heart because of how it came about and what it accomplished for me as a writer.

It came about because it was requested by the person closest to me in this life, Robert Allen Lowe. In quiet, intimate times, late at night, or sleepily awakening in some resort or beach front cottage, we would talk about our pasts as a way of getting to know each other better. Many people do that, but Bob would always say, "That's so unusual. I've never met anyone else who had that happen when they were eleven or thirteen." And how it had happened always needed a lot of explanation or context.

So, one day I decided to write it up. It came easily, and in a few weeks, I'd finished the first part of *Ambidextrous*, now titled, "Basement Games." Bob read it and agreed that it explained a lot. But what about so and so? And what about that incident or the other person?

So, when I had the chance between other writing projects and the work I was doing for SeaHorse Press and Gay Presses of New York, I wrote the second section, "A Valentine." That took the reader through my seventh grade in school.

Bob agreed that explained even more, especially my

long-term love for bicycles, go-carts, and speeding vehicles in general, not to mention my long-term love for adorably handsome boys, of which he was the most recent incarnation. But, he asked, what about . . . ? And so I ended up writing the third part, "The Effect of Mirrors."

"Mirrors" is about a very adult situation I found myself in—along with a female schoolmate with whom I was sexually experimenting—at age twelve and thirteen. And it was about how I suddenly understood something about the setting of our meetings, and about a rather grown-up realization I had that there were actually *three* people partaking in what I'd always thought of as a couple. That relationship ended. Shortly thereafter, a city-wide public school writing competition came about, and I was strongly urged to enter. I did so with that story, and so the last part of *Ambidextrous* is also about my first, harsh, baffling lesson about what can be written about and what can't, what is acceptable and what definitely is not. A lesson, I want to point out, I apparently did not learn since the book that included that story was then ignored, censored, burned, and excoriated, completing the vicious circle.

But the good that came out of it writing the book was immeasurable. Prior to *Ambidextrous*, the only time I'd been at all openly autobiographical was in my poetry, collected in *The Deformity Lover and Other Poems,* published by SeaHorse Press in 1977, which ended up selling over six thousand copies. Small stuff compared to the paperback half million of my novel *Eyes*. Or the more than quarter million sold in the Delacorte hardback and book club editions of *The Lure*. The difference being that the poetry was written in poetic forms: sonnets, songs, triolets, narratives. The content was always fitted to an appropriate, usually already existing form. (Although when adapted by two different musicians, the poems became sambas and rockabilly tunes and beguines.)

Foreword

My novels up to 1984 had all been fairly standard in form, if somewhat unique in style: third person, or, in the case of *Eyes* and *Late in the Season*, two different points-of-view were needed to get into the why of the relationships in those books. For *The Lure*, I modified the standard Flaubertian third person to fit an exciting plot and action. I called that "camera-on-the-shoulder." It's told omnisciently, but it's a faux omniscience: only what my main character sees, hears, thinks, postulates, feels and experiences. In the short novel, *Looking Glass Lives*, I interleaved a nineteenth century diary, written in the style and tone of that era, with a contemporary first person narrative until they completely dovetailed, which was the crux, the point, of the story.

With *Ambidextrous*, however, the first person narrative I used became something new for me: a more fluid and extremely intimate tool, telling the story as though I were telling it directly to Bob Lowe next to me in bed or on a beach towel or in a deck chair. It was more than first person; it was more like, "you are the only person I'm sharing this with, so listen closely." That allowed me to become the boy Felice, ages eleven to thirteen, undergoing the action, but also the grown up Felice, ages thirty-nine to forty, narrating. That meant I could comment, I could philosophize, I could wonder, I could express anger and sadness about action and characters from the past.

While writing *Ambidextrous*, I did what writing teachers always tell you to do but which is so difficult: I found my "voice." Or at least one of them. But I also found my instrument, the way a teenage musician will fool around for a while with various stringed instruments—from guitars to 'cellos—and then settle on, say, the viola. Having "found my instrument, found my voice," I would never lose it. I would alter it for the next two memoirs. I would flex it and experiment with it in my shorter memoirs, two volumes so far of *True Stories* about people in my life and our relationships. I would utilize another version for my Hollywood novel, *Justify My Sins* (also published by Beautiful Dreamer Press). I would never be unhappy when a reader, writer, editor, critic, or publisher told me, "You know I really don't like your protagonist (or main character), even though I'm fascinated by him." That's what I'm hoping for.

Once I got back into writing short stories, I suddenly had a freedom I'd never before possessed: I could easily, delightedly write from the point-of-view of weirdos and liars, self-serving rats and deluded characters, obviously dying and overwrought folk, near crazed and very upsetting characters—and *in their own voices*. In my latest book of fictional stories, I'm a thirties something married TV series show runner, an aging gay pretty boy desperate for security, a retired woman hoping for an end-of-life home abroad, a corporate human resources investigator, and a retired senior hoping to recapture a highpoint bike trip of his younger years. The feedback I've gotten tells me that those characters—villains and assholes, too—are in fact utterly believed, and in some cases, even beloved.

Can a writer ask for anything more?

11:52 p.m. PDT, 6/28/2023
—West Hollywood, CA.

"The world is so large," she said, "and a lifetime so short, and people so lovable and cruel and exciting."

Lawrence Durrell
The Dark Labyrinth

Basement Games

I'M TOLD BY MY PARENTS there was another girl in my life before Susan Flaherty: a small charming child named Ginny—the same name as my godmother who died young, alas, and whom I scarcely remember. My mother would pull out volume two of our three large photograph albums and show me pictures of Ginny and I, aged four and five years old. There we stand, myself and the daughter of our next door neighbors, in several snapshots. She appears delicate of feature, thin-skinned, fragile, her deep-set eyes (China Blue, I'm assured) hidden not only by the graininess of the unperfected black and white Kodak film but also by the somewhat large brow which shadows the middle of her face. Although I don't remember Ginny, I recognize her, of course. Not for nothing was I born on the final cusp of Aquarius, that most tenacious and eccentrically consistent of astrological signs. I recognize Ginny not in herself, but in other girls and women who would attract me in later years all of whom bore in progressively advanced stages the physical-and probably also the psychological-qualities which she fast brought into my life: Lois, Nancy, Lynne-Anne, Linda with whom I lived for two years in college and just escaped marrying, and finally Rachel, who fascinated me the most and with whom I also lived-even though by then I was ostensibly through with women.

If Ginny then is the base note of my love for women, her fine almost white hair the stamp by which I would later skip across a bar or party and thus into the orbit of yet another pale, slender lovely, then Susan Flaherty is the soprano line, the Ur-Siren, the temptress in my life: the flesh made tangible, a soft, padded surface with just so much give and exactly so much resistance. But even Circes need a fertile field over which to sow their enchantments, and Susan Flaherty's considerable charms, even at age eleven, would have been worthless if it weren't for the quirk of fate that selected for me, in the autumn of nineteen fifty-five, a class teacher named John Hargrave.

Even now I cannot think of this man without a slight flinch, an unconscious tensing of my fist, a small but apparent surge of adrenalin throughout my body. Were he to cross my path today—if he's still alive—and even hint at blocking my way, I'd knock him down without hesitation and stride on.

He was my fifth grade teacher; at least for two-thirds of the fifth grade. But he was a great deal more. He was my enemy, the first real enemy in my life. Though others may come along, we never forget our first enemy. More, he was my first true teacher. He awakened me from the dreamy innocence of my rather pampered childhood by showing me that life wasn't filled with loving family, kind adult friends, and mostly delightful companions my own age. After Hargrave, I knew that life was instead a deceptive tissue of the ordinary punctuated with sudden treacheries, unaccountable accidents, disagreeable discoveries, horrible little revelations. I knew that in this Kiplingesque jungle of tooth and claw that sweet, curly-haired, large-eyed, pudgy faced I could hate along with the best of the raptors. He showed me how to passively resist and thus to understand both endurance and the wells of my own stubbornness. Then he showed me the depths of my own inner violence, and exploded it so both of us (and the world) could see its force.

Without John Hargrave, I would never have become a rebel. Without having become an eleven year old rebel, I would never have walked consciously onto paths that would set me apart thereafter. Including that most sinful of childhood crimes-precocious sexuality.

You are thinking to yourself, he exaggerates. Motiveless malignity is storybook stuff. Squeers in Dickens, Iago in Othello. Where hostility exists, there must be a reason for it

I beg to differ. Not very long ago, I was in Washington, D.C. on a book tour, staying with a fellow writer and his friend at a charming townhouse in the Virginia-like Capitol Hill section of that city. Exhausted from autographing books sold from under my fingers, honored at receptions, adored by strangers. Important people suddenly changed plans to throw us a dinner party. It was at this dinner that I met a certain person. I won't describe him. He was the friend of our hosts and seemed to possess qualities that they found amusing and that I found despicable. He was intelligent enough to hold a room with his talk, yet he never talked except to complain and gossip and put people down, cleverly most of the time. He was unctuous and domineering, demanding, and yet pleading.

A dozen other guests were also present, so you would think I could ignore him. But he sensed the almost chemical dislike between us as immediately as I and sensing a masochistically fertile ground managed to place himself next to me at the table. I bore with him as long as I could, awaiting his sure to arrive attack. When it came, it wasn't at all subtle. "Of course, I haven't read anything you've written," he began, "but the only really important writers today are . . ." I let him ramble on. I waited until he finished and turned to me all expectation, for my response. "You're a fool," I said quietly, "and what's worse, a contemptible fool!" Then I turned my back on him to talk to my other tablemate, and kept my back to him the rest of the meal. By the time coffee and dessert were being served, I was out of my chair "visiting" others at the table, as far away from him as I could get, until it was time for us to get up and go to a local disco.

Out on the street, in the soft hush of the early September night, I heard the party within breaking up. My writer friend came out of the house and found me leaning against the fender of a car, smoking a cigarette. He began to discuss who would go with whom in who's car. "I don't care how we go," I replied, "as long as I'm not in the same car with ... "I didn't hide my contempt and all of my friend's promptings could not elicit from me what had happened.

Of course nothing had really happened: once thrown together, he and I would have somehow found a means .to hurt each other. Any incident would do. It would happen if we were the only survivors of a shipwreck abandoned on an ice floe floating in Baffin Bay, no help in sight. My friend pressed me on the subject: did I really think that certain people were naturally antipathetic as well as naturally sympathetic? I assured him in the words of the Son of Sam murderer, "Stop me before I kill again!"

Such madness is expected of grownups. But children too? Yes, especially when adult and child erect challenges for each other that neither can take with anything less than desperate seriousness, my war with John Hargrave began over a single fact which until then I and everyone e around me had taken for granted for years: I wrote with both hands. True, I favored my left hand, but not much. I would hold a pencil or crayon in each hand and begin to write with my left hand until I'd reached the center of a piece of paper, at which point I would switch to my right hand.

For a small child this method had several advantages. I could cover a quite large sheet of paper easily. I could use my entire upper body and both arms and hands in the act of writing, and thus not have to wonder what to do with that limp, hanging-in-the-way other hand and arm. And, I could, if I chose, be artistic by using two different colors of crayon or lead.

I'm not completely certain how I discovered this basic ambidexterity. I do recall that my brother and sister—one and two years older than I—would come home from first and second grade where they were learning how to read and write, and that I soon begged my mother for a pencil and paper so I could imitate them. This often happens among children close in age and I suppose they pretty much ignored me.

As they were gone all day at school while I remained at home, I would find their left-behind notebooks and primers and would continue my imitation. A chance primer, a stray sheet of second grade penmanship, gave me more than enough to do. By the time I was five years old, I could read better than either of them, and could print as well too.

The combinations of printed letters were consistently fascinating to me and I think that in the beginning I treated them as though they were little people—toy soldiers, tiny stick figure dolls. After a while, however, I no longer thought of them as animate, in the way our pet sheepdog was, or ants I spotted crossing the flagstones and attempted to deter from their preordained course by gently displacing them with a leaf or twig. I became enthralled by the aesthetics of printing out letters. Sometimes I printed only those letters which contained circles or arcs—C, D, G, U, B, P—and at other times, only letters which consisted entirely of straight lines, mostly diagonal lines—A, K, M, W, Z, X. Being able to put both circular and diagonal signs together and still have others recognize them was a revelation little short of thrilling. I would write out my little words—MOM, ZOO, WINK—and run with them to my mother, sitting marking a recipe in a woman's magazine. I would carefully watch her face as she read aloud the words I'd written, just as I had written them, as I had heard myself say them.

Her approval, a bestowed kiss for a good job, was never as wonderful to me as the fact that I had in some way made another person behave—if only for a few moments—exactly as I wanted them to by writing those simple and in some cases nonsensical words. I wonder if, in the long run, it isn't the heed to control others, to watch them perform your words as you wrote them, that forms the soul of the writer. If so, a playwright must be the most openly manipulative and daemonic of all our scribbling crew: his delight and despair at how actors read his lines suddenly becomes comprehensible. The poet, by this standard, is the least manipulative when he reads his words aloud; but as active a controller with his pictures and images and metaphors. The novelist . . .

As soon as it was obvious that I no longer needed my brother and sister to help me read and write, they stopped helping me, began to ignore me even more. Not "being in school" I was a bit cast aside, left on my own. Then I discovered that I didn't have to limit oneself to using only one hand to write but could use both, and using both I became more fully involved in the act of writing. I soon noticed this was unusual too: both my brother and sister only used one hand to write with. Though they scoffed at me and my "childishness," I knew better; being able to write with both hands therefore added to my private pleasure in the same way that having someone else read aloud what I'd written had added the public pleasure of writing.

By the time I got into school, no one paid much attention to how I wrote, only that I wrote very well. By second grade, I had graduated from printing, which I had mastered enough to play with, making tall, thin-letter words and short squat ones, words angled all in one direction, diagonals rounded, circles and arcs squared off-to script.

If you went to an American public school between nineteen-twenty and nineteen-sixty, you probably recall that manila frieze above the blackboards around each classroom which reproduced, about one foot high, all the letters of the alphabet in capital and small letter script. Each letter was perfectly-ideally-rendered. Each set against a barely visible grid-work of three horizontal lines-top, middle and bottom-by which you could gauge the correct height of your own line and sometimes, daringly (for lower case g's and y's and p's) drop below. I believe there was also a penmanship textbook with such a grid-work and we students had to imitate it as carefully as possible.

If printing was communication on a basic level—MOM, BEER, RIB, SLAP—script turned out to be more complex, and once mastered, far more aesthetic. Look at that word "aesthetic," for example-a word I didn't learn until high school. Only four vowels and five consonants, but they're both familiar and exotic. Little words such as "the" and "tic" within the larger word are simple enough. But can you imagine any other word in which they could possibly be put together? And the distinctly Greco-Roman "aes" that introduces these already known words opens up a new realm of literacy, lending ambience as well as meaning to the other smaller words.

Now print out the word AESTHETIC. It seems odd. The eye and the mind want to read it another way, and say ATHLETIC, which looks fine printed out. Now script the word "aesthetic" and enjoy the rhythm, the flow of three low letters, two high ones, another low one, another high one, with two concluding low letters-the open final "c" nicely balancing the initial closed "ae". Other words are tiny pleasures to write in script—"temptingly," "cripple," "enjoyment"—though they provide little real titillation when printed.

It's not clear to me which of my two adored teachers it was—Mrs. Mazey (I loved to write her name in script!) or Mrs. Holden—who suggested that while writing with two hands was fun, writing an entire line with one hand-of my choice-would be more pleasingly regular. It was true I soon noticed. All I had to do was write one full line left-handed, the line beneath it right-handed, to see that there were differences of angle and inflection that made my pages of script look almost frivolous next to the more dowdy if uninspired penmanship of my classmates.

Choosing which hand to use at the moment was not always easy. If I doted on the freedom of those lines achieved with my left hand—the slant, the spaciousness, the grace—I also liked the nearness, the self-containment of those I penned right-handed. As a result, I continued to use both hands while writing, sometimes doing my schoolwork one way, my homework the other. Recalling the two women, I now believe it must have been Mrs. Holden, my fourth-grade teacher, who suggested I limit my use of hands. In my memory she remains the more concerned, even the more affectionate of the two, if the more restrained in her outward show of emotion. Her ash blond hair piled high above her head, her close-featured pretty face, made her an instant object of whatever ten-year-old ability I had to admire. I did admire her and would do anything she even hinted at. Of all my teachers from Kindergarten to postgraduate courses, only two of the hundred or so people who taught me ever became objects of my adoration: one was Jerry Strauss, my junior high school science teacher, the other was Mrs. Holden.

I entered the fifth grade, and my life totally changed.

Perhaps now would be a good time to attempt to describe what kind of child I was at the time-based on my own memory and the recollections of family and friends. For I was to alter forever afterward.

The photographs in the family albums go a long way to show the baby, the child up till then. I was cute enough, and curly-haired enough to be an infant model then a child model for Macy's department store catalogues and advertisements: my first job. I was easy-tempered, according to everyone. Partly, my father believed, because of an odd illness I sustained at age sixteen months, and it's equally strange treatment. Even now I'm unsure exactly what this infant illness was, except that it was in some way "glandular." At birth I weighed ten-and-a-half pounds—a big baby—and in a year twenty-two pounds. Months later I was skin and bones. The only treatment possible at the time turned out to be a dietary rebalancing of my body's minerals, and although this was partly achieved by my ingesting a great deal of fresh seafood and thus large amounts of iodine, the treatment also required infusions of hops. The easiest way to get an infusion is by drinking beer. So, in album photo after album photo from the age of sixteen months to about four years old, I'm sipping from some adult's can of Rheingold or suckling the nipple of my own bottle with it's all too apparently non-milk contents. Little wonder I was an easy-tempered infant who seldom cried, who took photographer's directions without a murmur, who could be lifted and turned and adjusted exactly so and remain there ten minutes at a time, who sailed through the early, often traumatic years of early childhood without a hint of difficulty. I was little short of an alcoholic.

Yet this spaced-out glow continued for another five years or more. I was not moody or recalcitrant like my older brother; not colicky and anxious like my baby brother; not pushily outgoing like my sister. I was barely noticeable-to my parents, to my siblings, to myself. Life was lovely, if seen through an impressionist seven-and-a-half percent alcohol haze. People were uniformly good and all loved me to various degrees of intensity, from my parents to strangers. I wanted little and was given whatever I even appeared to wish. Unknown women on buses coveted me, everyone else-adult or child-seemed to want to befriend me. I might have been born of royal blood for the treatment I received.

Enter the villain. He was a square, heavy man. Not unhandsome with his large cube of a head and precisely ruled-out features, but bulky, somehow lumbering like a Hungarian anatomical drawing. His suits were dark, always pressed and clean, invariably pin-striped so quietly one had to peer to notice. They were square too, as though his tailor had despaired of ever instilling style never mind curves into the man and had opted instead for a cookie cutter pattern. I can't recall seeing Hargrave in shirtsleeves. I can't imagine seeing him smile. Not grumpy or hostile, he seemed more sad, even somewhat frustrated, than mean. Large he certainly was; hulking and bullyish he could become in an instant, but we sensed early on in the school term that he was not particularly interested in the class, in our lessons, or in school—never mind any specific child. At the time he couldn't have been more than forty-five years old, yet he wore the entrenched air of retirement of a much older man. Perhaps if he had been the type of a male teacher who feels easy among schoolchildren he might have taken us into his confidence or told us something of his past. No, whatever his past was, he never dreamed of bringing it up to illustrate some aspect of our lesson. Given this better than average group of fifth graders (ranked second academically among eight such classes), he was a strict disciplinarian, a steady character, a plodding teacher-and altogether safe. We all assumed this quite early on, and since no student with previous experience said otherwise, we were relaxed, off-guard.

Classes began the Monday after Labor Day that year and although it was clear to all thirty students that this would not be as stimulating or personal a school year for us as Mrs. Holden's fourth grade, we all felt that we would adjust somehow to Hargrave's plodding, and get through it with little trouble.

We did: all but me and one or two classmates who were close friends of mine either before or after the battle between Hargrave and I began. We opened our eyes for the first time to generational warfare and educational tyranny: an experience we would bring to fruition a decade later on campuses and in demonstrations across the nation.

The opening skirmish of the war was minor and inconclusive: no shot at Sarajevo, no torpedo to the gunwale of the Maine. It occurred during one of the few fully relaxed moments of our fifth-grade life—art class. These occurred twice a week, one hour before we were released for the day, when presumably our little minds were too over stimulated to learn anything considered really important.

In other fifth grade classes, art sessions gave rise to complex seasonal or holiday decoration schemes, to museum outings, to trips to local parks for outdoors draftsmanship. In Hargrave's class, whatever buoyancy we brought to these hours derived from the large, flaky, printed facade of the newspaper our teacher unconditionally erected between himself at his desk at the front of the room and ourselves at our fleet of desks beyond. Monitors handed around the chosen art medium of the day—usually colored pencils, or crayons, rarely chalks, messy creative tempera or aquarelles—and we were on our own. Art was one of the few times we were allowed to speak to each other in class, the only time the drop leaves between our desks were lifted up to make a larger workspace, suddenly making partners of two students previously isolated by aisles.

For me art class was as good as recess or lunch. Not only because of the extra little freedom but because I had a talent for drawing and enjoyed expressing myself in any art medium. Even Hargrave had enough sensitivity to realize that we were proud of our handiwork. The large blackboard at the rear of the room held weekly exemplars of our artwork along with stellar pages of book reports, perfect sheets of penmanship and high scored math exams.

There I sat at ten minutes to three o'clock on a gray early December afternoon about to put my signature to the upper hand corner of what I naively thought was a truly good colored pencil rendering of an autumn scene glimpsed just beyond the school yard's hurricane fence, when Hargrave wandered by my desk. Perhaps his original intention in stopping was to praise my work. If so, the second I reached up to write in my name, he said in a tight, gruff voice, "Do it right!" I must have turned to look at him in utter astonishment, because he repeated, "Do it right! Use your right hand."

I looked at the brick red pencil in my right hand, at the forest green pencil in my left hand with which I had been about to write my signature, and I couldn't make sense of what I'd just been told. If l signed in brick red the picture wouldn't look the way I wanted it to. The drawing was a tonal series of reds and browns and ochres, and I wanted to use the forest green signature to point out what color the drawing definitely was not. So I once more reached up to sign with my left hand.

"No!" he said, reaching for my hand and drawing it down so hard that my pencil point dug into the paper making a deep green rift before cracking off. "Sign it the right way!"

I switched the red pencil to my left hand and began again.

"With your right hand," he insisted.

"I always sign it this way," I defended myself. Right-handed, it would come out neat, cramped, inartistic.

"Do as I say!" he shouted into my uncomprehending face. Everyone in the class was now watching us. I was being shouted at and I didn't know why.

"It's my drawing."

He pushed me back against my seat and lifted the two other drawings sticking out from under my blotter, looking only at their signatures. "Who signed these?"

"I did."

"With your left hand." He almost spat the words out. I still didn't understand his question.

"Didn't you?" he prodded.

"Yes," I admitted, unsure what I was admitting.

Suddenly he addressed the class. "This is exactly what I was talking Here is a boy who can use his right hand as is right and proper and yet he insists on using his wrong hand." He turned to me. "Why is that?"

"I always use my . . ." I hesitated. I wasn't about to say "wrong" hand. "I always use this hand."

"Since when in my classroom?"

"All the time."

He turned to Suzanne Friedman, my neighbor and one of his favorites.

"Is that true?" he asked as though I had been shooting dope in the classroom wardrobe.

Solemnly, for Suzanne was as confused as I, she nodded yes.

"Why, boy? When you know it's wrong."

"No one ever told me it was wrong."

"I'm telling you. Who uses this hand?" he asked the class, lifting his left hand limply in the air. No one in the classroom did—or admitted so at the moment. "Does your mother?" he asked me. "Does your father? No? Then why do you? Just to be different. That's why, isn't it? And because you thought I wasn't watching. Isn't that why?"

"I do it because it feels right."

"It feels right," he repeated my words, mockingly. "Stand up, boy. Go to the file cabinet and open it with your left hand."

I did as instructed, as I would have done anyhow. "Now close it. And open it again with your right hand." I did.

"There doesn't it feel right that way?"

"No."

"It doesn't?" He was astonished. "Using your wrong hand you have to half turn your body and cross your arm in front of your chest to open the drawer and you mean to tell me that still feels right?"

What he had pointed out was indubitably so; yet it was also true that while I did have to make many small adjustments, that my body was used to doing them unconsciously, so I no longer noticed.

"This way feels correct to me," I said, using my left hand.

"Does it?" he sneered. "Then there must be something wrong with you boy, if the wrong hand feels right to you. God gave you a right hand. This is a right-handed world, turnstiles, can-openers, doorknobs, telephones, typewriters, everything is right-handed. Use your right hand in this classroom in the future. Sit down!"

I sat down, deeply indignant and embarrassed. A second later the school bell rang and we had to clean up our desks and leave for the day.

If the incident put me in a down mood walking home from school that day, the mood was gone by dinner time. Only when my father uncharacteristically asked me about school did I mention that my teacher had picked on me about using my left hand.

"Just tell him that you're naturally left-handed," my father said. "No one bothers about stuff like that anymore. Hell, even when I was in school, they understood that. No one's that old-fashioned anymore."

"But I'm not really left-handed," I said, trying to explain. I'm ambi . . ." I'd heard the word once but couldn't recall it.

"Ambidextrous," my mother said. "But that woman who tested you said that would change as you got older. She said that you were really left-handed. Remember?" she prodded, "that woman psychologist at Candlewood Lake who used to give you kids all those games to play with?"

"He's seen me using both hands."

"Then use the one he wants," my father concluded. The subject was either too trivial or too complicated to retain his interest.

"Not if he's left-handed," my mother put in. "Do what your father said. Tell him we approve of your using any hand you want to write with."

"Maybe you should use your feet," my older brother suggested. And that closed the discussion.

A more interested topic for my parents at the dinner table that night was our new neighbors, one house away, on our left.

They had moved in several weeks before, but my mother had just seen the family en masse that day and described them to my father using a hangover of the 'Forties slang they sometimes spoke together. "Oh brother! You should see them, Phil." "In the Welting Place?" "They didn't even paint it over before moving in. Six of them," she went on, "Him. Her. Three girls the kids' age. And her sister."

"I think I did see him," my father said. "In an aqua and cream DeSoto at the ESSO station last week. Seems okay.

"You'd like him!" my mother said meaning to be sarcastic. "He'll soon have a nose as red as your friend Bert."

Bert was a bachelor pal from father's early days with whom he still occasionally played stay-away-from-home-all-night poker games. Bert was reputed to be both a ladies' man and a heavy drinker. So, by allusion, was Ed Flaherty, our new neighbor, although it was never proven to me conclusively. My mother's illusions about Bert—known to us, naturally, as "Uncle Bert"—formed so complete and unshakeable a fantasy, so unchanged over the decades, that a month before her death, quite recently, she could tell me in total sincerity the following: After his divorced brother's death (Bert had lived with him five years) a few months before, and unable to cook or otherwise care for himself, Bert had perished of starvation. He'd been found in an apartment that had gone uncleaned for years, she added. Surely, she meant cirrhosis of the liver, given all his drinking, I asked. No, no, she insisted, it was starvation; he didn't even know how to open a can of beans. She couldn't be shaken out of this idea, couldn't be persuaded that people actually survive never mind flourish on restaurant and take-out delicatessen food.

My mother's facts might often be inaccurate, but her instincts seldom were. She could glance at a three-year-old in its mother's lap and declare the infant would come to a bad end. Nor would she be exaggerating much. I've heard her make such snap judgments over the years and have lived to learn of these infants growing up to become wife-battering embezzlers and weekend heroin addicts.

I was never able to confirm the future of Ed Flaherty or indeed the future of the Flaherty clan—who my mother instantly declared a "fly-by- night crew of one sort or another," although in their case, the night they spent on our block was more like two years. Still . . .

It seems necessary now to describe the block on which we lived, as a great deal of the following action takes place within its confines and is determined by its physical as well as its sociological (for want of a better word) set-up.

To drive along or past our block—as I suddenly found myself doing only five years ago in a successful search to find a shortcut off the packed Long Island Expressway to the Southern State Parkway on our way to Fire Island for the weekend—is to encounter a block in no way extraordinary. Sited low on that alluvial moraine that geologically divides northern from southern Long Island, our neighborhood block was a long, down sloping curve around extended lawns on a blackly tarred road which gently angled until the final tenth of its length, when it suddenly plunged steeply down into a more trafficked cross avenue. Even that cross street was local. One seldom saw any but resident's cars in the area. The houses were medium-sized suburban ranging from identical six-room "ranches" to ten and twelve-room Post-Victorians with numerous gables and three-quarter wraparound verandas, unattached garages, and workshops.

The alluvial deposit on which the entire neighborhood lay was rich enough to sustain huge shade trees as well as tiny stands of fruit-bearing ones. Because we were the first (or at most second) generation on this soil which had recently been farms, our little herb gardens and vegetable patches shot up as though they were the Salinas Valley. Flowers were even more spectacular. Every curve of the road was graced with mound upon blooming mound of Azaleas in the spring, balloon-like rainbows of giant Hydrangeas in the summer, all set against impeccably cut and raked lawns. My father was able to keep fig trees and Concord grape vines growing and fruitful through several incredibly ferocious winters (including the blizzard year, 1948); and with her "green thumb" my mother was able to bring to our table enormous Comice pears from three-year-old saplings.

Because of the great length of the street, we had many neighbors. Perhaps fifteen or twenty houses on each side. Naturally, not all, or even a quarter of those people were considered close neighbors. Our own next-door neighbors were on the one side few, quiet, and stand-offish, and on the other numerous, "nice," and gregarious. A few houses on either side of the road were filled with children our age, and this sometimes brought together families with little else in common. My older brother was best friends with a classmate who lived on the far northern end of our street more than a decade.

On late spring and early autumn nights sometimes as many as thirty children between eight and twelve years old could be gathered across from the Sevastano's house—the true geographical center of our block—for street games that had been developed on straight, short, Brooklyn and Bronx tenement grids, which we nonetheless adapted and played in our suburban amplitude of space, of vegetation, of places to hide during hide-and-seek. In the summer, most of us began to favor the northern portion of the street, because of the empty lots there, partly cleared by teenagers and grown-ups to make rough softball diamonds and football fields. In winter, the action shifted to the lower end of the block, where the street suddenly delved, making a perfect seventeen-degree angle drop for sleigh riding. Children from nearby streets were magnetically drawn for white loud wet afternoons. Sometimes a hundred or more were somewhere on that two hundred yard bump of snow-packed road.

It was exactly at this point of declivity on our block that the Flaherty house stood, closer to the road in front than most of its neighbors, and so with less front yard to go poorly tended over the three tenantships after the Weltings had moved. Both front and back lower floors were encased by dark meshed screen porches, which singularly blinded the view into goings-on within. During the Weltings' residence, the front porch had been lighted in July, May especially December, when elaborate Christmas displays filled its chilled length, complete with a second Christmas tree and wrapped pseudo-presents.

Child psychologists now understand how the infant's world expands by discrete stages from the warm surrounding flesh of the mother's body, to the three-dimensional block of crib and bassinet, to the larger acreage of the nursery with its attendant figures—parents, siblings, pets and dolls almost all equal—to the new world of other rooms, an entire house and yard—if any—until, presumably, the entire planet is obtainable through vacation jettings and daily horror casts on radio and television.

By eleven years old, my own world had passed those earlier stages although nearly another decade would be needed before I traveled by air with any naturalness. For all practical purposes, my universe was delimited to no more than six blocks in any direction. To the north, by a series of shops and stores that formed our commercial "town." To the east, by the elementary school I attended, its adjoining parklet and the house of a classmate. To the south, by the church my mother and sister still attended on Sundays, sometimes joined by my father and we boys, more often than not. Beyond this lay two movie theaters, one of which we children favored because of its all-day children's programs on Saturday afternoons which included three different serials: Flash Gordon, Tarzan and Buck Rogers, pirate and jungle movies, cartoons galore, and enough trailers to satisfy any cinephile, as well as inexpensive popcorn and candy. But that was already outside our everyday experience. To the west was the Lutheran church my older brother went to as a Cub Scout then Boy Scout; and beyond that a few blocks, the junior high school that he and my sister attended.

Aside from special visits—usually in the backseat of my parent's station wagon or as part of a small fleet of my peers on bicycles—to more distant places—this was my world. Within it, the long block I lived on was the center. It contained all the social, intellectual and athletic interests an eleven year old could possibly desire. 1 was just moving from one means of locomotion to another; from foot (and roller skates for speed and play) to bicycle. A roller-skating race on sidewalks could be sufficiently lengthy and interestingly exhausting if we merely circled our one block without ever crossing a street. Later on, once we began all but eating and sleeping athwart the handlebars of our Schwinns, this single block shrunk to one of a series of similarly shaped and sized blocks in a single neighborhood.

It wasn't too surprising that I should find the children around me sufficiently interesting. Growing up among so many siblings close to me in age meant that as a rule we were each other's best and worst friends and most common playmates. But I had other friends—shy, fat, red-haired Everett; quiet, thoughtful, pale-haired Gregory; wry, fast-talking, loud Ronnie. The girls were less interesting by far, and not only because they were girls. Ronnie's younger sister Janet Sevastano was attracted to me, but too small, thin, monkey-faced, and above all too closely linked to Ronnie. Rosalie Klein, who lived across the street from Janet and Ronnie, had the virtue of an already developing body—breasts in bud, long legs, dancer's posture—but her father was named Wolfgang, which was unforgiveable, and Rosalie talked too much. Then Susan Flaherty arrived.

She was the oldest of three sisters, each as physically different from the other as though they possessed different parents—which even the worst gossips on the block didn't suggest—instead of being the result of two parents whose combination of dominant and recessive genes, as we later learned in high school Biology, resulted in a wildly mixed possibility every time Mrs. Flaherty gave birth.

Susan was eleven years old, my age, with masses of curly hair orange as an October sunset at some times, the deep maroon of Japanese Maple leaves in high summer, at others. She was very pretty, with a minimum of freckles on her pale white face and neck, large, already luxuriantly lashed eyes the color of chocolate truffle centers in a

Whitman Sampler, a pug little nose, sensuous lips that almost seemed naturally lipsticked. She was medium sized, voluptuous in her jumpers, sweaters, smocks and skirts. I later learned that Susan Flaherty had quickly entered the masturbation fantasy lives of my older brother and his friends, displacing by her Irish beauty and reserve the known, brash, available Rosalie.

Beth Flaherty was a year younger than Susan, with short dark hair, a narrower more pinched version of Susan's facial features, though with bright Baltic blue eyes. She was almost painfully wiry, but far more active than her more feminine sister, quickly initiating street games, joining sports with boys years older. Beth was quiet, yet authoritative when she spoke. Smart, but also smart enough to keep quiet. Not really a tomboy, although her long lean limbs were hard and muscled as any boy's and as successful at sports, Beth easily established herself as Rosalie's rival on roller-skates and ice skates and bicycles and as her superior in street games and jump rope. She was the only girl I ever knew who could wrestle a boy to the ground and who would not cry when she was punched.

Where Beth was almost feline and Susan was softly rounded, their younger sister Kate was squat and sturdy. Her hair was the purest white blond, so bodiless that her mother kept it cut very short in a sort of "Twenties" bob, so that with her manly little body and square grumpy little face, Kate might have been a midget come into the family by mistake, or a changeling eking out the life of a girl in error. Kate tended to dress roughly compared to Susan's soft alpacas and tactile flannels and Beth's velvety corduroys and sleek polished cottons. She talked brusquely and took an oddly protective role over her older sisters. The wrong role, for Kate was as sweet as she was plain; as feminine within as she appeared not to be. She belonged among dolls and crinolines: A good jab during a game of

Johnny-on-the-pony would send Kate home in floods of tears. I could see Beth grow up to become an advertising executive, the adult Susan as a chanteuse, or mobster's moll or perhaps even a cool, casual brothel-keeper, but blond, boring Kate was a wife and mother in embryo. She belonged in kitchens and playrooms, among food-stained recipe files and over-crusted pie pans, amid yellowing diapers and ineptly mended toys.

The three Flaherty sisters hit our block like a delayed concussion. Kate's truculence, Beth's athletic skill, and Susan's beauty made them instantly famous if not instantly loved by all. My sister and her friends were utterly obsessed with the Flaherty sisters. They could think of, speak of no one for months. All-girl pow-wows in the form of numerous pajama parties were convened to discuss the fearsome trio. Long time disputes among the girls were suddenly mended as they closed ranks against the three outsiders. Councils of war were held almost daily: none of us had dreamed this disarray of girls could so quickly form so impregnably a front.

What made it worse, the Flaherty girls would not play with just any neighbor girl on our block. From the beginning they declined invitations left and right and formed their own little group, carefully selecting girls to join. Only one from our block, Karen Lucas, was ever invited into this choice grouplet. Naturally, Karen was immediately ostracized by neighbors who had played with her since they were in diapers.

The rest of the Flaherty club—as my sister and her cronies soon came to call it—were from nearby blocks, school friends, even girls from their previous neighborhood in the depths of Ridgewood. All this seemed astonishingly sophisticated to our sisters: over discriminating to their democratic little souls, oddly grown-up, elite. It was difficult to know exactly how Karen Lucas and the Flaherty

Ambidextrous: Basement Games

girls passed these hours together: speculation ran high. It was obvious that athletic Beth had little of an organizational nature—she spent too much of her time among us boys. Kate was deemed too young and too impolitic to be ringleader. Therefore Susan—the unnecessarily pretty Susan—had to be the club's headmistress: another reason for the gangly pre-adolescent girls to hate her.

For the rest of us, one result of this feminine polarization was purely social. Until then, our sisters and neighbors had been content to be our playmates. Now they suddenly broke off relations with us and arranged their own club. If in the past, in the middle of a summer street game we boys found we needed another player or even merely another base and we approached a group of girls sitting chatting on someone's porch to choose one, where normally they'd jump at the opportunity, they now sneered and told us they were "busy." Busy indeed, for a side benefit of this disturbing new genderization of our lives was that they were constantly putting together parties for every conceivable occasion. Daytime parties were given after school or weekend afternoons for birthdays, for holidays, for tea and cake—which often meant soda and cake—for listening to music and dancing, for Arbor Day and for any occasion you might name.

At first, we boys shunned these slapped-together events. But one by one we were somehow coerced, sometimes dragged by sisters and cousins to them, and word soon got around from those older boys who'd attended that at the dancing parties, one could "cop a feel" of a nearly nonexistent breast. So we began to attend merely to savor this new thrill. We were fed well with sweets and sodas, and treated far better than usual by the same girls who'd avoided or badmouthed us in the recent past. Even so, we boys bored easily. Even Rosalie's new fifteen-inch screen Zenith television set or Janet's new Webcor phonograph soon lost their allure. As for the girls themselves, who really wanted to cop a feel off Bobby Doria's sister? Once the goodies were eaten, we usually lit out for stickball or a game of "I Declare War." And the girls spent the next few days discussing the success of the party and planning another one.

Not without misgivings. They still hadn't managed to plant a spy in the Flaherty club or discover what arcane rites took place on the impossible-to-see-through back porch or that underground finished basement. They received a new shock. While continuing to exclude most of them, the Flaherty club opened its doors to boys!

My own entree followed soon after. One of my new friends in class, Edward Young, was invited to the Flaherty's one Saturday afternoon. The next Monday in the schoolyard, he told me three astonishing pieces of information. 1) The party which he and one other boy had attended with six girls was chaperoned only by Selma Flaherty, the girls' aunt, who left the basement halfway through the party. 2) The girls had given Edward and the other boy highballs with real—although minuscule—amounts of liquor. And 3) They had all played kissing games, which had progressed beyond lip-to-lip activities although he wouldn't say what this really meant.

Two days later, Edward told me that another party was to be held the following weekend, and I was invited.

As adults we tend to forget what it is physically like to be a child. The pain and pleasure that we now ordinarily feel so spotlighted, so precise that we can focus utterly upon the pimple of an ingrown hair in an area of a square an eighth of an inch, simply does not exist in childhood. With the exception of truly traumatic major afflictions, children feel a generalized hurt, an equally dispersed pleasure. This alters during pubescence as glands redistribute various hormones around the growing body. So, an eleven-year-old usually fails to understand how a grown-up can work on or play on with an illness or wound. Even an upset stomach completely dominates the child's body, mind, outlook, universe. It is the same with pleasure. A particularly delicious ice cream cone or chocolate candy is tasted not only in the child's nose and mouth, but right down to his toes, up the nape of his neck to the roots of his cowlick. As children, we are awash in sensations—even conflicting ones: the slightest caress of a fingertip can excite the whole body, the entire life.

All this as prelude to my first visit to the Flaherty house, where, within an hour, once Selma Flaherty had stumped up the stairs to her bedroom, we three boys and four girls were left to our own devices. Spin the Bottle was quickly run through and discarded for a new game—to me, at least—of who could kiss the longest. Kate disliked this game and was excused to go play with dolls upstairs. The rest of us settled down on large duck-covered pillows around the finished basement to play.

George and Susan claimed victory. Edward and Karen Lucas came in second. Beth and I, timid as we were still relative strangers, last. Our drinks had all been gulped and refilled during the kissing contest, so we still felt a bit high, especially in the winter airlessness of the steam-heated basement. Sweaters were soon removed. The girls wore brassieres. We boys took off our shirts. Then we switched partners to begin the kissing game again. This time someone dimmed the lights. I lay down on a pillow with Karen and began to kiss more comfortably, more confidently now that I knew what was expected. We kissed for a very long time.

When I looked up to declare Karen and I the winners, it suddenly seemed as though I were in another room, one where the contest was long- forgotten, replaced by another, far more intense game. The other girls' trainer bras were off. George had his hands inside Beth's skirt, and Edward Young's zipper was wide open, one of Susan's hands moving around within. I too somehow managed to get Karen's bra off, but she resisted my fumbling attempts—because unspecified? or because too specific? to get my fingers between her legs. I continued to stroke her smooth legs and thighs, as we sunk back onto the pillow into an endless kiss.

These facts do not describe the weightlessness, the flushed breathlessness I experienced. I did not know that the other boys were also unclear as to what all this was leading up to. I did know that our main interest lay in some unknown point beneath, between, below, somehow within; if asked, I couldn't say what it was, or what I would do when I found it.

Then we heard footsteps on the floor above—Selma walking to the bathroom, flushing a toilet, which caused us to stop momentarily and look up from what we were doing. It was then that I saw the first penis of my life. It belonged to Edward Young—and though it couldn't have been particularly large (while big for his age, he was still only eleven years old) it looked enormous, being erect, and in possession of Susan Flaherty's much smaller, chubby white hand. I say first penis, because while I'd probably seen scores before, without that single quality of erection which makes the organ a sexual instrument, they had been anything but impressive. We usually called it a wee-wee (the double diminutive decreasing its importance) and when we used it to urinate, that same word was again used, meaning in the symbology of words, that was its only admitted function. What Edward possessed and what Susan in turn possessed of Edward's was anything but a wee-wee. It was in my older brother's overheard and until then uncomprehended terminology, clearly a "boner." Edward himself was now an appendage to it. As Susan slowly raised and lowered her loose fist over its length, all pretense of kissing gone, Edward twisted and squirmed as he lay back on the pillow in helpless thrall to this object Susan had somehow or other managed to find and extract from his trousers.

Amazed, Karen and I stopped kissing and turned to watch. So did Beth and George. Our eyes, our still learning minds, focusing first on Susan's hand, then on Edward's face, as he moaned softly, reddened, whitened, reddened again, lifted up his head—it seemed involuntarily—from the pillow, his eyes glazed and almost popping out of their sockets, before he let out a guttural cry, fell back onto the pillow again, and managed to pull Susan's hand away. Still moaning, he quickly rolled over onto his front as though shot or stabbed, and to our stupefaction attempted to crawl away.

When Edward finally got to his feet, he was still almost doubled over. He looked at Susan with what might have been scorn or contempt. She continued to sit primly, looking at her hand with an almost abstracted stare and with no little satisfaction. Edward lurched off to the basement lavatory.

George and I jumped after him. After a few minutes of our knocking, Edward unlocked the lavatory door and let us in. He was sitting on the closed toilet seat, his handsome face was still very white, but gaining color.

"Are you okay?" George, his closer friend, asked.

"Yeah," Edward's voice seemed to have gotten deeper. "I'm okay."

"What happened? What did she do to you?" protective and suspicious George asked.

"You don't know?" Edward looked at us. It was clear we didn't have an idea. "She made me come."

George and I stared at each other in ignorance, then it occurred to the both of us at the same time. I asked first, "You mean that was sex?"

Edward nodded. "It's supposed to be inside her when it happens. But all the same that was it."

All three of us were silent with the implications. "Did it really hurt a lot?" I asked.

"Sure, it did. But in a nice way, too. Know what I mean?"

We didn't. It was a contradiction of all we had known and experienced: something either felt nice or it hurt, period.

"Is it still . . ." George hesitated, "a boner?"

"Nah. It's regular now."

He took it out of his pants and showed it to us. Sure enough, once again it was merely a wee-wee. It didn't look damaged.

A few minutes later, after we'd run out of questions, we three boys emerged from the bathroom. The pillows had been placed back in a single pile against one wall, the three girls were all buttoned up again, sitting on the overstuffed sofa, playing a game of "Old Maid" as though nothing had happened. Little was said to us, and in the guilty silence, we boys made our escape.

The next day at school recess, Edward told George and I that he would not be going back to the Flaherty club again. He gave no explanation why not. Later that afternoon as I was bicycling home from my friend Everett's house, our bicycles crossed paths and Edward asked me to do a favor for him. It all seemed very mysterious and I almost thought he had found a new group of girls. But no, instead he directed me several blocks away into the courtyard of St. Vincent's Catholic Church. We parked our bicycles and Edward led me inside the church.

I'd only been inside once before, for my friend Everett's confirmation. That Sunday afternoon, the building had been filled with people. This time, we were alone there, and the church was gloomy and quiet. Edward guided me to a middle pew and immediately knelt down. I followed him, still wondering what was going on. I looked around, instantly fascinated by the panel paintings of New Testament stories that I knew from the children's Bible our parents had given us some years before—intrigued by the sheer amount of blood and torture and suffering in these Catholic representations, compared to the more benignly banal ones in our Protestant book. Edward's face was almost hidden in his hands. Suddenly he grabbed my hand and held it tight staring at me.

"I had one again," he said, his face contorted in agony.

It took me a minute to realize that he meant he'd had another "boner."

"Did you come again?" I asked.

"No. I prayed to Baby Jesus and after a long time it went away."

"I thought you said it felt nice."

"It's a sin." He whispered, almost angrily. "It's a sin!"

"Who told you that?"

"It is. I know."

"How do you know?"

"I just do. Will you pray with me for our sins and so it will never happen again?"

I thought about it for a minute. "I'm not Catholic. I don't belong in this church."

"It doesn't make any difference."

"I don't see why it is a sin to have a boner. My brother and his friends' say they get them all the time."

"Then they're sinners too. Will you pray with me?"

"I didn't have a boner," I defended myself.

"Then pray for me. I'm a sinner."

I thought it was a bunch of baloney, but I said all right, I would pray for him. We knelt forward again, and he began to mumble. I also pretended to pray, but I really looked straight ahead into the chiaroscuro depths of the main chapel at the tiny rows of red and white candles flickering in front of the altar, casting living shadows upon all the gold and brass and silver and upon the carved planes of the—to me—weird statues of Christ and Mary and Joseph. Finally, Edward was done praying and we got up and left. I found myself thinking how difficult it must be to be Catholic and to have to think about sin all the time. In those few minutes, I'd lost some respect for Edward, whom I'd before thought a sensible boy. But he seemed satisfied.

Thus ended the Flaherty club's mixed gender social life. But not entirely. While Edward and his toady George kept away from the Flaherty's midweek afternoons, they somehow continued, if less physically demonstrative.

Susan never said a word, but both Beth and Kate kept asking after Edward, wondering if he were "recovered," all in such a mocking tone of voice that I found myself defending him.

"He's a big baby." Beth Flaherty dismissed him. "All you boys are."

"I'm not afraid."

"No?" she dared.

"Not at all. I'll come to your stupid basement any time. No matter how many girls are there. And no matter what we do."

A week passed after this challenge and I'd almost forgotten how I'd taken up Beth's dare when Susan Flaherty invited me to another "party." Only two people attended this little fete: myself, and Susan. It progressed fairly quickly from us drinking weak highballs to us French kissing to Susan's bra corning off to my pants corning down and her rubbing my wee-wee until—miracle of miracles!—it too became a boner, just like Edward's. Or rather almost like Edward's. While hard enough to qualify, mine just wasn't sensitive enough: or perhaps it was too sensitive. Susan tugged at it, she rubbed it, she stroked it, she did everything she could to it to elicit the preordained result. I lay back on the pillow and watched. Nothing happened. True it felt strange—as though something new and uncomfortable was suddenly attached to me. It was like a new leg or hand—something that refused to take mental direction. I did feel both lightheaded and congested in my lower torso, but nothing at all to provide her with moans and grunts.

Beth was called downstairs and she tried too. Again nothing. But I had survived their dare—so I made both Flaherty sisters take off their own pants and show me theirs. They did, with some trepidation, and though I wasn't allowed to touch, I inspected these barely existent organs a long time—enough to be able to memorize them for discussion later with my friends. When I finally packed my boner into my shorts and trousers and went home, it was with a feeling of triumph. It was obvious why girls would want to take boy's pants off and play with their boners; it was less clear to me why boys seemed so interested in taking off girl's undies to see—well, not much, as far as I'd been able to make out.

Susan continued to invite me over, continued to play with my boner while we kissed voluptuously, continued to ply me with cakes and cokes, and finally allowed me to touch her there. To my surprise, my touch produced an instant response—a slight rise, a tiny hardening of an area of flesh that I had thought pretty much like the rest of her. I soon learned that I could with the most delicate readjustment of one finger make Susan "come", with less obvious or violent results than those she'd provoked in Edward, still with results worth seeing. She also let me put my fingers inside her, where I cautiously probed around, following her directions—and again watching her reactions. Another time, when I had made her come several times, I lay on top of her, with my erection more or less at the area of her genitals, and bounced up and down a few times until she asked me to stop. I was fascinated to discover that she had come from this activity too, and lay panting and flushed. All I got out of it was the need to urinate.

Socially, Susan and I were now "friends", although I assume that I was more or less her stud, bringing her to orgasm by one method or another about four to six times a week. I don't know how it happened—blackmail I suppose—that Beth too became involved in our parties on a regular basis. After a week or two, I found myself manipulating both girls—sometimes together, sometimes one after the other—to orgasm. More athletic than her sister, Beth was less content to simply lay back. She preferred me bouncing up and down upon her, half wrestling with me for added excitement. Their younger sister Kate also joined in; although never alone, one of her sisters had to be present. Kate never let me get on top of her, and wouldn't be caught dead touching me in return, no matter how much Beth and Susan urged her.

I never mentioned any of these goings-on to Edward Young, who had become an altar boy at St. Vincent's shortly after our little prayer together; nor did I mention them to George nor to Everett, nor in fact to anyone. When my mother asked what I had been doing at the Flaherty's, I hedged, said I was "studying" or "playing:" neither answer was entirely incorrect or deceitful. One time my mother decided to ask what kind of games we played, and I told her mostly card games, Aces-up or Deuces or Old Maid. Another time, when she asked, I admitted on an impulse that we had once played Spin The Bottle, and she looked at me oddly for a minute.

My mother needn't have worried more than a brief instant. I was far less interested in any of the Flaherty girls that I was in Gene Autry, Captain Video, and Kukla, Fran and Ollie—after all, I was only a little boy.

I probably would have remained the Flaherty sisters' lover for the rest of my life—or at least for many more years—if two events hadn't occurred almost simultaneously. One concerned Mr. Hargrave and my ambidexterity; the second Aunt Selma.

Before I get into Selma and what happened to her, perhaps I ought to describe what was occurring in the fifth grade class from which I escaped afternoons to wallow in the odorless young flesh of three prepubescent girls, one dark-haired and lean, one blonde and plain, one redheaded and so seductive that I was content to bring her to orgasm after orgasm without enjoying a similar pleasure myself. For it was this divided nature of my life during these three months or so that gave each side of me—child and man—a particular force they would never again possess, even when circumstances began to fall more in my favor. I'm certain now that if my battle with Mr. Hargrave hadn't escalated as rapidly as it did and come to dominate my school life to the exclusion of all else, that I would probably have forgotten the Flaherty sisters' orgasms and gone on to become—if not quite an altar boy like Edward—simply an eleven-year-old boy, with interests of boys my own age—softball, cops and robbers, Batman and Superman comics, nature and astronomy. As it happened, only the almost daily manipulation to orgasm of three girls could satisfy my need for some kind of control; for my life had otherwise clearly begun to spin madly out of control.

After the art class incident, the next few steps in the Hargrave war were cautious ones. He would stop by my desk every day for a minute or two to watch me write. I would see him—if I weren't looking, feel him—coming and switch from left hand to right hand for his benefit, often starting a new page or paragraph; then when he had passed, switch back again. While this was fine for classroom notes which I could take home without showing anyone, it couldn't be done on tests which had to be handed in: the difference between my writing with two different hands was too obvious.

In the past, I'd written right-handedly as deftly as left-handedly. But now, because I didn't want to do it, it became more difficult. My usual neat right-handed script became as loose as my left-handed script; then looser. It also took longer. I would still be writing long after those around me had finished a test—even when I knew all the answers. Unsurprisingly, I began to receive poor penmanship grades for each test or report I handed in. This slow decline went on about a month.

The next step was more traumatic. One day I developed pains in my right hand similar to rheumatism. By the middle of the school day, I was down in the nurse's office, my mother was telephoned to come pick me up. The nurse gave me two children's aspirin for the pain, my mother two more that night before I went to sleep.

The following morning the pain persisted, increased. Instead of going to school, I went to our family doctor, who inspected my hand, took X- rays, and asked many questions: had I fallen, banged my hand, caught it anywhere? I hadn't and if I had no reason for my hand to hurt so badly neither had he. Still, he decided to treat it as a type of bursitis, and he placed my arm in a sling, advising me not to use it for a few weeks and to bathe in Epsom Salts every night.

Mr. Hargrave was incensed when he saw my right hand suddenly dysfunctional. Grudgingly he said I might as well use the other to write with, which I easily did. But he stared at me with obvious annoyance during tests and reports as though admitting that he might have lost this fray, but he promised he would be less easily defeated in the future. He also used another weapon in his arsenal—he barred me from art class, my favorite subject, making me read while other students could paint or draw to their heart's content. I was furious at the tactic, but I wouldn't give him the satisfaction of knowing it and never complained.

When, finally, I couldn't keep the sling on any longer and returned to class without it, Hargrave came to stand by my desk ten minutes at a time to make certain I wrote the way he wanted. It wasn't easy. My right hand seemed now to belong to someone else. It did things the left hand would never do: it dropped bottles of tempera on the classroom floor, it got caught in cabinet doors, it let notebooks and packages slip and fall, it broke pencil points and made brand new ballpoint pens run out of ink. Hargrave wasn't fooled. He brought to class a small, hard, rubber ball to strengthen my right hand. He wanted to see me using it whenever I was not writing.

Somehow or other, that hard yellow ball also managed to slip out of my right hand at crucial moments: once smashing the glass door of the art supplies cabinet. Hargrave took the ball away, saying I had used it enough. Instead, he gave me extra penmanship lessons to "help strengthen" my right hand. These were to be done on the front blackboard while the other students had art class.

Naturally my resentment grew. So did my rebelliousness. Behind Hargrave's back I would switch from right hand to left while writing the blackboard. This went on until he noticed one student unable to hide his merriment at my trickery. Hargrave turned, I was caught and made write more lessons.

Meanwhile, at home, I continued to complain about his treatment, with no satisfactory response from my parents. My father thought Hargrave's yellow ball a "good idea." He had no comment about the extra lessons on the blackboard or the loss of my favorite class in school. Besides, there were other, more pressing matters to occupy my parents at this time. My older brother had become a somnambulist—that was serious business. One morning he'd been found sleeping in the front seat of our station wagon, three floors away from his bedroom. Another sleepwalking venture had taken him clear out of the house and across the street, where he'd been discovered, curled up, sleeping under a hydrangea bush when Mr. Kalman left his house to go to work at six-thirty a.m. That was truly frightening: my brother could have kept on walking and been hit by a car. Doctors were consulted. All sorts of therapies advised.

My sister also developed problems. She had begun menstruating and for some reason that managed to make her—and my mother too—constantly upset and angry. They would suddenly erupt into argument with each other over any trivial matter.

My younger brother also added his woes. Six-years-old and in the first grade, his first Patch Test—routinely given to spot early signs of tuberculosis—had come back positive: the only one in the school. No matter how much he ate—and it was plenty, enough for my father to nickname him "Crunchy"—he remained skin and bone. He was tested for anemia and for the same glandular condition which had unbalanced my early infancy, all with inconclusive results. Instead, my parents decided on a regimen to fatten him up.

Who knows what other problems my parents were then facing: business doldrums for my father; disinterest in their sex life for my mother; whatever they were, they were too much for my own little problem to compete with. On occasion, whenever I became too despondent, my mother would take me aside and plead with me to be a "good boy" and to not make trouble. She was tired, she said, she had too much work just picking up after us. The last time she made her plea, she revealed why she was so tired and irritated: she was pregnant again. I would simply have to learn how to cope with Hargrave myself.

I loved my mother then. It's difficult to write a sentence like that from a perspective of so many decades later, following so many misunderstandings between us, so many abandonments (mine); after divorces (hers) marriages (again, hers); after stunning revelations about sexual activities and drug use (mine) and a public Coming-Out (again, mine) in magazines that she couldn't ignore (her comment was: "Why didn't you hire a sky-writing plane?"); after reconciliations and in-depth discussions; after a new friendship had been forged between us, this time as equals, adults; and after her death. But it was true then. If there was one constant in my life as a child, it was that my parents loved me, and because she was on the spot the most, that my mother loved me, no questions asked. She, in return was completely worthy of my equally unquestioning devotion. She might occasionally be cross or less than completely wonderful, otherwise she was nearly perfect. She washed and fed me, groomed and clothed me, listened to my wishes, intuited my wants and needs, persuaded rather than coerced me, explained things to me, treated me as though I were older and more understanding than I really was, so I would attempt to fulfill her ideal of a son. I had been an easy birth and aside from my various strange, minor illnesses, an easy to care for child compared to my brothers and sister. Now that I am middle-aged, I find it difficult to believe that such a perfectly understood and responsive relationship could exist between us for so long. But it did, and since I was brave, grateful and loving, I decided not to add to my mother's troubles at this difficult time in her life. I'd fight my battles alone.

This proved difficult, especially as the weeks went by and Mr. Hargrave stepped up his attentions to me. He hit on the idea of tying my left hand behind my back in class so I couldn't use it to write. Impossible you say? Downright Dickensian? True, but it happened, and no one stopped him. Naturally, under this restraint I became fidgety, talkative and surly, all in a quiet way. I continued to be even more clumsy than before. My penmanship degenerated into mere scribbling, unreadable even to me. Those subjects in which I had previously excelled—math, science, history, English—were now worthless to me: I was all but failing in them. Nothing I did at home or at school gave me or Hargrave any satisfaction.

Perversely, Hargrave saw all this not as the failure of his strict regimen, which it was, but as a result of my own stubbornness in refusing to cooperate; and he grew more intolerant. Every day as we filed into class and sat in our assigned seats, he would look over the class with his usual indifferent stare, then glower at me.

I began to retaliate in the only ways I knew how. If I was Hargrave's prisoner inside the school, outside we were more equal. I discovered his phone number and began calling his home. Whenever his wife answered, I. would say that I was the older brother (deepening my voice) or even sister of someone in our class and ask if I could speak to her husband clarify a lesson we had been given. When Hargrave picked up that receiver, I would hang up, certain I'd interrupted his evening and annoyed him. Whenever I called and Hargrave himself answered, I either hung quickly or made rude noises into the phone. Once I blew a whistle.

He never knew it was me, or if he suspected he never said anything. But he did increase his tortures. He kept me in class after school, writing penmanship lessons on the blackboard, day after day. When my mother asked why I was always late, I lied to her, said we were working on a special project in class.

After a week of my being kept after school every day, I decided I had to retaliate in a more noticeable way. My revenge centered around Hargrave's car. One day instead of going directly home from school, I followed him, hiding behind trees and other cars until he arrived at his parked car—an unattractive tan two-door Ford coupe—the cheapest model available that year which he probably could barely afford on his teacher's salary. The following morning I left for school early and walked around the block until

I located the Ford coupe. Holding my skate-key tightly in my fist, its pointed end out, I moved alongside the car until I made contact and gouged a twelve-foot-long scar into the side fender, bumper to bumper.

Again without being certain I was the culprit, Hargrave attacked. He added to my tied-up left hand and loss of art class and daily after-school penmanship, another, at-home penmanship lesson, and a book report every week. He also called on me first in class, and when I knew the answer he would keep asking me questions which became more and more detailed and trivial until he arrived at one I wouldn't know—at which point I would receive a demerit and more homework.

Naturally, I found a new way to get back at him. I cracked a soda bottle on the side of a curbstone and placed the thick broken edge under the front tire of the parked car so it was deeply hidden, so angled it had to make a nasty gash as soon as the Ford moved forward. Hargrave was an hour late the following morning. He never said why.

Triple homework for me. And I failed every subject on my report cars and was given behavior reprimands in every category provided. I couldn't take such a card home, and convinced my sister to forge my mother's signature on it. At home, I told my mother I'd lost the report card. She believed me.

Hargrave had run out of legitimate ways to torture me, so he began insulting me in class. He had me stand in front of the room and would verbally downgrade me a half hour at a time: I was stupid, I was sloppy, I couldn't write, I needed a haircut, my shoes were old and poorly polished, my trousers needed cleaning, my shirts needed ironing. This proved to be a fatal mistake on his part for two reasons. First, I was as well groomed as any boy in the class; in fact there were some truly poor and neglected children in the room who were all too conscious of the old and poorly cared-for clothing they were forced to wear to school. Second, I was a popular, well-liked boy and as soon as Hargrave's attacks became personal enough where the students could form their own opinions, rather than academic where clearly he had ail advantage, my friends took my side and turned against him. Volunteers—even among girls—dropped to nil in his class.

I suffered his insults and humiliations. My classmates continued to treat me as an equal. In some cases, at lunch and recess, they would go out of their way to show their support by sharing a particularly fine dessert or game with me. My closest friends were angered and more and more demanded that I tell my father and have him come to school to "pop Hargrave one right on his kisser."

The next time Hargrave called me up in front of the class to begin his daily attacks, Lillian Bauman, one of the more sensitive girls in the class, couldn't stand it anymore and burst out crying. Hargrave asked two other girls to have her taken to the nurse's office; but she wouldn't budge. When he tried to do it himself, she burst into hysterical screaming and a female teacher from the next room had to be called in to calm her and take her away.

When they were gone, Hargrave seemed genuinely embarrassed. He realized from the glares that greeted him how much he had lowered himself in his students' eyes and how many potential enemies he had in the room. His response was typical of the weak: he sent me to my seat and pretended nothing had happened. Then he promised to give us art class for the rest of the afternoon. Even I was to have art—for the first time in two months. I never made it past lunch period. Seeing poor little Lillian so hysterical, my anger at my own treatment grew. I couldn't swallow my food. When I did manage to get down half a chicken salad sandwich, I became nauseous and began to vomit. I was brought to the nurse's office and then sent home. I later found out that while Lillian and I were gone " that afternoon, Hargrave had tried to bribe the class into silence, promising them a field trip to the Planetarium if no one told what had brought on the two illnesses.

I decided I couldn't put up with Hargrave any longer. The next day I refused to go to school. I even contrived to work myself up to a quite spectacular nosebleed as an excuse. Even so, it was clear that my mother was having one of the worse days of her pregnancy; it was all too obvious that she wouldn't be able to bear having me around. So—holding an ice cube wrapped in a hanky against my upper lip—I staunched the blood and said I was feeling better: I would go to school after all. I could tell she was relieved, and although she remained vague and headachy, she put extra cookies in my lunch box and sent me off with a note to excuse my lateness.

En route to school I usually walked to the end of my block, turned the corner, hopped the two short ends of parallel longer blocks, crossed the street, slogged along another long block, turned that corner and completed the one last long stretch that led to the school, which sat on its own freestanding square block. The middle of the second long walk was cut by several empty lots a bit hillier than their surroundings. I suppose that explained why houses hadn't yet been built there. Though it was a fairly rough terrain for the neighborhood, a shortcut through the lots had been worn down by decades of schoolchildren. And while it was a bit wild, it was hardly unattractive to us, except in the wettest weather when it was muddy and usually avoided.

In the spring, rangy forsythia, honeysuckle vines and tall gone-wild azaleas flanked the path; robins and sparrows and blue jays constantly flew about our heads during late May and early June when they were nesting. Off in one distant corner of the lots, someone had laid out a small vegetable garden where neat rows of Romaine lettuce, Beefsteak tomatoes and summer squash grew. It was a pleasant place to walk through in good weather: quiet, pretty, a relief from the regularity of sidewalks and suburban houses. I loved it.

That morning, holding a handkerchief up in case my nose began to bleed again, lugging my books and unfinished homework (quadrupled) and my note from my mother, I was miserable. As soon as I was inside the lots and out of sight of anyone on either street, I stopped and sat down. It was later than the time I ordinarily went to school, and no other children were around. It was very quiet. Not even a sparrow chirping. Two yards away, a woman was hanging out sheets on a clothesline. I heard the high-pitched metallic shrieking of the clothesline gears as she pulled it and the dull slaps of the wet sheets flapping. I saw everything around me with a clarity I'd never before experienced—never before suspected. I knew with equal clarity that I was trapped, doomed.

My life was unreal: a nightmare during school hours, an unending orgy during late afternoons and weekends. Somehow or other, I had been displaced by tiny, irreconcilable steps from being my mother's beloved son, a model student and a good child into a sulky, ill-tempered, nose-bleeding, tire-slashing, fender-mangling sexual fanatic. I hated it. Somehow, I'd lost something wonderful, something tender and lovely, that I could hardly recall any more—my childhood. I knew who was to blame for this—Mr. John Hargrave, the Satan of my life. He'd tempted me out of virtue and into every bad deed short of theft and murder, and I'd fallen without a fight.

I began to cry. Then, thinking that might bring on the nosebleed again, I immediately stopped. I considered my alternatives. I could run away, although to where and for how long before I was caught I had no idea. Having little experience of life, I was certain running away would certainly lead me deeper into a life of crime, probably ending with me strapped into the electric chair as nearby power lines sizzled. Another possibility was even more desperate. I could walk over to the four-laned, heavily trafficked Braddock Avenue, and when I saw a speeding car coming my way too fast for the driver to stop in time, I could run into the middle of the street and kill myself. A third possibility presented itself: I could fight back. Not by stealth and cunning as I had been doing so far, but openly, defying Hargrave and everyone else, rebelling, demanding that I be treated like the adult I had somehow been tricked into becoming.

As I thought more about this last option, my anger grew. It didn't need much to fuel it, given all my recent humiliations. But just thinking how snidely Hargrave would probably receive my mother's note, how mockingly he would read it out loud to the class, infuriated me. I realized that I was small by comparison with my enemy, easily outmaneuvered, under-powered, with no influence whatsoever-and I despaired. If there was a God how could He let this happen to me? I'd been good, not bad; true, not false. Any wrongs I'd committed had been forced on me by circumstances, not because I liked doing them. I turned my eyes up to the pale blue, blank, unreflecting morning sky, and shook my fist at it, daring God to account for His actions against me.

When I received no answer, I became even angrier, and dared God to show Himself to me and fight it out, one to one. Still no response, although in the second after my challenge I half expected the azure sky to rip open and lightning to strike me dead. Now I knew better. I'd gotten no answer, because He wouldn't dare show himself. He was ashamed. If He existed at all! I pondered: a world without God, with ineffectual parents barely able to help themselves and their children, a world with no one to help. It was a terrifying place to exist in. I was more frightened than I'd ever been, not by some bogeyman but by the reasoned-out realization of nothingness. I decided in that moment that if all that I had believed in before was meaningless, then I was enough. Only *I* existed for certain. Only *I* could be relied upon to help myself. I *had* to fight back.

If illness couldn't stop him, neither could obedience satisfy him. I watched the clock out of the corner of my eye, noting that I had only one more hour of school to get through. I thought since his anger had taken so long to get going because of my lateness, that somehow it would not fulfill itself until the allotted class time was long past. What I didn't count on was that free of its normal time-frame, his anger might gallop on ahead. At a half hour to three, when he called out "Art. All third in the row students get the materials," I too, third in my row, stood to go to the art cabinet in the back of the class.

"Not you!" he shouted. Everyone in the class knew he meant me. "You come here and write yesterday's lessons on the blackboard."

I didn't move. He had so counted on his authority that he returned to his desk without looking back to see if l was following. After a while, he realized that I hadn't moved.

"Well, what are you waiting for?" he asked. I didn't answer.

"I said to come to the blackboard and write yesterday's lesson. The lesson you were supposed to do at home."

I knew I couldn't, wouldn't. I'd made my decision in the empty lot and I would stick to it, no matter what happened. "No," I said firmly.

"No?" He couldn't have been happier; open insubordination was exactly what he'd been looking for.

"No. I'm not writing any lesson on that blackboard. Not today. Not ever."

This was more than he had bargained for. "Come here," he said, red faced now, with barely restrained anger.

"No."

He stood up. "If you aren't at this desk by the time I count to five . . ."

I walked to the wardrobe, opened a door, took out my jacket, and walked toward the back classroom door.

"Where are you going?"

I had my hand on the back door handle. It turned.

"Come back here! Where are you going?" he shouted.

I turned and faced him. I put on my jacket slowly, and saw thirty frightened children's faces and Hargrave's looming bulk ready to go into action in an instant, his face almost purple with anger. What really annoyed me was that not one of the other children moved, he'd cowed them so much. I despised them at that moment, all of them, along with him.

"If you step out of this classroom," Hargrave shouted, "You're not coming back."

"Go to hell! Go to hell, where you belong, *you Devil!*"

What had come out of my mouth in that instant shocked me as much as anyone else. I froze with the import of my words.

Hargrave started for me. I knew I had to get away and get something between us. I opened the door and got outside then I slammed the door shut with such force it seemed to explode. The small four-paned glass windows at the top of the door shattered inward. I could see Hargrave throw his hands in front of his face as the glass blew in. I ran for it.

As I raced, classroom door after classroom door all down the corridor was flung open as teachers stepped out to see what had happened. By then I was in a total panic and wildly skidding past them charging down the metal stairway and almost flying out the school's side door. I kept running until I was blocks past my house. Only when I had reach Hillside Avenue did I realize where I was and stop to catch my breath. Then I turned around and very slowly walked back.

My mother wasn't at home, which was surprising and slightly upsetting. I wondered if she had gone to the doctor. In a way it was a reprieve-I wouldn't have to explain what I was doing home from school early. It would be another forty-five minutes until my brother and sister, would arrive home from the local junior high school.

It's difficult to recall a time when suburban houses containing valuables were left unlocked. Our house was locked. The front and kitchen doors were locked from the outside- but I didn't even try them. Like most other houses on the street ours had a two-car garage which held so many cast-off refrigerators, early air conditioners, so much gardening equipment, summer lawn furniture and discarded toys that only one automobile-usually my mother's station wagon-could fit inside. The garage was connected to the house by a shed-like equipment room, containing the gas and water heaters. This room was narrow, tall, with one tiny high window. Once, when we'd come home from a visit to some relatives late at night and my parents realized they hadn't remembered to take the house keys, my father had lifted my older brother up to the little window, managed to get it unlatched by sliding a piece of thin cardboard between the window and the sill, and my older brother had gotten in. By half-shimmying, half-stepping against the oil burner on one side and the hot water heater on the other, he had managed to reach the floor. An adjoining, seldom locked doorway led from the boiler room to the kitchen pantry. So, we'd gotten in.

I used to enter the shed from the garage whenever I was bored or otherwise alone. On rainy days we children would sometimes noisily fight each other on the top floor of the house where our bedrooms were located, loudly raucous enough to disturb my mother. Defending her sanity, she would divide us up-usually sending one or two of us into the garage. There was plenty to keep us busy. We would fool around going through the big square cardboard boxes that contained our Christmas tree ornaments, or we would play cards lolling in the lawn furniture and pretending it was the sultry middle of August. At other times we were more restless and would place planks of wood on our roller skates and setting down on them zoom around the concrete garage floor. The heater was generally off limits, even a little frightening. Only one other area of the large house held such awe for us, my father's clothes closet. off the master bedroom, with its trapdoor to the roof. The constant humming of the water heater was somewhat comforting as it sounded a lot like our little cat, Puppy, so named because he didn't seem to believe that he was a feline but rolled over, retrieved sticks, chased cars, bit rather than scratched, never hissed but did try to bark, and in general acted like a dog. Every once in a while, the oil burner would suddenly ignite, sounding like a real explosion and we'd all run for it. Even worse, once the oil burner was going it eventually snapped on the water heater with an ominous series of metallic clacks and dings that reminded us of the robot monsters in the Flash Gordon serials—it even looked like a rather evil, if so far stationary, robot.

    Thus, more fears were added to my uncertainty that I would get into the window and down the other side, to which was added my anxiety about the outcome of what had happened in school. Surely, I'd be expelled and sent to reform school, where all the worst boys (and mental defectives too) went. My parents would hate and disown me. My friends would never see me again. Instead of playing with toys and roller skates, I'd be chopping rocks for highway projects, stamping out license plates until I was old as my grandfather.

Depressing as these thoughts were, I still felt neither less angry nor less justified in my actions. I only hoped I could persuade my mother how pressured I'd been. I sat on my lunch pail against the shed among her dahlia bulbs and thought I would like to die.

In the midst of this despair, I heard my name called. Not a shout so much as a loud stage whisper: it came from the vicinity of the Flaherty's house. I stood up and walked across the Doria's backyard to the Flaherty basement window, which I now saw was slightly ajar. Through the soiled screen I could barely make out Susan's face. Was she sick?

"I had a sore throat, but I feel fine now. I was just bored with school and didn't want to go. Want to come in?"

"Anyone else home?"

"My mom's out playing Canasta. Only Selma's here. Come in. I'll open the door."

This was an old fashioned double trapdoor angled into the side of the house and surrounded on all sides by bushes, now just twigs. I'd never seen it open, and quickly went downstairs, pulling the doors shut behind me.

"Where is she?" I asked, meaning her aunt.

"Upstairs sleeping, I think. Want a Yoo-Hoo?"

This was a chocolate milk soda we kids loved and which my mother wouldn't let us drink because she'd somehow or other discovered it contained not only too much sugar but also as much caffeine as a mug of coffee. Yoo-Hoos were the staple drink of the Flaherty girls' socials; open wooden crates of them—full and empty—were stacked in one corner of their garage. I now wonder how much the imbibing of this drink went toward the girls' general gabbiness, excitability and sexual stimulation.

We each took a bottle of Yoo-Hoo and went to the sofa. The familiar room was dim so that Susan could watch the tiny, asymmetrically placed screen of their black and white

Motorola television. I asked what she was watching and Susan said casually, "A story."

It was an adult's program: women in tight black cocktail gowns with linguine-thin shoulder straps, "Italian-boy" close-cut hairdos and dangerously high-heeled shoes. The men's jackets and trousers looked baggy enough to hold two of them. The men themselves were tall and dark-haired and blank-looking, quite dull by comparison with the femme fatales surrounding them and certainly not worth all the cunning these women exerted on their behalf. I knew this was one of the seemingly endless open-ended soap operas my own mother watched religiously, *Search for Tomorrow* or *As the World Turns*. Years later, she was still watching them. Once, when I'd been living on my own for some time and used to go home for tense infrequent Sunday dinners, I brought along a friend who had been an actor on one of these programs. I thought it would give my mother a thrill. Little did I knew that George had played a judge's son, a drug addicted ex-con whose main function on the program was to knock up girls from good families then leave them for dead in flaming convertibles. The minute George and I stepped in the front door, my mother's eyes widened, I innocently assumed with pleasure. "You bastard!" she muttered and I had to throw myself between them until she calmed down.

I'm not certain which program Susan was watching but she was enthralled with it and this gave me the opportunity to look at her for what must have been the thousandth time, yet which somehow felt as though it were the first. Doubtless the traumas of that day-the sudden awareness of my predicament on the path to school through the empty lot as devastating as the vision of Eternity that was said to have toppled St. Paul from his stallion, my decision to no longer be oppressed, its explosive repercussion a few hours later in class-all this had forced me to look at everything around me with a sense of foreboding uniqueness: as though I were memorizing it all for long future reflections in a cell. The only comparable sensation I can now recall happened some dozen years later, an hour or so into my first LSD experience, when I'd pulled out of The Great White Light dissolution of self and reconstructed the universe little by little by surrounding hints and clues of sensory evidence. That too would pass into almost total forgetfulness yet also leave its irrevocable effect upon me. Nor should it be surprising that Susan Flaherty would be the object of my new regard. She and I shared a private hidden little world of limited yet important activity in as flagrant disregard of the world's conventions as I had defended in class. She was as much a rebel as I.

Not that she looked it at the time. On the contrary, she'd absorbed her time and place and culture so completely as to be a sort of mini-icon of contentment and normality. She sat on the sofa with her pants legs up under her just like Terry Moore did while being photographed for Screen Queens or one of the other movie magazines the Flaherty girls read with page-crumpling avidity. Instead of La Moore's chinchilla chubby, however, Susan's top that day was yet another of those 'Fifties sweaters so fluffy that girls who wore them seemed engirdled with peach-colored or ice-blue nimbuses, or a friendly if indeterminate species of mammal. The Flaherty red hair she alone possessed among her generation had been combed out so that it was clearly "tresses" rather than just hair, in imitation of one of the popular redheads she admired—Arlene Dahl, Rhonda Fleming, Susan Hayward—I was never certain which.

Her bare feet, the pointed precise manner by which she would bring the lightest of finger tipped touches to select her favorite chocolate out of the spacious Whitman Sampler and never be surprised (as I so often was) by an unexpectedly embedded pecan-half or oversweet mint cream, suggested poise and self-containment to a polished degree. I sipped my Yoo-Hoo until I made the honking swallow that signified I'd reached bottom, whereupon she extended a hand to take my bottle away without once glancing away from the television screen. Then she took my hand and put it upon her chest.

I sort of massaged this area—touching more sweater fluff than what it contained—for a while, until Susan lifted her sweater, revealing no trainer bra (she'd been at home all day) but her two small pink-nippled, erect breasts. I caressed these until at a station break she moved us into a deep kiss that ended a millisecond before her program resumed live coverage. But a new concession had been semiconsciously made as she slipped her slacks down and guided my hand to the cotton panties between her legs. Although she continued focusing on the program with the compulsion of an onlooker driving past a car wreck, I could tell from her hesitation over the chocolate box that she was not totally undistracted.

The next station break was longer, and when it ended, our kiss was once more precisely broken, my own trousers were down around my ankles, her hand wrapped around my eleven-year-old erection. I managed to get her panties clear of her bottom, no easy task. She now paid little attention to my efforts. I noticed that one chocolate—a long triangular raspberry cream shaped like the *Merrimac*—remained kissing her lips a longish until she gulped it down with a sigh.

During the next commercial we lay down side by side, she on propped-up pillows still facing the television screen, her grip on my erection as actively rotational as before, I next to her with half my hand inside her, my fingers thrumming as though I were playing "I love coffee, I love tea," the only tune I'd ever managed to learn to play, one handed-on my grandfather's old standup piano in Western Rhode Island. Her small sighs were more frequent now, the chocolate box abandoned on the floor, the last candy streaked across her chin where I lapped it off. I removed my hand from her vagina and managed to get on top of her. Unstopped, I settled onto her pillow-soft thighs, then angled up and down trying to find the most comfortable location for my erection which suddenly seemed very much in the way. I didn't have to do much. After a few seconds it seemed to slide into a suddenly all-enveloping new place: warm, wettish, tight. Her continued relative indifference to my shifting about—she never left off watching the TV—didn't phase me a bit, concerned as I was only with these new sensations. True she continued to sigh with some regularity, a good sign, I thought. So, thinking it was now or never, I pushed further inside her and watched her gulp a bit, trying to say something. She even turned away from the TV screen and toward me once, some word trying to escape her Whitman-smeared mouth. Finally she managed to get it out, "Nina Foch", but I was no longer listening or caring, I was feeling burning heat, icy cold, my back so rigid for a minute that my toes curled back into cramps just before I collapsed on top of her, melted away on a floe of hot cheese and loganberry jam with whipped cream, dotted with just a hint of chocolate.

I don't know what had made Susan suddenly look at me, or what she had meant by mentioning the actress's name. But it had been enough to cause my first orgasm and I couldn't have cared less.

A minute later, she looked up again sharply. I had returned to my senses enough to sense her concern and looked up too: in time to see her Aunt Selma poised in mid-step on the stairway leading down to the basement staring at us, her ungainly large hands like stricken birds fluttering about the front of her body as though she was about to take off. Then Selma was gone, clumping up the stairs and into the kitchen.

Susan roughly pushed me off. I let myself slip out of her, looked at my lower body for any kind of physical indication of my brief if incredible experience.

"You have to get dressed and go," Susan said.

That was clear to me. "And Aunt Selma?"

"Don't worry about her," she said, already dressed, the television set turned off, the Whitman's Sampler picked up and its two layers of double candies set in place before the lid was shut—she was that methodical.

"What if . . . ?" I began.

"I'll talk to her," Susan said, efficiently. Then in another more warning tone of voice. "By the way, don't tell anyone you lost your cherry to me today. Understand? Promise."

I promised and was let out the double doors onto the sidewalk, where I quickly caught up with the tail end of children just returning home from school. My brother and sister had already let themselves into the house with my brother's key and were in the kitchen arguing over the details of the note my mother had left while eating Oreos and drinking milk out the jelly-jar glasses we kids had to use because we broke so many of my mother's better glasses.

Their argument might have lasted until my mother returned home (from a doctor's appointment the note said; she'd picked up my younger brother already) if it wasn't for the police siren that intervened, shrieking down our quiet street directly to the Flaherty house, carrying every neighbor child who'd just gotten indoors back out again onto lawn or stoop to see what was going on.

The policemen were let into the house and a clot of children gathered on our front lawn-as close as they dared approach the police car or the Flaherty's house. We were all treated to another, longer sounding, higher pitched siren from an ambulance careening down the street. The extended Caddy all-metal station wagon stopped on a dime, inches from the rear bumper of the police car, and two white-suited men leapt out, ran up the outside stairs of the Flaherty house and went inside.

By now, we'd all moved closer. Some children surrounded the two cars, while the rest of us clustered on the Doria's front lawn, when suddenly all four men came out of the house, two carrying a gurney so covered over with white blankets we could barely make out who was under it (the body was too long to be Susan's, I thought). As they hustled it into the backdoor of the ambulance, the policeman shouted at the boys who had leaned in through the open window of the police car and found the siren mechanism. In seconds, the ambulance was closed off and shot wailing up the street; seconds later, the police car too was gone. Many children ran after the cars. I did so half-heartedly. I turned around after only a few feet to catch a glimpse of red hair and an ice-blue fluffy sweater, as Susan shut first the screened porch door then the white wooden door behind her.

Children know a great deal of what goes on among the adults in their lives: from overheard conversations they are not supposed to understand or from the way some people are treated by others. If children don't always act on that knowledge or appear to forget it, it is usually chance: adults are intrinsically less interesting to nine or ten-year-olds than other nine or ten-year-olds. So it was that any halfway perceptive child in my family could interpret the lives of certain grown-ups from our parent's brief, enigmatic statements. It was obvious to us that the Caruso's next door were having financial problems sending their twin sons to Pratt University simultaneously, despite Bill Caruso's successful beauty salon business. We also knew that Rosalie Klein's parents had been separated more than once; the wildly named Wolfgang—a large, balding, dumpy man with a Charlie Chaplin moustache—was, unexpectedly, a ladies' man. I've mentioned my mother's deep suspicion regarding my Uncle Bert; and her assurance that the Flaherty's-husband and wife-were alcoholics, gamblers, high-livers, both of whom had to work not merely to raise their three children and not only to pay the expensive mortgage on their house, but more importantly so they could spend their weekends in total debauch.

But when conversation turned to Selma Flaherty, silence of a peculiar sort ensued, that special kind of taciturnity accompanied by head nodding and occasional sighs that suggested unspeakable sadness. Selma herself gave little proof of a tragic destiny. Unlike her dashingly handsome paper-thin brother, she was both dowdy and plain. While he could occasionally be induced to peal out some current or traditional song—"Danny Boy" or "Oh my Papa"—at neighborhood gatherings, his lush tenor thrilling every female within aural range, Selma was soft-spoken to a fault. If her sister-in-law was an elegant dresser—I recall small square hats with peasant quills flying and nattily tailored dress suits—Selma was seldom seen in anything classier than an old cardigan half buttoned over a floral printed cotton housedress.

Her face was squarish—like that of blond little Kate—her eyes a watery blue and usually unfocused; her walk if not quite shambling was at least somewhat erratic-like a marionette only partly attached. Still, she was kind to children, never yelled at us and above all never told us what we should and shouldn't do. We liked her. Even so, it was clear that, in my older brother's fourteen year old terminology, Selma was playing "with only half a deck." He hinted that he'd somehow or other discovered that she had more than once resided in a ward at Creedmoor State Hospital, which we occasionally biked past, quickly, as though mental illness were contagious. He also knew—again he wouldn't say how—that she'd once worked in a girdle factory, a fact that caused instant mirth whenever we thought of it.

So it wasn't all that surprising, I suppose, to learn that after she'd come upon Susan and I *in flagrante*, the poor woman—who after all was more or less chaperone and *duenna* as well as housekeeper and general slave—had spiraled into spasms of guilt and certainty of retribution. Intending suicide, she'd gone into the kitchen cabinet, pulled out and promptly swallowed the remaining contents of a half gallon of liquid laundry bleach. Found by Susan minutes later, her pink housedress as ruined as her throat and esophagus by the lethal fluid, Selma had fallen to the kitchen floor, writhing in agony. Cool as I would have expected (following her *sang froid* after intercourse) Susan called the police and ambulance, and following their instructions, had attempted to flush out her aunt's throat with brimming pans-full of water. And to a large degree she had succeeded. Selma lived—although her vocal cords were half burned out—and the kitchen was awash, the sink overflowing by the time the policemen arrived to relieve Susan of her first-aid chore. Selma returned to Creedmoor State Hospital for another, somewhat longer than usual, visit then was an outpatient for another year, until the Flaherty family once more lifted roots and disappeared forever from our block and from my life.

By then, however, they were as good as gone for me. The Flaherty girls never again invited me to their basement. I never again spoke to Susan, who became reclusive when not in school, more mysteriously unavailable, and more beautiful with each passing week. Years later, talking about the family with my older brother and sister, I was not too amazed to hear my sister expound a theory that most of the Flaherty women—wife, sister, and oldest daughter—were lovers of the slender, well-dressed tenor.

My mother arrived home from her doctor's appointment in good spirits and with grocery bags in the back of her station wagon, just as our street was beginning to clear of groups of neighbor children. She had missed the local excitement but had arrived home to provide me with a new terror. Despite my first taste of sexual intercourse and the thrill of a near suicide two doors away, I couldn't forget that only a few hours before I'd utterly destroyed my academic future in the middle of the fifth grade. I hadn't told my siblings about this—not trusting them to not use it against me in some fit of minor annoyance and ruining my few chances to figure out what to do next. But my mother didn't notice my sudden quietness. She even ruffled my hair, and called me "Junior Pie," her most extreme term of affection. I went up to my room and fell into an exhausted sleep.

My sister awakened me in time for dinner, held at the kitchen table hours before my parent's own quieter, later dinner in the dining room my father worked late that night. Subdued and still sleepy as I was, it was obvious from my mother's odd little glances at me that she knew. Every spoonful of soup, although needed if I were to dine for the next four year off reform school gruel, tasted to me like a spoonful of the same laundry bleach that Selma Flaherty had imbibed, luckily for her all at once. I managed to get through dinner without any major incident, dessert and all, and was about to run upstairs again when my mother asked me—not my sister as was usual—to stay and help with the dishes. My siblings went up to do their homework, and for once, I almost wished I had triple homework to do.

As she washed and I wiped our supper plates, she didn't ask me what had happened. Instead, she began to talk to me about her own girlhood. I loved these stories: both my parents had grown up in a small town in New England during the 'teens and 'twenties and the world they'd inhabited as children always seemed inescapably charming—and lost—to me. Suggestions of its continuing influence were apparent every time we visited my maternal grandfather's home and what remained of his once huge farm and orchards in Rhode Island: enough still, that with many early photographs, we could piece together how delightful a life it had been, despite all the material comforts they'd lacked and which we children now possessed so unthinkingly.

"Do you remember that goat?" my mother asked.

I said I did. When she was young my mother had been frightened by a Tuberculosis scare. No penicillin or sulfa drugs existed at the time and it was an incurable, usually fatal disease. She'd been told to drink goat's milk to build up her health; it was evidently three times as rich in nutrients as cow's milk. The only way to obtain goat's milk daily was for my grandfather to buy a goat and keep it on the property ready to be milked. It seemed to work: my mother never developed the dreaded disease, neither did she develop any fondness for the life-saving animal.

"I hated that goat," she told me. "Even though it was always kept on a tether, every time I went to pick vegetables in my mother's garden plot, it would come after me. Every afternoon. Sometimes it managed to chew through that rope and it would chase me right into Grandpa's house. Usually, it just tried biting and kicking me. I had to be so careful when I was gathering tomatoes and squash and cucumbers for my mother. Oh, that goat drove me crazy! Yet, at the same time, I knew I couldn't ask my father to get rid of it, because I needed the milk it gave if I was to stay healthy."

I listened quietly. I didn't say a word back. We finished the dishes and she took my hand and led me into the living room. Still holding me tightly she sat down awkwardly, wearily, my future sister—she would turn out to be short-lived, dying after only three weeks—very apparent in my mother's stomach.

"I got a phone call today from the Vice-Principal of your school," my mother said, looking me in the eye. "What *happened*?"

I hesitated at first, but she kept on insisting, more sternly, that I tell her, so I poured out the months of agony, of tortures, of humiliations, of extra work, of taunting and deprivation that Hargrave had subjected me to; never once mentioning my own retaliations, naturally. The recounting of each terrible moment in class with him refueled my anger.

"Why didn't you tell me?" she asked.

"I *did*. I tried. You told me to try to be good, remember?" I defended myself. "I didn't want to bother you."

"This is very serious," she said. "You damaged school property."

"I'll pay for the broken glass. I have allowance money saved up."

"That's all very well, but how will you pay back your teacher for what you did to him?"

I stared at her uncomprehending. What I did to *him*?

"We have to go see your Principal tomorrow morning. I want you to tell her that all this is going to stop and that you'll be a good boy again."

It was clear that despite the detailing of my sufferings she still didn't understand. I tried again to tell her what had happened: how he had tied my hand, how he made me write on the blackboard while the other children could paint and draw, all the homework I'd been given, how he'd made fun of my clothing and appearance. She interrupted me sternly. "Enough! We're going up to the Principal's office tomorrow and you're going to apologize."

"He hates me," I found the wit to say. "He hates me worse than your goat *ever* hated you. I never want to see him again. I'll never go back to his class. Never. *Never. NEVER!* I'll kill him first. I'll *kill* him. *I'll KILL him!*"

I began pounding my mother as though she were Hargrave. She managed to stop my punishing little hands, held them, looking at my face with the most pained expression I'd ever seen—as though I were a stranger.

"You don't want to kill *anyone*." She declared with great certainty. "Do you hear? I don't ever want you to say that again."

Through my anger and tears I said quite clearly, "Then I'll run away from home. I'll go to reform school. I'll go to prison. I'll go anywhere. But I won't go back to his class. Never. And if you make me, I'll kill him."

"Stop now!" she said, alarmed by the wildness of my ranting. "You're just a little boy. You won't kill anyone."

"I will. I swear it."

"You're too young to swear, too," she tried to make it into a joke. "Now, I'm going to let go of your hands. Promise you won't hit me again."

"I'm sorry. I didn't mean to hit you, Mommy. I love you."

"What's happened to you?" she wondered out loud. "What happened to my little boy, my little Junior Pie?" Then, suddenly realizing how deep the waters were that we now treaded together, "What are we going to do.?"

"I don't want to be bad. He makes me bad. I was never bad before. Please don't make me go back. I'll . . . I'll kill *myself*, like Selma tried to do, with bleach. I will. Only I'll make sure no one is around to find me until I'm good and dead. And I'll drink gasoline too, to make sure."

Now she was more alarmed.

"Don't say that. You're not going to do anything of the kind. We'll talk to your Principal tomorrow. We'll do something, have you put in another class." She enfolded me against her big stomach, her soft hair, her smell of Lilac eau de cologne. "I'm sure she'll agree to it. But you'll have to promise to be very good from now on. And," holding me tighter, "you must never even think about killing yourself. That Flaherty woman is sick. She didn't know what she was doing. You're not sick like her. Just angry. God would be terribly unhappy and angry if you tried that. And so would I. Do you understand?"

"Please help me," I pleaded. "Don't make me go back to his class, please!"

"We'll try. And I still have to talk to your father. But you have to promise to behave."

"I promise," I said, crossing my heart.

She continued holding me another few minutes. Then said, "Now go upstairs. I want you asleep when your father comes home. And tomorrow, I'll wake you late. We don't have to see the Principal until eleven o'clock."

I kissed her and went up to my room, but I couldn't sleep for hours. I brushed my teeth, washed my hands and face, hung up and folded my clothing—determined to be a good child in every way—and lay in bed wondering what would happen the next day at eleven o'clock. My mother loved me and believed me. I was certain of that. But she wasn't a very forceful woman. She constantly gave in to my father, even when it was obvious to all of us that he was in the wrong. In her few arguments with friends and neighbors, she usually backed off first, withdrawing altogether—a method of behavior I would despise for years to come as weakness until I'd become mature enough to try it once and discovered how much more this tactic accomplished than my usual face-off aggressiveness. Still, she was on my side—I hadn't given my parents a spot of trouble so far. And I was sure I had frightened her with my suicide threat: only a truly desperate child of eleven would speak like that.

So I was still awake when my father's Pontiac pulled into our driveway. I waited what I thought was a prudent amount of time before putting on my slippers and bathrobe and sneaking down the staircase leading into the dimly lit living room. That room opened onto the dining room where my parents now sat, having coffee and dessert, so I didn't have to go more than halfway down the stairs. Hidden, I could usually hear every word they spoke in the dining room. But tonight they were talking quietly, and I wasn't even sure my mother had broached the subject until I heard my father's exasperated "Not him too. What's with these kids, Anne?" A rhetorical question: it went unanswered. I heard more mumbling, then my father asked: "Where did he learn such a thing?" and my mother's murmured explanation-in what must have been recently garnered detail about Selma Flaherty's suicide attempt. Evidently my mother went on to tell him what I'd earlier narrated of my treatment at Hargrave's hands, for he suddenly expostulated, "Let me go up to that school and see who pushes who around," followed by my mother's "Please, Phil, we've got to handle this right. Fighting isn't going to help" followed by more conversation too quiet for me to make out. Eventually they concluded some agreement. I was to be "spoken to" by my father, but not punished. I was also to be "carefully watched" by my mother, lest I make good on my suicide threat. My freedom would be curtailed—my father managing somehow to find blame for all this on how "wildly" my mother allowed us to run free, although she was as strict a mother as any I ever met. It all sounded both supportive and problematic to me. And indeed, two days later, on a Sunday afternoon, I was "spoken to" by my father who warned me not to cause my mother any more trouble, or else: and he lifted a powerful-looking hand to make his point.

It was a strange experience to wake up late the following day, to be given breakfast alone after my siblings were off at school, as my mother listened half-heartedly to a radio program and looked worried. It was already warm although still early March, and my mother ate a little, drank two cups of coffee and complained of a headache. But she sent me up to my room to get cleaned up and dressed and I didn't have to wait long before she too was dressed, and we drove the few blocks to school.

It was even eerier going through the school building at that hour of the morning. We had to go to the second floor where the Principal's office! was located, a floor I'd seldom been on in my career in that building. I'd gone from kindergarten and first grade on the street floor directly to second and third grades on the third floor, and then been in classrooms the top floor. My mother and I went into the school through the double front doors we children never used, into the large marble-lined foyer with its murals of improbable scenes from American history painted by out-of-work artists during the Depression—the entire building was an F.D.R. era project: marble floors, fine mahogany paneling, beautifully, carefully done. We ascended the long, curving staircase that half spiraled up from the foyer and which I'd never used before. I held onto my mother's hand, to "help her" up as she was in her seventh month of pregnancy and easily fatigued. At the top of the stairway lay the main administrative offices, three smaller ones flanking the Principal's office, into which my mother was announced and ushered, while I was placed, uncomfortably (my fate being decided within) on an adult-sized chair in the waiting area for what seemed hours.

From where I sat, close to a door open onto the corridor through which indifferent, mostly female adults came and went only half glancing at me, I could feel the hushed regular silence and response of surrounding orderly classrooms: a sudden burst of group laughter issuing out of the tilted transom windows of one classroom door, silence again as the students were hushed. I felt totally apart from it all-school, class, students, teachers-even in the middle of it, and I yearned to once more be accepted, integrated into that life. Conflictingly, I was also determined that I wouldn't apologize to Hargrave; I would never return to his class. I'd already learned too well the lesson of the previous day's revelation in the empty lot. Nothing could possibly change our enmity now.

Bored, anxious, I tried to divert myself by watching the Vice Principal's secretary filing student records. Then she too got up and left the office. I was alone-and from where I sat I could neither see nor hear my mother and the Principal. But by leaning back in the chair, I found that I could see a bit through the smoked glass panels on either side of the office door.

What I saw at first relaxed me—my mother, arms outstretched, pleading for me. Until I realized she wasn't pleading at all, but showing the Principal the black and blue marks I'd left in my angry pounding of her the evening before. This was a bad sign-indicative as it was of a truly bad l child, one who would beat his own mother. I felt even more alienated and alone.

I don't know how it was in your elementary school, but in mine the Vice-Principal ran the show. Mrs. Strang was a woman in her mid-fifties, with the build of a drill sergeant, the straight, iron-gray hair of a Mother Superior, and the eagle eyes of a factory inspector. Despite her girth, she had the energy of a woman half her age, and was all over the school building and grounds, appearing when you least expected her, and always to point out something wrong or to haul off some misbehaving child. She'd been known to pounce on and slap sixth grade boys her size, and to be able to control obstreperous assemblies with a single word. She was a terror; probably had served as a prison warden before getting a job with the Board of Education; and we all feared her, with good reason.

But if this bold, interfering middle-aged woman was a known terror, the Principal was a distant, and thus utterly unfathomable one. Mrs. Thomas was in her late sixties, perhaps even in her seventies, a tall, straight, regal woman, slender even in the near-shapeless pale-hued neck to ankle dresses she favored, with a tiny head partly hidden beneath an enormous powder-puff of flyaway white hair.

Her walk—the few times we students ever saw her—was regal, slow, sometimes aided by a thin ferrule. Her voice was quavering but her speech was clear and her words were precise as a paper cut. She always wore a sort of key ring on a very long leather thong invisibly attached in some cunning manner to her beltless dresses. The keys looked dangerous, as though they were used to lock children into airless dungeons. I'd seen Mrs. Thomas only a half-dozen times in my school life, never spoken to her or been noticed by her, and considered her beyond the merely human.

I was naturally nervous when her office door opened and my mother signaled me into the room. Even more anxious, when my mother left the room and closed the door behind her. I'm certain I trembled.

"Come closer," Mrs. Thomas said. "Don't be afraid."

I walked around to her desk as instructed and she immediately took both my hands in a close but not tight grasp. Her face was very old, and I remember thinking almost pretty. Her eyes were pale gray and seemed kind. Her nose was tiny, even a bit pert. Her cheeks and the skin around; her eyes and unlipsticked mouth were furrowed.

"I do not like to think that any child in this school is unhappy," she began. I didn't respond. "Are you happy here?"

I shook my head no. Then considered a bit and said, "I have been happy here. When my teachers . . ." I weighed my words, "When my teachers liked me. Mrs. Holden, Mrs. Mazey . . ."

"Yes, but that was earlier grades. You're in the fifth grade now."

"Are you going to send me to reform school?"

"Do you want to go to reform school?" she asked.

I shook my head, no.

"You must pay for the damage to the windows."

"I will."

"And you must do something good for the school, too. Do you like gardens?"

I said I'd never thought of gardens before.

"We have a garden group here. I want you to become part of that group and help beautify our school."

I said I would like that. Her conversation was so elliptical that I wasn't certain what else had been decided.

"Mr. Hargrave told me he's never had a more badly behaved student than you."

I set my lips together, determined not to speak.

"Your mother tells me you don't want to be in his class."

Grimly determined not to speak now: even if I were tortured.

"Well, he doesn't want you in his class either."

Which was fine by me.

"Do you want another chance?" she asked. When I still didn't respond, she said, "If we put you into another fifth grade class, you'll have to behave all the time."

Relief of a sort. But whose class? Mrs. Dennis was reputed to like girls far more than boys, and Miss Witter's students were said to be somewhat backward.

"An incident of this seriousness will be a blot on your school record," Mrs. Thomas added. "But you may make it up by good behavior and hard work for the next year and a half."

Now I said, "Yes, Ma'am."

"All your previous teachers thought you quite intelligent and capable. Perhaps you were bored? Perhaps you found the work in Mr. Hargrave's class a little too easy?"

I didn't know how to answer that.

"Mrs. Campanella has had experience with high-strung children. You know that you are a nervous, high-strung boy."

It was the first I'd heard of it, but I said nothing.

"It says so on all your records," Mrs. Thomas explained,

pointing to a batch of rectangular yellowish cards on her desk. "And *very* intelligent. All that in my opinion is the sign of a boy who could make a real mark on the world some day. Many talented people have had troubled childhoods, you know."

I'd never in my life been spoken to like this and it made me curious about exactly what kind of future I would have.

"Do you possess any special talents?" Mrs. Thomas asked.

"I like to paint and draw," I said, wondering if that was what she meant.

"And you're quite good at it, too. Would you like to grow up to be an artist?" She asked, and now I'd lost most of my nervousness.

"Yes Ma'am. Very much."

"You know that artists often have the most difficult lives of all. And the most rewarding. My brother was an artist. He's long dead. But there is glory to be had in art," she went on, "even an immortal name to be made." Stars swam in front of me at her words. "But first, you must get through school. First you must be as good as the ordinary, so that later on you can be better than ordinary. You must achieve high grades and the best behavior record. Then you will be able to go to a high school especially for artists."

"I'd like that."

"I'm going to place you in Mrs. Campanella's class. Five-one. You'll have to work hard. Those are the best students in the grade.

I tried to recall who Mrs. Campanella was. Of course, her name was easy enough to remember; it was the same as the famous Dodger catcher. Wasn't she a small, plump, bustling woman with a classroom on the opposite end of the U of the school building from where Hargrave's room was? I'd never heard anything bad-or good either, for that matter? about her.

"Thank you for giving me another chance," I said. Mrs. Thomas let go of my hands and I stepped back. "Is that all?" I asked.

"Unless you want to kiss me to thank me for my trouble."

I did kiss her, on her dried up old rouged cheek, my face enclosed in the fine wispiness of her abundant white hair. Oddly, she didn't smell like an old lady, as I'd expected. She hardly possessed any fragrance at all.

She pried me away gently. "Go now."

As I reached the office door, she added softly, "Don't forget the garden club. It meets on Saturday afternoons at twelve noon."

In the outer office, my mother was talking to Mrs. Strang. They stopped when they noticed me. My mother asked if my talk with the Principal had gone well and I said, yes. I also said that I was to go to Mrs. Campanella's class and that Mrs. Thomas had asked me t join the garden club, and that I thought Mrs. Thomas was the best school principal in the world. Then the previously nasty, mean Mrs. Strang turned out to be as nice as she could be. She had collected my textbooks and notebooks from Mr. Hargrave and gave me some to carry and carried the rest. I kissed my mother goodbye, and she was relieved. Then Mrs. Strang took my hand and walked me up two flights of stairs to the fourth floor, explaining some of the scenes depicted on the murals.

Although she was initially wary of me, Mrs. Campanella didn't treat me any differently than any of her other students, all of whom she liked, and she helped open me up as a student, an artist, and gardener (she was the faculty head of the garden group) in those remaining months of the fifth grade. She promoted me to six-one the following year, which she ended up teaching; and under her care and teaching I blossomed into a near-perfect student: a state that would continue through high school.

I only saw Mr. Hargrave once more close up (rather than the many times I saw him at a distance across the schoolyard at recess or in the auditorium at assembly). It was a year later when I was a trusted member of the school's honor guard, holding one of the four flags (school, city, state and country) the day before Veteran's Day as our group went around to each class room in the building where one boy read a statement, and everyone saluted the flag.

Susan Flaherty was there too, at the desk directly in front of Mr. Hargrave, a site reserved for his favorite student each year. When she raised her left hand, to salute I could see through her pink fluffy sweater how much her breasts had developed in less than a year.

Hargrave seemed relaxed in the early summer weather, his shirt top button undone, his tie slightly loosened, his suit jacket off until we stood at attention, when he put it on. He took it off again when we left the room. I don't think he recognized me. Susan Flaherty didn't look my way once or in any way give a hint that she knew me.

A Valentine

WHEN FRIENDS TELL of their elaborate vacation plans I'm often shocked to a rare speechlessness. One will be rubber rafting for a week down the Colorado River with two companions, hiking equipment, mountain scaling tools, and schemes for endless strenuous activity. Another plans to ski across Alberta for six days, with nightly stop-offs at small cabins listed on unreliable, out-of-date guidebooks. A third has a program for an archaeological dig two weeks long, four hundred miles outside Cuzco. Part of the fun, he claims, will be getting to the tropical jungle where he plans to search for ruins.

My idea of a vacation is quite different. I long for a soft bed, temperate weather, one beach and one Olympic-sized swimming pool within a five minute's leisurely stroll. Food should be abundant, excellent, easily prepared, or better yet prepared by someone else. The latest books, magazines and recorded music ought to be within fingertip's reach when I awaken from my third spontaneous nap of the day. Entertainment—a disco, a bar, a cinema—should be nearby and of high caliber. Attractive, well—dressed, charming members of at least three sexes ought to be plentiful. I'll restrict my activities to swimming, snorkeling, dancing, shopping, dining out, fucking, and taking long slow patrols along surf lines and country lanes. Many such resorts exist and I can't understand why a human being of my acquaintance would pass his or her well-earned rest from employment in any other manner.

I recently attempted to analyze how this ideal vacation developed in me and I arrived at a startling conclusion: it derives from my childhood, between the ages of ten and fourteen years old, from those days in which I was home ill from school. Since then I've grown too driven to spend more than a day in bed for even the severest flu, the wildest infection. Following minor surgery a few years back I grew so antsy in the hospital, I roamed around the building, I.V. tubes dangling from a portable metal rack, until I found my doctor and persuaded him to let me sign myself out, two days before he wanted to let me go. That evening I attended the Black Party at the Flamingo, and while I couldn't do more than sit and watch the goings-on, I felt where I belonged—and doing something. In those earlier days, a cold, a virus, an infection served as an excuse to take a vacation from the difficult pre- and early-adolescent strains of school, friends, and family: occasions which set the tone for the future.

Like many people who have unexpectedly arrived at the ripe age of forty while others around me have succumbed to auto accidents, strokes, heart attacks and bizarre cancers, I was only a moderately healthy child. Not that any terrifically dangerous illness came my way. Not at all. Yet throughout my youth I was assailed by an astounding variety of weird diseases which never seemed to alight on anyone else and which invariably sent my doctor hunting through medical texts, sometimes merely to find a name for the condition.

I've already mentioned the still unexplained glandular disorder of my infancy. This was followed by a period of good health, punctuated here and there with typical childhood setbacks—measles, mumps, colds. But around the age of ten my weight once more began to rapidly alter, no doubt fruit of my earlier metabolic problem. I'd be underweight two years at a time, then suddenly overweight for another two years, then underweight again. All this, despite little change in my eating habits or my activity level. I began to develop strange allergies—to strawberries, my favorite fruit; to tomatoes; one year to honey, the next to white bread. These allergies are now gone—but I still haven't lost the instant ability to become allergic to unexpected foods: a cup of miso soup might do me in for a week, a papaya may suddenly prove near lethal. Such occurrences are rare now, when I was a child they seemed every day. One afternoon in class at the end of one school year my upper lip began to swell. By the time I'd arrived home it was twice its normal size. My mother searched in vain for the telltale red dot of an insect's bite. That night as I slept, the lip continued to grow, and grow and grow. I had visions of it so large it would extend over my mouth like an ungainly pink flap I would have to hold open to eat or speak. Other than this, I felt fine: no fever, no other symptoms. After a week, during which I remained at home, mostly alone in my bedroom wondering what I had done to deserve such an eerie fate, watching other, luckier children play outside in the lovely June weather, my lip began to shrink back to normal. It was never outsized again, and no doctor then or since has ever been able to tell me why it happened.

For a child to be mildly ill is a wonderful time. You doze on and off all day in your bed, which you only get out of to have the sheets changed or to go to the bathroom or to be quickly sponge-bathed and have your pajamas changed. Your bed becomes a world—the limits of your touchable universe. All is placed within hand's reach: medicines, fruit juices, tissues and handkerchief, reading matter, crayons and paper, notebooks, toys, sometimes a radio or nowadays a portable television with its remote control panel. The curtains are kept half-closed; the door to your room only left two inches ajar, so little noise will awaken you if you're sleeping; yet so your call downstairs to your mother can be heard clearly. You lie surrounded by plumped up pillows and an expanse of blanket and quilted comforter whose patterns madly danced during your fever dreams, but which now become—with a bit of work—whole mountain ranges and valleys for your attacking armies of pencils and erasers, your defending garrison of picture books surmounted by a box of tissues. If you're bored, you can clear the bed, flatten out the humps and have an endless ecru plain in front of you, broken only by your lower body and legs, flat spots to form temporary little seats for your mother as she kisses your forehead checking for fever; for your siblings and friends to gingerly perch upon as they quietly say hello, they can only stay for a minute but they wanted to bring you: 1) A giant get-well card signed by your classmates. 2) Copies of *Forum* or *Scholastic* and *Popular Mechanics*, your favorite magazines at age twelve. 3) A prized doll whose healing powers your sister swears by, which she leaves nearby. 4) A new toy truck your younger brother received as a birthday gift and wouldn't let you touch for months, which he now guiltily lays at your side explaining all its intricate working parts, embarrassed by his concern. 5) The beloved person of your new friend whom your other, closer, friends have persuaded to visit, even though you wouldn't have asked him yourself, your relationship being too fragile to withstand such a demand—and who proves to be as handsome and winning under these conditions as you suspected.

    In the middle of the sixth grade, with Mrs. Campanella once more my teacher, the horrors of Mr. Hargrave and the fifth grade almost forgotten, the three Flaherty sisters all but invisible, I developed an odd, tenacious little stomach virus which laid me up more than a week—and all the above happened. The new friend was Ricky Hersch, who lived a block and a half away. His cousin Gregory had persuaded Ricky to come see me. Ricky brought but one item besides his slim dark grace, his silver-green eyes and comic book princeling face—a flat, folio-sized book about fighter airplanes. Both of us were embarrassed by the situation. Even though I'd had my mother brush my hair and had cleared my bed of its five-day accumulated debris, I felt I looked my worst. He of course felt like a young hero for having given in to his usually unprepossessing cousin's demands.

Far from being afraid of catching whatever I had, Ricky assured me he would even sleep in my bed with me (oh joy!) to prove it—a test I didn't have the nerve to accept.

Instead I watched as he flipped open the big rectangular folio and talked about German Fokkers and Messerschmidts, Japanese Zeroes, British Hornets and other wonderful looking single and two-seater airplanes painted navy and silver or gray and red or yellow and green, like giant dragonflies—though far deadlier. He also invited me, when I was well again, to visit his bedroom, until then forbidden to me, where he would show me his score or more of hand-built models of the airplanes in the book.

With the cunning of a lover I was clever enough to ask Ricky scads of spontaneous questions, not about him and his life (which I desperately wanted to know) but about the firing power of the B-17, the true durability of the flimsy-looking pontoons on the battle-modified China Clipper. So successful was I that when Ricky took my hand to say goodbye, to hope I'd be well enough to see him the following weekend and to admit "you're okay, after all," we both knew it was as close to an admission of mutual passion as boys our age could possibly make.

Left alone, I looked though the book he'd left and soon actually became interested in the planes. I'd been in one airplane already, a Cessna six-seater on a short flight with my father. Ricky had flown five times he told me, once on a large passenger plane from Washington, D.C. back to New York. I could picture Ricky and I high in the clouds in the double cockpit of a Zero bomber (my favorite I decided from its bright colors and svelte lines) that we'd stolen from the enemy, diving and strafing the bad guys. I daydreamed and dozed until dinner time when I was awakened to homemade cream of mushroom soup and pumpernickel bread decorated with melting flowerets of butter, and later, when I'd eaten that (slowly: I ate, moved, thought slowly when ill), a mug of milky sweet tea and a translucent china bowl half-filled with butterscotch pudding. 1 read, listening—or thinking I was listening—to the sound of the television set downstairs, where my brothers and sister were splayed out on the carpet, partly watching *My Little Margie* and *I Married Joan* and partly doing their homework. After my father came home from work and made his obligatory, tender bedside visit, I dozed again, never fully falling asleep until long after all of my family were in their bedrooms, tucked in for the night. As though by being ill, I had somehow become guardian of the upstairs of the house, an area unused by us children during our normal days except to change our clothing.

Anyone who has lived in a large house must know what I mean. Those who have grown up in small apartments and cottages may not. There is something in an oversized, underused house that produces almost a presence. Animals sense it almost upon entering; whether it has been lived in constantly and is thus filled with many distracting odors or if it has been abandoned for decades, in which case another, muskier, drier, older, fainter presence pervades. Children also sense it. What accounts for it? Large masses of unmoved air in corridors and rooms? Air risen to the ceiling with nowhere else to go? Or something else?

Our house in the suburbs of New York, though newly

built and first occupied by us, had its stranger aspects, and it was from these that we, and especially we children, required the protection of someone upstairs ill; temporarily aligned with those oddnesses and so able to disarm them for us. Chief among the experiences and never really settled by the time we moved years later, was my father's clothes closet. This had a trapdoor which opened to the roof. It was so high that even my father needed a chair to reach up and unlatch the door, but we children were in mortal terror of going into the closet. Only a mile and a half away from Creedmor State Hospital for the Insane, and we were certain that homicidal psychopaths escaped there with regularity, scaling the steep sloping roofs of houses like ours to crawl into hatches and clamber down into the very closets we would be asked to fetch clothes hangars from on dark nights when our mother was out of earshot, two floors below at her iron mangle watching Jack Benny or *Your Show of Shows* on television, oblivious to our screams as we were torn limb from limb.

A more mundane if equally baffling mystery surrounded the lock on our bedroom door. When we moved into this house, my older brother and I were given the large front bedroom, my sister a smaller nearby bedroom, while my infant brother was placed in a dressing room adjacent to my parent's bedroom. After some reconstruction more rooms were added upstairs as well as down: an upstairs playroom and another small bedroom. Somehow, during the construction work the floors on one side of the second floor were thrown into a slight although distinct angle. As a result the doors to the two larger, north—facing bedrooms slammed shut whenever they were left open. In addition to this, the mechanism of my and my brother's bedroom door somehow or other developed another malfunction, one we were never able to totally correct all the remaining years we lived there, although dozens of stopgap methods were attempted. There were two door—to-jamb mechanisms: a push-in latch and a lock latch. The latter would suddenly lock and could not be opened by turning the doorknob even though this was supposed to be the way to unlock it.

We would rush home from school, run upstairs, change into play clothing, and turn to find the doorstep knocked over, the electrical tape over the lock mysteriously missing, and see, hear, groaningly feel the door slam closed—and locked. The only remedy we ever devised was to insert the blade of a butter knife and somehow jiggle the lock open again. Why only this edge and no other would do, we never found out. Worse, even with a butter knife the door could only be opened from the inside of the room. If for some reason the butter knife wasn't in its usual spot on the dresser top (my mother unthinkingly brought it downstairs, someone used it instead of a shoehorn and bent it) we would have to stamp on the floor and shout for help, have someone lean out of my sister's bedroom window with the blade in hand, as we leaned far out of one of our windows to reach it, and following anywhere from a few minutes to half hour of finessing the knife blade, the lock would suddenly snap open.

We would tape it over doubly thick, fit sticks, nails, matchbooks to jam the lock mechanism. It always came untaped, unjammed, ready to lock us in mysteriously. We left doorstops of various sizes and shapes nearby; they always managed to be kicked out of place, under the bureau or a bed at the crucial moment when the lock became unstuck.

Who could doubt that some malicious spirit ruled this doorway? We didn't. We respected its ability to suddenly stop us from errands and play alike with neither rhyme nor reason——and through its enigmatic operation, its inexorability in our lives, we became a little more attuned to the motiveless madness, the absurdity that nowadays seems to rule everyone's life.

At the time, of course, it was an exception; all accidents and extraordinary events were. The everyday course of life went on with a placid ordinary inevitability that I now understand was merely transitional, utterly dominating and credible as it seemed then. If, once I'd settled into the sixth grade, I never longed for the horrifying excitements of my long guerilla warfare against Mr. Hargrave, neither did I yearn for the lubricious afternoons after school two houses away with my fingers thrust deep into the small, odorless vaginas of the Flaherty sisters. Sexuality had been new and different—like one of the half-dozen new flavors of ice cream our local Howard Johnson introduced that year: blueberry, peachwhip, fudge ripple, butterscotch, and almond—and in the long run, I assumed, as important. Summer arrived, almost ended, and we went away until late August to a North Shore mansion with undiscoverable secret passages. When we returned home I retained the same classroom as the year before, the same teacher (we were all pleased that plump, enlightened Mrs. Campanella had been "promoted" with us), a few new students in our class, and the magic of a hand-me—down Schwinn bicycle from a friend of my parents. It was to become the focus of my waking and dreaming life.

The September of my twelfth year began almost indistinguishable from late August, and it must have been the longest gentlest Autumn I ever lived through. In terms of precipitation and temperature it was utterly serene. By late October, we were shocked when our mothers insisted that we button up our light Windbreakers for post-dinner street games and bicycle rides. By Thanksgiving, we still hadn't had frost; the next week we had a fleeting cold snap, followed by five weeks of Indian Summer. The huge oaks, elms, maples, English planes and hickory trees changed colors one species at a time, then softly wafted their stunning palette of hues onto still green lawns, still un-iced sidewalks and roads unpitted by snow salt. Late afternoons and lingering warm evenings, hundreds of teenaged boys could be counted in a fifteen-minute circuit of our neighborhood, each raking deep red, pale orange, golden green, gleaming brown leaves into almost purely tinted cones on the curbside strips of grass that abutted the street, to be collected later, hauled off or burned in fragrant, thin-smoked fires. Every morning to, and every afternoon from school, Gregory and Martin and James Kallas and I would wade through color after Autumn color of leaf mounds, one side of the street per day, the four of us reduced to three as our path neared first Martin's house, then to two as we veered past Gregory's house, until James and I reached my corner, and separated.

We were never a real quartet of friends. An alliance of sorts had been formed between James Kallas and I in the second grade. My friendship with meek, wide-eyed Gregory Taylor had begun and never really ended in my aborted fifth grade class with Mr. Hargrave. Martin O'Connor had been in Mrs. Campanella's fifth grade class when I entered after the Hargrave debacle.

If all three were my friends, they weren't necessarily each other's best or even second-best friend. Gregory was pretty much under the influence of his family, a large one filled with brothers, cousins, and sisters. Martin's buddy was Richard, a goggle-eyed, crew-cut boy I found both unattractive and vulgar. James was from a newly émigré Greek family which had left Cyprus during the Partition: my mother befriended his mother and learned all sorts of wonderful recipes from her lemon-egg soup, stuffed grape leaves, braised lamb and flaky, honeysweet pastries. James was the most uprooted in his family. He was meant to be a shepherd or farmer, and the wild eccentricities of his new country and its inhabitants continually floored him. "Can you beat that!" he would exclaim whether he was facing a barbecued hot-dog or the forty-foot tall mutant ants of *Them*, that year's horror film.

We four boys were loosely bound together by shared interests—ourselves, primarily. Even timid Gregory possessed at least one special talent, which made each of us individual, valuable among the great wash of boys our age. We also shared a certain adventurous spirit which combined with the ecstatic new mobility of bicycles allowed us to explore the expanding world around us. I never told my parents that one Saturday afternoon, when we were twelve years old, that the four of us bicycled out to Huntington and back, a trip of fifty miles. We never told my siblings how well known we four friends were to boys two and three neighborhoods away, in Belaire and Douglaston, as we rode around light as air looking for stickball games to win, boys to fight or befriend, small gaggles of girls to jeer at or assault—four bikes can cause instant havoc in the largest of girl's groups around a jump rope. Every park, schoolyard, empty lot and soda shop in a ten-mile radius was our domain. We ruled it indifferently, not with the Hun-like rapacity of Junior Cook's gang, five blocks away, but with curiosity and a superiority born of our special qualities.

We would alight at some stickball match in Cambria Heights and not seem in any way extraordinary. Gregory and James Kallas were short; only Martin was tall. The only physical specialty among us, at first, belonged to James Kallas. He was so dark he looked almost Turkish, and he still spoke with a thick Mediterranean accent that other children made fun of—until he stood on home plate and belted out home run after home run with an unvarying, almost mechanical skill until every Spaulding among a dozen boys had been batted out of reach up into second and third story rain gutters or deeply nestled inside high telephone wires.

Gregory's talent was quieter—most of the time. He was

a naturalist at ten, a chemist at eleven, a physicist at twelve years old. "Want to see something interesting?" he would modestly announce and we would follow him to an isolated section of Alley Pond Park where he would set off homemade depth charges in the water that sent eruptions of willow, mud and a few old fish exploding into the air. Or he'd calmly put together different colored powders into an oaken tube he'd fashioned, tamp it down, point it, light the fuse and blast a large rock face to smithereens. His sulfur bombs were the best in the county, perfect for tossing at small groups of Junior Cook's gang (although never at Junior Cook himself) if we spotted them on foot or at rest. And Gregory's dog turds wrapped in tin foil with a phosphorus fire package on top were great hits every Halloween. We would hide in the bushes across the street and watch some hapless person respond to a rung doorbell, observe them spot the fire in their doorway, see them stamp it out and come up with a shoe, sneaker, slipper full of shit. Thanks to Gregory.

Martin's talent was his knowledge. He had perhaps the greatest capacity of apparently trivial information of any child or adult I've ever met: and unlike the usual idiot savant, Martin possessed the connections too. If you entered a datum and demanded an answer in a specific area, Martin would come up with it. He was as smart as Robbie the Robot in Forbidden Planet and always offered all sorts of useful extra information. He was the navigator of all our longer bike trips, the map, guide, and Cicerone. We would say, "All right, Martin, PS. 109 in Hollis" and he would tell us the building's address and layout, the size and shape of the schoolyard, who would most likely be there at what times, and he would throw in whose brother or sister among our acquaintance attended the Junior High School. Or we might wonder whether to go to a movie on a rainy Sunday afternoon, and Martin would know what features, cartoons, episodes of Flash Gordon and Tarzan, even which trailers were showing, and their times at all six movie theaters within bicycling distance. He also gave us his opinion of the programs and of the quality of the popcorn sold—both for eating and for throwing at the movie screen from the highest balcony. Martin solved sports statistics questions with a barrage of information that floored other kids. Not only would he tell who won the World's Series in 1953, but in how many games, and which team won which games; and would also tell us Duke Snyder's and Phil Rizzuto's batting averages for those games, as well as their averages broken down season by season in relation to the other player's highs, lows and the league averages for those years.

Among this group of whizzes, my own abilities were less obvious. I was the social glue among them, of course, and initiator of all actions and reactions as a group. I was the plan-maker, the friendliest and most adept at meeting new people and so the spokesperson. I possessed but one physical talent—speed. On foot, on roller skates, on ice skates and especially on a bicycle, I was fast! I could start a fight with a much bigger boy, circle him, throw a surprise punch, and get out of harm's way. By the tune he got up off the ground I was two blocks away.

Then I began to fiddle with the primitive sprocket gears of my bike and with the chain and brakes. I saved up my allowance and bought narrow, silken-smooth Michelin tires in place of the slow, safe balloon ones that had come with the Schwinn, so that my appearances and disappearances became swift, unpredictable. I was the scout on our longer trips. the distraction who would weave in and out of rival boy's bikes until my slower friends (especially James on his beat-up old machine) were out of danger. Within a year of getting the Schwinn, thanks to my adaptations and mechanical experiments—fruit of my intense reading of magazines and books about European racing bikes and the French Grand Tour—I was the champion racer of my area. Boys from miles away biked over after school or on weekends to challenge me. All but one rode back clearly defeated.

One would think that a quartet this well-fitted for preadolescent life would last forever, and it's true that we remained friends until Junior High and even beyond. It helped that we were good students, smart, freedom loving, not known as troublemakers and so free from parent's pressure to disband. That was until I met Ricky Hersch and all ordinary interests—friends, school, family, hobbies—became tinged with, then dominated by, and finally completely absorbed within the passion he introduced into my life.

It would take several months for me to recognize how much out relationship caused me to lose, to miss, cumulating on St. Valentine's Day; and then only when I could no longer avoid seeing the truth. His effect on me would last decades longer. Only a few years ago, when I unexpectedly saw an ex-lover of mine (the "love of my life") at a *vernissage* did I realize that. He was standing against a wall, and had turned into profile—the greatest profile in New York I always thought, right off the cover of that matchbook portraying a bearded cowboy that read, "Draw me and you too can become an artist." And I thought to myself, Lord if that doesn't look like Ricky Hersch. Only when he turned toward me, noticed me, and his face softened with recognition did the time warp slam shut and whom he actually was shift into place. Even then, as we talked, I kept thinking how precisely he resembled what Ricky Hersch would look like grown to twenty—four years old, and the previously inexplicable attraction, the intense sexuality we had experienced together was somewhat explained.

I'd be lying to say I recall when Ricky Hersch first appeared in my life. Undoubtedly he was in the background for some time, as I was in his periphery for years, as he was part of the large Taylor clan which seemed to fill every available room of the rambling house where my friend Gregory lived. We met not cute but hostile. I remember it well because it was the occasion of one of Gregory's experiments—one designed weeks before to solve a problem on the extensive, mostly wild Taylor property: field mice.

The three-story rickety house was one of the first erected in that section of our suburb. Martin claimed it had been built in the eighteenth century when it was known as the Gossage Farm, but the original edifice must have been torn or burned down and had been replaced by a mid-nineteenth century structure. It was painted an off-shade of green during those years (Russian Green in fact, though no one knew that at the time) with pebbled gray slate on its scores of roofs and dormers. Built off the ground upon a fieldstone foundation only partly hidden by a cement coating, the house possessed a half-dozen porches and out buildings which during the Twenties and Thirties had been attached and appropriated as sewing rooms, laundries, pantries and extra bedrooms as the Taylor family grew. The Hersches had come to live there at the death of Ricky's father in the Korean War, after he'd sired a "baseball team" (my father's term). Ricky was the eighth, considered the baby.

This old house would have been a remarkable eyesore in the neighborhood if it weren't situated rather far back from the street and if it hadn't been pretty well covered by a small stand of obscuring hickory trees—grown enormous by the time I was a child. Further hiding the ramshackle main house was a concord grape arbor of some size and yield (and beauty when in full leaf and fruit, from August to October) attached to a trellised-over garage extension; and even more extraordinary, two dozen of the largest, hardiest and most colorful azalea and hydrangeas in the area (blue heads of flowers the size of a tricycle wheel)—the envy of my mother and other gardening hobbyists. Deeper within the acre of Taylor property other botanical splendors abutted scenes of utter dilapidation: a lilac tree that had drifted up into the telephone wires suspended enormous flotillas of perfumed purple blooms that shaded the Taylor's unsavory pet graveyard; the backyard compost heap once declared a public menace gave onto three Comice pear saplings which almost curtseyed by October they were so heavy with large luscious yellow fruit.

Naturally in such a disorganized place field mice would set up nests, construct warrens, thrive. There seemed to be a sufficient abundance of fruit, garden vegetables and flowers for Taylors, Hersches, and field mice to coexist peacefully together. Then there was Gregory's aged grandmother who hadn't stepped out of the house, or in fact beyond the backyard veranda, in five years since the day she had stepped directly onto the body of a particularly plump field mouse which she had instantly killed and which had sent her spinning back into the house, screaming. Mr. Taylor and the older Taylor and Hersch boys had declared war on the helpless animals with varying results. Poisons and traps in an incredible variety of sizes and methods of mutilation were laid down monthly with little or no effectiveness. The field mouse population continued to thrive.

All this was nonsense to Gregory. He and his friends had nothing against the small gray-brown creatures. To us, their fugitive existence was simply another allure of the Taylor property as a play area. The yard was filled with children no matter the time of year—although it was most enticing in summer when it was most alive with toads, turtles, the numerous Taylor cats and Hersch puppies. It was also the coolest spot in the neighborhood because of all the shade trees. But, tolerant as Gregory was, he was foremost a scientist, so, for a period of six months those few field mice still alive in the traps were carefully killed, preserved and dissected until he knew every capillary and nerve ending. Later on, once he discovered the properties of what he called "Greek Fire" (i.e., the diesel fuel kept in barrels behind the garage for use in the mostly inoperable pickup truck Mr. Taylor owned), he decided on a more elaborate enterprise: the mass extinction of all the mice.

His plan had the elegance of a fine scientific experiment and the spectacle of a Cecil B. DeMille epic. He proposed digging tiny ditches connecting all the areas on the property where mice had been seen or their warren holes suspected of being. These ditches were to be filled with Gregory's potential fire and set alight. He enlisted our help in the scheme and we readily agreed. It was one of those long Autumn weekends with nothing more inviting to hold our attention and we all looked forward to seeing come true his vision of ringing the yards with a sizzling mouse-toasting fire that would last fifteen minutes at the most and be otherwise unperilous. Gregory had verbally pictured the plan to us in images so sensational they dwarfed the Dresden firebomb photos his shell-shocked uncle Joe from upstate New York had once shown us.

It was a hazy afternoon promising a shower by sunset, when we were all ready. The small central ditch in front of us was filled with diesel fuel and the surrounding ditches were sprinkled with it. We'd already been given a test display, seen how the fire charged along a narrow slot of ground gathering force until it intensified into a powerful beam of destruction that could enter a pinhole opening in a mouse warren and explode it with a soft, fleshy burst of sound, scattering dirt and decimated rodents. We were excited by the prospect of running alongside the ditches watching as one after another of the mouse communities—hated now because slated for death—exploded. Ricky

Hersch biked into the yard right onto a ditch and rocked the front wheel, collapsing the carefully constructed earth battlement.

Gregory all but collapsed with the sudden frustration of his grand plan for extinction by his cousin's unthinking *deux ex machina*. Martin, James Kallas, myself, Billy and Andy Taylor and even Cal Hersch, Ricky's old brother jumped up from where we had hunkered down awaiting the conflagration and began shouting for Ricky to "get off there, stupid!" Which Ricky refused to do. When we ran up to him and attempted to explain what we were trying to accomplish, it was obvious from the sneer on his perfectly modeled lips, the disdain in his pale green eyes, the toss of his long mahogany hair that he knew very well what was going on and why. And though he didn't give a damn about the mice—he scarcely gave a damn about his family, Gregory more than once had told me—it amused him to see his cousin's scheme so easily ruined. "It won't work anyway," he said.

That meant to me that Ricky wanted to humiliate his cousin—and my good friend Gregory—yet again. Enraged, I pushed through the group, shoved Ricky off his bike, and commanded the others to rebuild the ditch so the experiment could continue.

I didn't see but I certainly felt the punch Ricky landed on my back when I turned to help them, a punch aimed at my kidney. I fell onto the ground, but managed to grab one of Ricky's legs, bringing him down too. Soon the field mouse holocaust was forgotten by all as he and I began to punch, wrestle, slug, slap each other with the cold ferocity of grown-ups who've hated each other for decades. Feeble attempts by the other boys to stop us gave way to cheers and shouts. Soon kids from nearby yards and streets ran to watch us knock each other down, get up again, then knock each other down again, moving clear around the property until we were at the front of the house. There, just under the third-story window, we continued, until Ricky's mother, who'd been washing windows, broke us up by emptying a pail of soapy water on top of our heads.

Wet, groggy, black and blue, bleeding, surrounded by friends and protectors, I staggered to my feet to see Ricky do the same, ready to square off again, although it was clear that neither of us would be able to throw a punch if we tried. I hoarsely shouted, "And if I hear you're ever bothering Gregory again, I'll annihilate you!" By then Mrs. Hersch and two of Ricky's older sisters had come downstairs and were trying to hustle him into the house. Ricky was still able to stand his ground for another minute to yell back, "And I'll decapitate you if you try," before he was pulled up the back porch steps and inside.

Right then I knew I'd won our fight with a word—a word I'd heard in one of those by now forgotten Grade-B Sci-Fi films I'd recently seen—a word better than Ricky's word, more unusual, more appropriate, possessing that magical sense that words still hold for children as they do [or primitive tribesmen.

I remained at the Taylor's long enough that afternoon to watch Gregory's experiment succeed. Then James Kallas took me to his house, where his Aunt Damita (who didn't speak English) salved and bandaged the worst and most obvious of my wounds and bruises so that when I finally got home my mother could easily recognize that I was out of mortal danger, and so yell and threaten me with a week of staying in my room (which she soon forgot) with only half the passion she would have expended if I were truly hurt.

A week later, as the temporarily retightened quartet walked home from school, I asked Gregory if his cousin had bothered him any more. He said no. Then added, "But he wants to race you." Before I could say I would race him any time, Gregory added darkly, "through the underground road of the new shopping mall."

This was a real challenge and it was obvious that Ricky wanted revenge for my good word which had defeated him. Hillside Mall was a partly-finished edifice built on what had been a series of abandoned lots, which when completed—some said it would take another two years would be the largest shopping mall on Long Island. The central core of buildings was almost a mile long and all deliveries were to be made through a road that ran beneath the mall, directly to scores of storage basements. The entire area was fenced off, forbidden. We'd bicycled around it dozens of times and knew there was only one weekend watchman. While he had a formidable reputation, he couldn't be all over the site at the same time.

We were most attracted by the long sloping tunnels which dipped into darkness at each end of the mall. Junior Cook and his henchman Mike Bayley were the only kids we knew who'd ever biked into that tunnel and they reported that it was long, straight, dark as pitch, except for small ceiling-hung lights every few hundred feet. In their recitations, long after the experience, awe and a sense of danger overcome by the slimmest margin was apparent. If fourteen year old toughs felt that way, you can imagine how we would feel. And that was to be the location of the bike race between me and Ricky Hersch! Naturally, I told Gregory I'd take up his cousin's dare, and my friends began to discuss what kind of flowers to place on my grave. But I didn't set a date for the meeting and almost a month went by before Ricky did, which built up my confidence. It could only mean one thing: Ricky was as afraid of the race and location as I.

During that month the impending race was all but forgotten in our settling into the sixth grade. Three years before, our public school had been stripped of its seventh and eighth grade classes as the city's Board of Education finally moved into the second half of the twentieth century. Gone were the old eight grades of elementary school, from kindergarten toddlers to fifteen and sixteen-year-old seniors able to drive to school.

Instead, intermediate schools between elementary education and high school were devised to carry the three wildest, orneriest and—in many cases—sexiest years of transition. This left twelve—year—olds as seniors in our school. From being freewheeling, thoughtless kids, we were suddenly thrust into positions of authority and responsibility. We became the honor guard at all school functions, we were monitors in cafeterias, assemblies and school yards. We ran the audio/visual equipment that brought the various "educational" film strips (we called them strip films) and movies to lesser-grade classes. And we were suddenly being told that within a few months, all this idleness and play and ease we enjoyed (!) would end. The minute we stepped into our future Junior High Schools, we'd be on, being evaluated, guided, winnowed out for good and bad toward those elusive goals that led to specialized vocational or academic High School, and from there into the job market or on to college and the professions.

Mrs. Campanella attempted to make this difficult period as tensionless as possible, but even she could do little about the immense amounts of English grammar we'd never learned or long forgotten; nor could she brighten up the dusty three chapters per week of *The Return of the Native* and *A Tale of Two Cities* we had to plow through that year. She was ambitious for us. All of us to one degree or another, and her best students most of all. Since our class was the first—six-one out of six classes in the grade—and thus supposedly the best the school had to offer, we were the litmus paper of the entire faculty: the test by which they would be judged by other, further-along schools and faculties. To aid us in mastering all we'd supposedly already conquered and were sure to be tested on, she took a new tack that she'd learned teaching that previous summer in a progressive school in Connecticut. We were broken down into study groups of six to eight students for each subject. We shifted about during the day into different seats in the room where we gave reports, devised projects, reviewed each other, and were tested. Since this was an old public school, our desks were nailed down in rigid rows, front to back in the classroom. We couldn't group desks in circles and rectangles as she preferred. We remained at our usual desks for less than one-third of the day, when we had "general lessons." The rest of each school day we formed and reformed smaller groups. And it seemed to work. Our class tested as highly as we were supposed to by the year's end.

An unexpected benefit of this new mobility was that we came to meet, work with, and know children in our class who had been pinioned by alphabetical order four rows and five seats away. I no longer had to be friendly only to Martin O'Connor in front, Jeannette Rogers in back, with Allison Struthers on my left (Gregory Taylor behind her), and Jimmy Larchen to my right. Now I dealt with students whose last names began with A and G and Y. My old buddy Edward Young shared science and art with me now because we were more or less equally skilled and interested in these subjects. I shared social studies and math with the two nicest girls in the class, Nancy Carlson and Lynne-Anne Fribourg. Martin was also in this group along with Suzanne Friedman and Myron Goldblum.

Among us we possessed the smartest boy (Martin) and the smartest girl (Suzanne) in class, as well as the prettiest girl (Lynne-Anne) and the ugliest boy (Myron) in the grade. I always wondered if this was the kind of heterogeneity Mrs. Campanella had been looking for when she told us that such groups besides helping our studies, would also teach us "social skills," a term none of us had heard before, and which I'm still not certain I really understand. The only social changes that occurred was that Nancy became the only female (part-time) member of our four-boy gang: mostly because of her bicycling ability, her readiness to join us in our milder "daring" stunts, and the unfailingly ample pastry supplies in her mother's kitchen—our first and sometimes last stop on any biking excursion. Nancy was never my "girlfriend" as some other boys attempted to prove. Indeed, after having wallowed in nubile female flesh the year before, I hadn't even kissed a girl since, never mind intentionally touching or even addressing one—except Nancy.

If I had wanted a girl I needn't have looked any further than Lynne-Anne Fribourg. She fit my physical type to perfection—a pale beauty with small features, fjord—blue eyes, hair yellow as thread, the physical grace of a young Isadora Duncan, the fashion sense—given her limited means at twelve years old—of a movie star. Her face was as clear as pane glass. When she blushed you could see the redness quickly gather under her skin then slowly dissipate again. Her legs were long, her small breasts perfectly sized for the slightly frilled Peter Pan collar blouses or ash-mauve cotton sweaters she favored. Lynne-Anne was shy, quiet, slow to anger, intelligent, easily amused, never prudish, friendly. At rest she was immobile as a statuette, when active possessed of a steady stream of graceful energy. Humbert Humbert would have slit his wrists following a ten-minute téte a téte with Lynne-Anne; she was as completely incorruptible as she was charming.

By all the symmetry of our simple justice, Lynne-Anne belonged with Edward Young, grown taller and handsomer than ever. We selected the two of them to represent our class in special assemblies merely because they looked so well together. But Edward had sworn off girls, telling me the last time we discussed it that he wanted to remain "pure" for when he met the right one, whom of course he would marry and with whom he would live happily ever after. Meanwhile, Lynne-Anne's extracurricular life seemed to be completely woman-oriented: she was surrounded by girlfriends, sisters, female cousins and aunts. I think her father was at home at times: if so he was the only male in the Fribourg house. And while she was always cordial to Edward Young, she gave him or other boys little thought. I would sometimes catch her looking at me or at Martin (whose brightness and store of facts she admired as much as we did) with the slightly disgusted somewhat indifferent gaze of a Park Avenue matron who has come out of the Waldorf and happened upon a bum urinating against the wheel of an adjacently parked stretch-limousine.

If Lynne-Anne was physically near-perfect, then Myron Goldblum was beast to her beauty, hunchback to her Esmeralda. Undressed for gym class, his squat, powerful body was a sight to alarm even our aged teacher Mr. Brown ("Mac" to us sixth graders), who claimed to have been in a Japanese POW camp and seen comrades mutilated and beheaded daily. It was fine by Mac when Myron's gym shorts were being laundered or were lost (or more often stolen) and Myron had to wear his long pants—although the teacher wouldn't tolerate such a lapse in any other student. Myron's chest was broad and thick, like that of a middle-aged man; he had no apparent lower torso, a fact obscured by several layers of baby fat within which could be detected the intimation of a navel and the hint of genitalia thankfully not yet too developed. What we saw of Myron dressed for class was bad enough: powerful shoulders, shoulder blades so thick they budded toward the inevitability of a double hump, short thick arms with blotchy skin, nubby fingers with extra wide fingernails (yet capable of great dexterity—he once showed me the tiniest hand built crystal radio set), a neck that didn't seem there at all, a square head with tight curls the color of—Martin once decreed with his unerring accuracy—"dog shit two days after a visit to the Vet." Myron's facial features were equally hopeless: a bulbous nose, fat cheeks, the largest pair of lips that I'd seen on a Caucasian, and small, almost beady, close-set eyes the hue of someone's ready to discard suede jacket.

It would be a pleasant irony to report that Lynne-Anne was a ditz or a bitch and Myron a gentle saint. But these O'Henryesque twists are seldom credible for a good reason: a child's personality is usually closely allied to his physical self during the years of acculturation. Thus fat boys are generally sissies or slobs or bullies; skinny girls usually tomboys or manipulating tattle-tales. How can they be otherwise? That's how we expect them to be. So, Lynne-Anne, treated like a princess out of a Nordic fairy tale by father, family, friends, teachers, and at school, was sweet tempered, and Myron was a ratfink bastard, avoided by us outside of school. Naturally Lynne-Anne went out of her way to be kind to Myron, with that slightly aloof courtesy of a woman petting the calf she has just selected to be slaughtered for tomorrow's veal roast. Whereas Myron, showing equally rare forbearance, didn't once trip or "accidentally" wound Lynne-Anne as he did every other girl he came near, and was never once overheard calling her a "dimwitted broad" or "half-titted nincompoop"—his general appellations for the female gender.

These tolerances and restraints between the two, while cause for comment among us, were never viewed in any other light, and we in their group knew as little as the other twenty-four in the class of the underground currents being forged by the duo over the map of "Pieter Stuyvesant's Olde Nieuw Amsterdam" and long division problems, currents that would explode into view later on with the force of Gregory Taylor's "Greek Fire" among the field mice.

But I wouldn't have been surprised to discover that everyone else in Mrs. Campanella's sixth grade class but me knew what was going on, untrue though this was. For I had MADE A DISCOVERY sometime shortly after the fight with Ricky Hersch and this discovery was to keep me entranced and so, fairly oblivious to anything else. I had found a book that I liked. More, I had found a book that opened up a new, glorious and heroic world to me, and I read it again and again, falling more deeply inside that world, rejoicing when I discovered there was a second book almost as good by the same author. Since this had never happened before in the seven or so years that I had been reading, it was an event of some significance. You may have already guessed the identity of that first book—*The Iliad*; this is how I discovered it.

Every year we were required by school to see a dentist. This was fine with my parents who constantly tried to get us to take care of our teeth and who now had an outside excuse to step up the pressure. Earlier on it wasn't such a problem. Our teeth came and went with dreamlike regularity. But by the time we were ten or eleven years old, all the teeth we had in our mouths were what we were going to have for the rest of our lives (save those "wisdom teeth" that we were told we would "earn" later on): they had to be cared for. At about this time, my father discovered a "new" dentist. I put quotes around the adjective because while he may f have been new to us, he wasn't so to anyone else.

On or just past the age of retirement, Dr. Brichter combined an obnoxious personality, a dislike for children, and a love of his antiquated dental equipment that made visits to his office occasions of fear beforehand and regret after. His reign of terror lasted four long years. By then a dentist who lived closer, with up—to—date equipment, a penchant for dispensing painkillers and an almost maniacal adoration of young adolescents took Dr. Brichter's place. Dr. Towerbridge would feed us candy in the anteroom, inject us with Novocain in the outer office long before it was needed and in doses to make us swoon, then guide us into his Super-Duper Palace of Dental Care, where he topped it all off with a mask full of nitrous oxide he must have set on "stun." There, as we oozed in and out of consciousness, he would take care of any caries. clean our gums, caress our bodies, and occasionally, discreetly masturbate himself. None of us ever cared, should we be alert enough in those few moments of consciousness within his inner sanctum to realize what was going on. All that mattered was Dr. Towerbridge's friendly manner and the pink cloud of painlessness. It was paradise compared to Dr. Brichter's chamber of horrors, where Novocain was only administered for "big problems," i.e., never to us, and where one could count the rotations of the antediluvian drill as it buzzed in our mouths, grinding our brains to talcum powder.

The one consolation of going to Dr. Brichter was that we did it as a group and so were supposedly strong in our unity. This mattered not a whit once you were alone in his chair, prey to his more violent fantasies. Believing that to await the torture was worse than the torture itself, my brother and sister always took advantage of their seniority to make me go last. As far as I was concerned this was slightly beneficial, as Brichter would have already worked out his sadism on the others and so not bother much with me.

Since this often meant that I had to sit in Brichter's outer office for up to eighty or ninety unforgivably lost minutes each visit, I soon discovered that right downstairs from the dreaded office was a better place to wait, a small branch of the New York Public Library. Not much more than a storefront, it couldn't begin to claim to possess the row upon row of gleaming blond wood shelves and millions of volumes of our own local library. But it had its own advantages: 1) There was no separate children's and adults' rooms as was so rigidly enforced at our local library. Here a few shelves held the more standard children's books, but we could wander about the place and sit at one of the octagonal distressed-oak reading tables with any magazine or book we'd selected to browse through. 2) Because so few people came into this branch, the two female librarians soon came to recognize me by sight, and one of them, pleased by my seeming desire to read grown up books and by my ability to do so, stamped my library card "Adults Section," which allowed me to take out any book not only from her branch, but I later discovered from my own library too—with the proviso that the book selected might not be taken out if it were found to be too grown up.

It was one afternoon while nervously looking through the books on the "just back" shelf of this library awaiting the time until my sister would come downstairs to tell me it was time to leave this sun-filled, book-warm place and ascend the two flights of fifteen stairs to Dr. Brichter's Hall of Horrors, that I saw *The Iliad*. At first, all I did was flip through it, intrigued by the title, which was clearly not English (although the text was) and by the odd non-English names of the characters mentioned in the captions to the illustrations—names like Apollo and Helen, Diomedes and Priam, Ajax (I laughed: it was the same as the pot cleanser my mother used at home) and Achilles. The translation was in prose and though I never again found that particular volume, I often considered it the best. The book contained a glossary of names at the back, a simple, readable typeface (Garamond, I believe), and the elegant layout of each page perfectly matched the size and shape—six inches by eight inches—of the volume.

More importantly, the black and white line drawings by John Flaxman made in the late eighteenth century were among the most beautiful I'd ever seen. Recall that I'd always considered myself an artist. The purity of line and the suggestion of volume, the carefully selected detail, the sense of space and dimensionality this draftsman had achieved with such restraint and limited means fascinated me. I took the book out of the library based on the drawings alone, and I was already imitating them on scrap paper upstairs when I was called into Dr. Brichter's office for my ordeal.

Headachy but with the book held tightly in my lap, I sat behind my brother and sister on the bus home and began to read the captions more closely. "Sleep and Death conveying the body of Sarpedon to Lycia" was one, "Zeus sending the Evil Dream to Agamemnon" was another. "The Descent of Discord," "Hera Commanding the Sun to Set," "Poseidon Rising From the Sea," "The Judgement of Paris," "Achilles Mourning Patroclus," were others. I wanted to know, had to know, who these strange people were, what they were doing, and why. Nowadays well-paid, highly professional writers are hired to devise book flap inner and paperback back-cover copy that will enflame us to pick up, purchase and read their wares. This was accomplished for me by far simpler means—a gaggle of strange names, and even odder concepts. Who was this curly-locked, bearded Poseidon driving his chariot and water snorting horses like a submarine out of the ocean depths and then—somehow—riding the waves? Who were Sleep and Death? They seemed to be women able to fly, and to carry large bodies. Who was this Hera that she could command the sun to rise and go down whenever she wanted? Who was Achilles—and what was his relationship to Patroclus?—that such bloodshed should be extracted for a single death amid so many decades of carnage?

I began to read from the beginning: "The anger of Achilles, I tell, and the innumerable troubles this brought to the Greeks." I was hooked. I read on, hating to close the book, to get off the bus at our stop, to eat dinner or to go to sleep.

Ambidextrous: A Valentine

The next day was Saturday. Instead of phoning my friends to find out what they were doing, I stayed indoors reading. I read on throughout the weekend, not understanding all—hardly half—of what I read, but needing more. When I finished the book, I began to read it again. This time I put together names and action more closely with the illustrations (a habit I've never lost; I still keep an Atlas near my reading chair, and refer to it often when reading to make sure I know where everything happens). I had to understand all the complicated relations among the characters.

I had read the book three times when I went back to Dr. Brichter. My siblings thought I must be crazy as I hurried them along our way, anticipating the visit so much. As soon as we arrived, I went back downstairs and told the librarian how much I'd liked the book, and asked if I could take it out again. I could, she said. I could keep it out three more weeks. She told me Homer had written another book, unfortunately out on loan to someone else. She promised that if she were at the return desk when it came in, she would hold it for me. I reread *The Iliad* a fourth time, and hot on the trail of the author's other book, tried my own library, where I found a copy of *The Odyssey*. When I'd read that book three times and both volumes had to be returned I made a major decision. I had to have them with me all the time, not in a place ten miles away, where at a stranger's whim, they might be missing when I wanted to read them. I persuaded my older brother to take me to a bookstore in downtown Jamaica where, with my saved—up allowance, I spent the royal sum of two dollars and ninety-five cents each for copies of the books—naturally, with the Flaxman drawings.

Neither my parents nor my siblings paid much attention to all this. I'd already moved away from my brother and sister simply because we'd all reached ages where, unless we were forced together, we went off with our own friends.

They had no idea what I liked, hated; enjoyed, didn't; wanted, dreamt of. They never thought to ask me what I was reading. My older brother had worn a particularly sour look when I made him take me to buy the books—he had gone hesitantly, and never mentioned it afterward. He was already fifteen. All he could think of was cars. My sister, at fourteen, was at the beginning of dating. All she could think of was seventeen year old boys. As for my parents, they seemed oblivious. In the months since the problem with Mr. Hargrave, I'd behaved myself, created no new problems, and had brought home high grades from school—unexpectedly high this first third of the sixth grade. They were content that I had "adjusted," although I knew I'd done nothing of the kind. On the contrary, I'd turned the world my way, conformed only to the extent absolutely necessary to coexist with mere mortals. Didn't Homer's two books tell me there was a place, a time, a race of men and women and gods and goddesses who thought as I did? Who acted as I would love to act? Who made elaborately beautiful speeches of adoration, revenge, explanation, apology, as I thought right?

From what I'd seen of the world around me by age twelve, it was base and hypocritically dishonorable—money-grubbing and tawdry. When it wasn't absurd (a state too grand for everyday life), it was usually ridiculous. I treated my friends as Achilles had treated his allies, and my enemies with the same code of ethics. Any other way was a sham, a betrayal of man's inner nobility. My father's corns and their treatment, my mother inadvertently burning the kitchen curtains with a pan of frying breakfast sausages, my sister's lengthy phone conversations with her best friend about Roger Withers and Sam Duke, my older brother's refusal to speak at home, his general gloom and then his Jabbering with his pals outside of the house—all of this seemed a clown show to me. I couldn't wait to get

Ambidextrous: A Valentine

away from it after school or on weekends. and be with my friends. Even if they hadn't read Homer. they behaved like the heroes of old, with clear-cut motives, easy to understand actions. They seldom thought of their own self-aggrandizement. This disparity between those I lived among. and what I yearned to be. reached a snapping point one late Sunday afternoon as I lay on the old sofa reading *The Odyssey* once again.

My father passed through the room, shambling in his slippers, and asked what book l was reading. Eager to share. I handed Homer over. He sat on the sofa and leafed through it. Excited, I tried to explain the story. I thought I made as fine a case for the book as anyone could. He didn't comment, which was unusual, he just gave the book back to me and went upstairs.

Later on that evening I overheard him mention it to my mother, when they assumed I was out of earshot. The conversation went like this:

He: Did you see that book your son is reading all the time?

She: It's about time someone in this family did some reading. Did you look at it?

He: He's only twelve years old.

She: He has no idea what isn't showing.

He: I never saw pictures like that until I was old enough to vote. All bare-assed like that.

She: It takes place in Greece. I guess it was too warm for clothes there.

He: I don't see your friend (meaning Donna Kallas) going around bare-assed like that.

She: She's so skinny. Who would look?

Laughter.

I didn't know whether to scream or die of embarrassment. They were discussing the two greatest epics in Western Literature (I knew: it said so in the introduction) as though it were Cub Scout smut.

But I did look at the drawings more carefully to see what my father was complaining about. True, both men and women were fairly unclothed, but that was because they were so beautifully modeled, fleshed, proportioned. They didn't have to hide their beer bellies, their fat hips, their deformed feet. Yes, the women's breasts showed: but only in outline. I'd walked in on my sister a month or so before while she was palpating her breasts in front of a mirror (to make them grow?) and they hadn't been outlined: they had volume, heft, slight differences of color, nipples! And Flaxman might have drawn buttocks, but never genitals. Besides, I knew what genitals looked like. I'd seen three small vaginas for months last year, explored every aspect of them with fingers and eyes. What was a drawing of one compared to that almost clinical knowledge I'd had? And who cared? That was life, everyday life. This, this was Literature, Art, Flaxman, Homer! The drawings might be idealized, but I was certain someday I would see faces and bodies as beautifully proportioned as wonderfully muscled. It was an ideal, as Homer's warriors and gods were ideals. Ideals were all that mattered.

I began to draw on the sly; drawings inspired by Flaxman but perversely disproportionate. I would copy an illustration of a woman, say, half-turned away from the viewer, one arm in the air, the other at her side, her lower torso draped. But I would swell or elongate her breasts. Or I would draw another woman, facing forward, wearing a short chiton, holding a long spear. Then I would remove the kilt-like skirt and add in her genitals where I knew they belonged, then draw them separately on another piece of paper, outlined by the hint of a V of thighs. Then I would make that V larger and larger, until it completely filled an eight-and-a-half by eleven inch sheet of paper and became almost unrecognizable, abstract. I drew men too, narrowing their waists until they were absurdly small, or ridiculously squaring their buttocks, or extending their shoulders enormously until the men were top-heavy. Sometimes I drew slender large-breasted women, then added male genitalia. Or I drafted out robust, chunky warrior men and gave them sharply-pointed breasts, large nipples, buttocks so huge they looked like kids bouncing about in a potato sack race.

I hid these drawings, naturally, but I looked at them often, adding outrageous new details, feeling a strange pleasure in the monsters I created. Until, one day, wondering what my father would say—not about me, but about poor Homer's nefarious influence upon me—I destroyed them all. Yet the drawings provided me with a draftsman's needed sense of anatomy that would see me through years of art classes right up through college. Even now I can lay down a dozen quick sure strokes and make an individually unique male or female face and body.

Then, having accomplished God only knew what, I dropped it. I put Homer aside, for a moment of later desperation. He would save me then more gloriously than I could dream possible, he would pay back my love and attention, my belief in his vanished or never—existent world; and in so doing, he would bring on a more sinister delusion: a belief in the potency of the written word.

Children are the best anticipators because of their impatience, their unsteady grasp of time—it's entirely psychological, subjective; and clocks are the biggest liars—their construction of futures and emendations of those futures all conspire to aid them. Watching a child anticipate, we feel certain he'll be disappointed with the banal activity when it arrives. Hasn't that happened to us innumerable times? Or has it? Children need an actual acknowledged catastrophe to be disappointed in a plan or project they've invested so much in. Amazed, we observe them sincerely delighted in seeing for the fifth time a full-length cartoon they know half the dialogue and all of the action to. They clearly haven't forgotten it, yet it has become in some way new, unexpected, unparalleled in their experience. Some Zen Buddhists believe that if we could all honestly recapture this enchantment with what life offers as though it were always new, we would not become children but wise men. We'd live forever, balanced on the ingenuous edge of security and the unprecedented.

Greatly as I and my friends had anticipated the bicycle duel with Ricky Hersch at the unfinished Hillside Mall, detailed as we were our various, ever-altering scenarios for what would occur there, none of us were actually prepared for its eventuality. This might explain our surprise—and my own momentary consternation when Gregory met us in the schoolyard after lunch the Monday after my parents' "discussion" of my reading and told us that Ricky wanted to speak to me. At first I was certain he was going to back out. But when the four of us went to the deepest recess of the paved school playground where Ricky's cohorts from six-three hung out, I knew he wouldn't be able to back out if he wanted to. Nor, surrounded by my own friends, could I. We locked onto each other aloofly; the other eight or nine boys kept their distance but remained well within listening range.

Ricky opened up by saying, "I see you're all healed up."

I countered offhandedly, "There wasn't much to heal up."

His green-gray eyes narrowed a bit as he inspected my face. "No? Well there'll be plenty after Saturday."

"I'll race you anytime. Any place."

"Under the Hillside Mall," he quickly said. "Saturday at four in the afternoon."

"That's fine," I countered, watching for a reaction.

None was forthcoming, but his pretty face did seem to soften a bit, and for the first time I noticed how dark and straight his eyebrows were, except over his left eye where the fine hair was devilishly raised in a tiny mischievous caret.

Ambidextrous: A Valentine

"Good," he said. "I'll meet you there."

The other boys quickly gathered as Ricky and I stepped apart. They too agreed to meet at the entrance to the mall on Saturday. All of us would be needed on bikes, they thought, to keep track of the watchman and to distract him from the race if necessary. One of each of our friends would have to be stationed at the tunnel entrance to make sure we set off together, two more at the exit to declare the winner.

My only concession to the race that week was a complete overhaul of my bicycle. I wanted nothing to fail me. I inspected the French racing tires to forestall any rips in the thick outer brushed-silk grooves, the slender rubber tubes within. I reset the sprocket gears and tested them at different settings until I found a combination that would start off slowly in first gear, sail into a strong cruising second, then give me a lightning jump in third for the last lap of the race. I cleaned and polished the gears until they shone. I tightened and polished every connecting bolt on the bike. I stripped off the front basket, the front lamp, even the tiny tool kit. I experimented with the seat and handlebars until I'd achieved as angled-in a relationship between them as my body could fit. Aerodynamics meant speed and I intended to be riding almost horizontal—just like the prizewinning French bicyclists. I removed the fenders—mudguards, my mother called them; at the speed I expected to be traveling others, not I, would have to watch out for splashes. A month before, I had installed a small handbrake attached to a back wheel drum that cost $25.00 of my allowance money, and found that it, rather than the old foot brake, gave better control in sharp turns. Fearing that in my excitement I might instinctively hit the foot brakes without meaning to, I disconnected them.

To test out this almost-new speed vehicle, I took a long ride out to a huge concrete paved parking lot connected to a shopping mall in Manhasset, similar to the one where we would be racing and there ran the bike through its paces, tuning myself at the same time as I tested its abilities in u-turns and sudden descents. It required some getting used to. Right after the race I would have to change some of the alterations back: a hair-trigger response was the last thing I wanted when dawdling around the neighborhood. But it felt marvelous: for the first time I understood how a machine and a man could be a single integrated unit bent on one aim—winning. By the time I was done, it was dark and I had to ride home without a horn or headlight, through side streets, extra alert to any unexpected traffic. That night after dinner and television, I quietly went down to the garage to check if the machine had sustained any damage during the difficult testing. None.

Martin, James Kallas, and Gregory arrived at my house at three the next afternoon. We fooled around for a half hour. then got on our bikes without a word and rode to the mall. Ricky's friends were already there. One had been there on and off all day and had been chased off by the watchman earlier. He described the man as a "linebacker, a real bear." No one had seen the watchman since they'd arrived although they hiked around the place twice. One boy was still out in case the watchman made a last-minute appearance.

Ricky showed up wearing an over-large old leather jacket that I recognized as having belonged to his father, the dead G.I. I guessed it was supposed to be his lucky charm. Its cracked brown shine set off his pale skin, his dark straight hair, the tiny commas of red high on each cheekbone. I thought I'd never seen a handsomer boy. For a minute I wished we didn't have to be opponents but could be friends. Knowing that could not be, I made another wish, that Rick Hersch would never grow old: would always remain as he was that afternoon.

We shook hands, then Martin and one of Ricky's friends rode over to the exit. The scout approached to say that all was clear—no sign of the watchman. We all rode to the entryway, peered into the, dark unknown at the end of the open ramp, all of us hesitating with one excuse or another, half-on, half-off our bikes, pedaling idly around in small circles, talking. When Gregory spotted a gray Chevy coming our way, both Ricky and I said: "The watchman!" He turned to me. "Let's do it!"

"*Now!*" I answered.

The car closed in fast. We heard someone shouting "Hey, you kids!" out the window. But we were ready. On the mark . . . Go! We swept down the incline into the tunnel as we heard our friends yelling and speeding off above.

If ever for a split second I believed in any concept of Hell, it had to have resembled that almost soundless, incredibly fast race under the uncompleted mall. We both hit a light bump at the bottom and as our bikes easily jumped over it I could make out what seemed an endless nothingness, dimly lighted by yellow ceiling lamps within chrome casings placed so far apart that long stretches of darkness lay between. Streaks of puddles from the last rain suddenly splattered under our bike tires, the carcasses of rats and cats and who knows what other animals lay alongside them, sometimes right in the oil-slicked water. With each flicker into then out of the distorting vague lamplight, I was able to make out shadows: the side walls we sped past sketched with damp mold, chalked with the names of prospective businesses they would become cellars for. A few concrete loading platforms. A parked truck facing us (we flashed around either side). Walking, we might have seen more, been able to read the names of the stores, clearly identify and thus negate the sinister ambiguities of these features. But I had popped into second gear as we'd landed and I could hear the madly regular pedaling of Ricky's feet as we raced along the rugged concrete road, swaying slightly every now and again as a sudden gust of fetid air struck us from God alone knew what quirk of ventilation or atmosphere. was already half-nauseous with the close dampness, half blinded by the ever-changing light. short of breath from exertion, unsure most of the time exactly where Ricky was (I thought just behind me). After he switched into his cruising mode. all that told me I wasn't alone in that unexpectedly eerie long tunnel was the sudden unsyncopated ghost of splash as he followed through each puddle.

I knew I was ahead: my bicycle had been primed to win and my legs were pedaling so fast the gears spun out twice—but I coasted, lifting my feet off a second until they caught again. I was so in rhythm with the bike they always caught exactly right before the bike could slow down. I thought I heard voices ahead, wondered if it were another distortion like the light, the air, the wind currents—inside the tunnel. Then I thought saw a steady growing glimmering ahead. I prepared myself to shift into third gear for the ascent, glad to be getting out of the place. I sped into a new kind of light that I knew had to be from the outside. When I looked around, I could barely make out Ricky. I felt a bump beneath the tires just like the one we had hit landing, and I was about to go up, out of the tunnel. I'd won!

Looming in front of me, above me, was a huge bulk of shadow. At first I thought it was far off, another parked truck perhaps, and I prepared to get around it. Then it seemed to turn, turn around and become a recognizable figure—the dreaded watchman. He must have seen us ride down and drove to this opening to catch us.

My bike shot up into his large, swearing face, and he threw his arms out and began to zigzag so I couldn't get past. I aimed for the space between the far side wall, and he threw out one paw and tried to grab the handlebar. I was going too fast for him to hold on, but he exerted enough thrust to add a new vector to my direction and to send the bike into a sharp swerve, directly into the wall. I saw the bike lean over, begin to fall beneath me. I couldn't stop, it was going so fast, so out of control. I didn't even have time to put out a foot to somehow brake myself—the normal reaction in such a situation. I gripped the handbrake and it squealed like a dying animal as the wheels slid on the pavement. The bike and I impacted the wall straight on. With my left arm raised to cover my face, I flew right over it, hearing the metallic clangor of the bike on the other side. Astonished, spinning over the wall, hitting the pavement: I actually saw stars—blue, yellow, red stars against a black satin scrim—just like characters in comic books when Superman or Batman socked them. I heard yelling; the watchman was furious. Everything fell away—sight, hearing, touch.

Only for a second. I opened one eye, couldn't open the other, and saw the huge man above me, both hands on Ricky's shoulders. Ricky stared down at me, horrified. I thought—this is the end, I'm a goner and closed my eyes. Everything in my body felt broken. I blacked out again.

I could hear Ricky's voice very close to my face: he must have knelt down. He sounded frightened. "I think he's still alive. I'm not sure. You look."

"He'd *better* be alive." The gruff watchman sounded frightened too.

"Look!" Ricky said.

"No." The voice backed away. "What the hell were you kids doing down there in the first place? You're not supposed to be here, damn you!"

"I saw you grab him," Ricky said, with amazing *sang froid*. "I was right behind. I saw you grab him. If he's dead it's all your fault. I'll testify in court."

"*What*? You weren't supposed to be *down* there."

"If he's dead," Ricky repeated, "you're going to be in real trouble. You deliberately grabbed him. You killed him."

I felt hair brush my lips: Ricky's hair from its silky length as he leaned over to listen for my heartbeat. He must have found it, because he suddenly whispered, "Can you get up? If you can move, jerk your right leg."

I didn't know whether I could get up or not. I knew I didn't want to be dead, so I jerked my right leg.

"He's alive! His leg moved!" Ricky said excitedly. "You'd better call an ambulance. Quick! If he dies because there isn't medical help, you'll really pay for it!"

The watchman must have come closer, because Ricky said: "No! Don't move him! Don't touch him! You might make it worse. I take First Aid in school. You aren't supposed to move an accident victim. His guts might fall out or his neck and back could be broken."

"Jesus!" the watchman said. "Stay here with him. There's a phone in an empty store I use as an office. Don't move him. You goddamn kids. All I need now is a lawsuit. Or to lose my job because you little bastards had to come here and race your . . ."

His mumbling became more distant, was finally gone.

"Can you get up?" Ricky asked. "If you can, you'd better do it right now."

I opened my eyes, saw gray sky, attempted to move. Ricky helped me to my feet. "Anything broken?" he asked.

I wasn't sure. I nodded no though my left leg was killing me.

"Quick," he said. "We've got to get out of here before he gets back or we're really in Dutch."

He pulled my bicycle up from where it had crashed, and placed it more or less under me. "Understand?" he asked me.

I nodded again, wobblingly gripped the slightly askew handlebar—my poor bike!—lifted myself onto the seat and almost fell off. Ricky held the handlebars and urged me to try again. I did. The bike wobbled badly on the right side. He saw it, and gave me his bike, then took mine.

"Come on! Let's go!" he whispered. We pedaled across the shortest distance of open paved parking lot into some trees separating the mall from the next street. "Come on!" he insisted. Painful as it was for me, distressed as I was by the condition of my bicycle—the handbrake completely gone, the seat awry, the front wheel spokes bent—I had to laugh seeing him ride it like a clown in the most distant ring of the circus. It kept pulling to one side, and he had to constantly lean the other way. It couldn't have been easy, but he did it and kept looking back to urge me on.

We got through the trees and I followed his shortcut through someone's backyard onto a single lane macadam road through a section of one-story cottages I'd never seen before. Then over an unused railroad track half hidden in tall grass, through empty lots onto another single lane street I wasn't familiar with.

Only when we'd gotten onto our side of the Cross Island Expressway did I feel safe enough to give into the chills and trembling that had begun to take hold of my body. We rode along the service road. I swerved onto one of the endless lawns that fronted the expressway, almost crashing into a tree. I fell off the bike clutching myself: I'd never felt so cold in my life.

"What's wrong?" Ricky asked. I rolled on the ground, shivering. He got off my bike and dragged me through a stand of trees into what looked like a secluded dale. I couldn't speak through the chattering of my teeth. "Holy cow!" he said, looking at me. "You must be in shock!" He ran out, came back with the two bikes, then dropped beside me, whipped off his father's leather army jacket and placed it over me. That helped warm me, but I still shivered. He thought a minute, then decided he had to do more. He carefully lay down next to me on the grass, making certain to fit himself alongside my entire body. I clutched at him from under the jacket and shivered until I thought my teeth and bones would break apart and fly out of my body in all directions.

The shivering stopped. I felt warm. I opened my eyes, and turned to thank him. No words came out. But Ricky seemed relieved and he moved all over me, touching my arms and legs, checking for broken or fractured bones, he said. Under the jacket his hands roved, across my ribcage, my back, up my neck. Everything worked, he said, matter-of-factly. I was just "shook up by the fall. Got up too quickly."

When I was able to speak, I said, "I didn't want to race you."

He seemed surprised. "Why not? You won! You're the best bike racer in the county. Everyone knows it."

"I didn't win. I fell."

"You didn't *fall*. He knocked you down. That big fuck!" The last spoken in real anger. "Of course you won the race. You were the first one out of the tunnel If I were first, he would have grabbed me and knocked me down instead."

His logic was too impeccable to deny. I began to shiver again and he came under the big jacket with me again and huddled close. "Don't talk. We're just going to stay here until you feel better. All right?"

He remained there almost an hour until I was filled with looking at the corners of his face, filled with the texture of his long dark hair—every strand tinted an identical black walnut—feeling its soft texture across my face when he leaned close, filled with his boysmell and boybreath and the strength and security of his arms, all within the slightly nutty-scented, hot sheepskin ambiance of his father's bomber jacket, until I was no longer trembling and beads of perspiration had broken out on his forehead.

Unwillingly I told him I felt okay, honest. Completely

relieved, Ricky threw off the jacket and once again tested me for breaks or fractures or sprains. We discovered some lollapalooza bruises, one gash the length of my left leg, another on my left forearm, a bump on the side of my head: none seemed serious. Ricky acted like a doctor in a movie, making me stand up, bend over to touch hands to toes (I couldn't; got dizzy). He asked if I could ride. I thought I could, sore as I felt. So he banged around the front of my bike with a bolt-tightener from his tool kit until the spokes were more or less straight, the wheel less bent, the seat re-angled. We got on the bikes and slowly rode back home.

A block away from the Taylor house, we saw almost a dozen bikes parked around the huge front yard Hickory tree. Ricky motioned me to stop. I wondered why.

"Back there you said that you didn't want to race me?" he asked. "Why not?"

I shrugged. "I don't know." I looked into his startlingly colored eyes. "I guess I didn't want to see you have to lose."

He blushed and seeing that, I did too: we both realized the admission I'd just made.

"What a jerk! When we tell them what happened to us, no will even bother to ask who won."

I could already see him calculating how to tell our story most dramatically. We would ride into the Taylor yard and I would all but collapse. Our two groups of friends would jump up and ask what happened, where had we been so long. We would collaborate on a fantastic story, beginning with the truth (which was interesting enough) but really elaborating on what we'd seen or thought we'd seen speeding through the tunnel. I'd let Ricky take over and relate how I'd been stopped by the brutal, stupid watchman and how Ricky had outwitted him and gotten us away.

"You're right, I guess," I said. "But don't tell them how I couldn't ride anymore and fell down and how you had to put your father's jacket over me and all. Or I'll tell who won the race."

"You do and I'll tell them not only how you needed to be held like a big baby but that you kissed me."

"I didn't! That's a lie!"

"No. But you wanted to. It's the same thing."

"I didn't. And it's not the same thing."

My feelings exposed, I felt trapped, aware that I was blushing, angry that he had read my thoughts and emotions so easily, so correctly.

"What's the difference?" Ricky said airily.

It was later that night, after dinner, as we sat in the living room watching television, I in the midst of my family for once oddly all there, that I wondered how long Ricky and I would keep those secrets. A week or so later, in math class, I let myself imagine what it would have been like if I had kissed Ricky, and let myself be kissed back. I was determined to find out.

That was pretty much the history of our relationship when I came down with the bad stomach virus and stayed out of school for a week and asked Gregory to have his cousin come visit me. I didn't really want Ricky to see me weak and vulnerable again, but it would be a good excuse for us to be alone again—which I badly wanted.

As soon as I was recovered I took up Ricky's offer to see his model airplanes. More sensitive than I to what our new friendship would entail in social complications, Ricky chose a Tuesday afternoon when his cousin Gregory would be away at a Sea Scout meeting.

I'd been in the Taylor house before, of course, but not beyond the large sit-in kitchen and Gregory's bedroom. He shared this large second floor back room with two older brothers and we were constantly interrupted by their comings and goings, which wasn't much fun. But Ricky had his own room at the very top of the house, a slope-roofed former attic room that was hot in summer and cold in winter. I don't think the room made a great impression on me at first, except by how out of the way from the rest of the house and huge family it was—a separate stairway with a door he usually kept closed rose up from the third floor—and by how high up it was. Ricky showed me the thick branch of a nearby Hickory tree he used to scale up to his window when he didn't want to be seen.

Once I had sat there a while, it was a wonderful, almost ideal boy's room: part sanctuary, part playroom, part treehouse. The furniture was spare: a narrow single bed placed directly under the apex of the dormer, with a high tiny window at its head and two larger windows on either side; a small, kicked-up looking cherry wood bed table; a big rattan rocking chair with checkered blue and white pillows. Ricky kept two dark green metal Armed Forces footlockers under the bed, containing, he said, his best toys and other goodies he would show me later.

What made the room truly special, delightful, were the twenty balsa wood model airplanes hung from tacks on the sloping ceilings—models of Fokkers, Messerschmidts, Zeroes, Stukas, B-14s, B-52s, even the X-l, the jet that Chuck Yeager had recently flown in breaking the sound barrier. All the models were beautifully painted the same colors they'd been in the big book Ricky had loaned me, with carefully delineated details—decals, numbers, markings, flags, window trim. Each model hung at a different level, some at hand and eye level, others high above our heads. They softly spun, bobbing in the wind, so fragile at times that a stray air current, even our breath would set them turning into some new aspect of their constant ballet.

We sat on the bed and Ricky let me inspect a still unpainted seaplane he was building, its unsanded pontoons like big feet. I asked all sorts of questions about it. He answered me but seemed distracted. I became aware that I was sniffing the air, smelling a subtle, pervasive odor I was familiar with.

"Like it?" Ricky asked, smiling shyly.

Not sure whether he was asking about the bedroom, the model of the seaplane in my hand or what, I said I did. Ricky got up and locked the door. Before joining me on the bed again he located a key wedged under the drawer of his little bedside table and opened one footlocker. I was so busy examining the abundance of bottle caps and tiny boat models, war medals, and gun slugs in the locker I almost didn't notice him pull out a slender yellow and green tube with a white cap until he brought it to my nose. Then, so I would have no doubts, he unscrewed the cap. I immediately recognized it as the source of the odor in the room, but stronger, sharper.

"Like it?" Ricky asked again; again I was unsure what he was asking.

"Sure."

He unfolded a number five sized brown paper bag he'd kept in the footlocker and carefully inserted the tube inside it. When he pulled the tube out again and screwed back the top, I could see a long dribble of almost clear glue on the rectangular open bottom.

"Here," he said handing me the bag.

I didn't know what he expected me to do.

"Didn't you ever do it this way?"

I shook my head.

"It's better this way. You get more fumes. Don't sniff too much at once, okay? This should be enough for the two of us right now."

I looked into the bag again and, feeling like a horse with a feedbag on, put my face inside. Foolish, I thought. But when I pulled my head out a minute later, Ricky nudged me back in. I saw the afternoon light filtering in through the irregular paper weave of the bag, and continued wondering what I was supposed to be doing.

I didn't have to wait long. Ricky gently pulled the bag off my face saying, "My turn now."

I saw the brown bag disappear from in front of my eyes, saw the room come back, saw everything in the room shake and shatter, felt my head spin as though I had been standing up and revolving in a tight circle. All I could do was fall back onto the bed, looking up at the ceiling, the models, everything around me shaking and disappearing. Even the bed beneath me seemed to disappear. I was floating on air, on a magic carpet.

"Great, huh?" Ricky said, a thrill threading through his voice. Then he fell back next to me.

We lay like that for a while. I still didn't know what I was experiencing. He chuckled every once in a while. My head seemed to clear a little. Ricky sat up and offered me the paper bag again. This time when I put my face inside, I inhaled deeply, and heard him say, "It's better than cigarettes, huh?" until I fell back on the bed and he had to laugh, taking the bag off my face and putting it on him. Then he was next to me on the bed again, laughing quietly, and I felt miles up in the air along with the X-1 jet flying through the stratosphere, zooming faster than sound.

It seemed natural the third time we did it that when we fell back onto the bed we would face each other; natural that we would stare at each other, touch each other's faces—his small straight nose, his horizontal eyebrows except where one lifted suddenly, his mouth; natural finally that we would not be content with staring and touching, but begin to kiss.

We kissed long after the high was gone. My experience with the Flaherty club had made me a terrific long-breathed French kisser. When we broke away from each other, Ricky laughed a little and said, "Wow! Jesus Wow!" then sat up to sniff from the bag again. I joined him and we began kissing sitting up, then wrapped our arms around each other and slowly floated down to the bedspread in a kiss that seemed to last forever and to merge us completely into each other so that we were pilot and copilot zooming lightning swift through the lower atmosphere, high as a meteorite.

We might have stayed there kissing for hours, but we heard shouting downstairs. Ricky sat up, said "Damn!" got up, opened the bedroom door and yelled down, "In a few minutes, huh? I'm with a friend." He closed the door, came back to the bed, sat down, took me in his arms and said, "You see, I said you wanted to kiss me." We kissed without sniffing the glue and for an even longer time, our hands all over each other's necks and backs and ears, our tongues deep inside each other's mouths—those soft pink caves, where we explored every crevasse, perambulated every ridge, tried out every taste bud of spongy tongue. We only stopped when the shouting downstairs was loud enough for me to make out the words.

"I better see what my Aunt wants. She sounds like she's about to bust a gut," Ricky said. At the door he asked if I wanted to borrow one of the models. I took the dragonfly-colored Zero.

"Come tomorrow," Ricky said, half-whispering, his hands over my supersensitive nape. "After school, okay? And don't tell Gregory."

I walked the block and a half home feeling like never before, as though I had been flying in the clouds with Ricky, the same way that Wendy had flown with Peter Pan in the animated movie I'd seen the year before: only they had never kissed while flying. We had. And Ricky was better looking than the Disney version of the flying boy.

The wonderful mood lasted until dinner when my sister began picking on me. When I went to bed, I couldn't help but notice a small yellowish stain on the front of my jockey undershorts.

"Looks like you peed in your pants," my older brother said, as I inspected the stain. Then he corrected, "Or jizzed."

I didn't know what he was talking about. I changed my underpants and stared at the yellow and green model airplane Ricky had let me borrow as if it were a talisman of our friendship. I went to sleep and didn't have to dream.

The next day after I'd finished my homework and dinner, I went to the Taylor property. Our pre-arranged signal had been emended at school recess, so I would visit him later and more secretly. Ricky hung out his window, whispering encouragement as I negotiated my difficult first time climbing the Hickory tree all the way up to his room. Once there I was rewarded with a sight: the second Army footlocker had been unlocked—the one containing what Ricky had promised was his "best stuff."

"Want to see what's inside?"

Naturally I did. I sat on the bed as he opened it and eagerly pulled out 1) A deadly-looking bayonet with what appeared to be a rusty stain which he assured me was "commie blood." 2) A defused grenade that still looked deadly—when it didn't resemble an under-grown unripe pineapple. 3) Two cans of K-rations, one for "Ham" a second for "Mixed Vegetables." 4) An old but well-preserved Army hat with patches sewn onto one side of the crease.

He also took out a large leather wallet which contained photographs of his father—the Korean War hero—who much resembled Ricky, especially when Ricky tried on the overlarge hat at the same angle as his father had worn it in some snapshots. There were other photos of his father and his buddies in uniform: against the side of a bleak, sun—stroked mountain, their arms over each other's shoulders, the sun's glare icing the fenders of the auto they leaned against, frosting their foreheads perpetually young. One photo had script on the back.

"That's Tony Warner," Ricky said, "My dad's best buddy."

After Tom Hersch's death, Tony Warner had brought back the two footlockers and had personally given them to

Ricky, whom he knew was his father's favorite. That wasn't too long ago. Ricky had been eight then and he remembered how great Tony had been. Warner still wrote him several times a year and Ricky got Christmas and birthday gifts from him, even though Tony hadn't been able to remain but had gone back to Encino, California.

"What's this say?" I asked, trying to read the back of the photo—a smashing studio portrait of Tony in uniform complete with army cap rakishly angled, a shy smile, large light eyes.

"Can't you read? It says, 'From the best bj buddy ever."

Ricky looked at me.

"Don't tell me you don't know what that means. No? Well, maybe you'll find out some day."

"Does it mean like the best of friends?" I tried.

"It's that, but it's more than that. Maybe you and I can be bj buddies sometime. Would you like that?"

"Is it like blood brothers? I asked. It was a concept I knew from a multitude of grad B adventure movies.

"Better than that. It means you and your buddy are the absolute chosen friends to each other, and no one else can ever be that. It means you'll do anything for your buddy."

"Like lie for him and be tortured and all?"

"And keep secrets together that you can't tell anyone," he added mysteriously. "It means you're closer than a mother or father or brother to your buddy. And if you have a wife, it means you're closer to your buddy than to your wife."

I accepted this wisdom without much effort. After all, I'd kept secrets from my parents and family without having a bj buddy, and I didn't have a wife. It seemed a cinch. I was waiting for him to open another drawer, deeper inside the locker. He didn't. He put the gear back into the box and closed it.

"What's in there?"

"More photos. You'll see them later, okay?"

I agreed. Once the footlocker had been locked and placed under the bed, Rickey went into the other one and come up with the airplane glue and the paper bag and we began sniffing it and kissing again. During one momentary break I watched Ricky's hand range all over my lower torso and legs. "No broken bones, fractures or sprains," I said languorously, aware that my words were slurred.

"No? What's this?" he asked. "Looks like a boner to me." He played with it through my corduroy pants, then we sniffed more glue. It was dark out, almost eight o'clock. I said I had to go home.

Visiting Ricky the next two nights was out—Thursday I had a test to study for and the next night we went to dinner at my aunt and uncle's in Richmond Hill, which took all night. On Saturday afternoon I was back in Ricky's room. The minute I got in the door, he carefully locked it behind me and swore me to secrecy. [wanted to see the photos in the lower shelf of the footlocker didn't I, he asked. I said I did. Then I had to swear not to tell anyone what I would see. If I did tell Ricky warned, he would never let me in his room, never let me have glue, never kiss me, never talk to me, never recognize me again.

I swore to all he asked and he slid the photos out of the drawer, removing them one at a time from a worn-looking manila army envelope. These were also snapshots of men in uniform, or at least partly in uniform. Most seemed to be army men, but there were two marine MPs and even some sailors. All the photos seemed to be of men in the same position, sitting in a big stuffed chair with shirts and even hats on, but no trousers. All the men were sitting fairly casually, except for the fact that they were all holding their erections.

"Now, that's a boner!" Ricky said of one photo in an excited low-toned voice. "And look at this one!"

We went through all the photos, and when we were done, he pulled out another envelope-full, but would only show me one photo. It was of Ricky's father, and he wore no clothing but an askew army hat. He sat on a sofa, his legs up, his knees pointing at the camera. Someone's hand was reaching into the picture to grab his cock. He smiled at the camera.

The glue appeared suddenly and in no time Ricky and I were sniffing and kissing. This time Ricky began rubbing me all over. He pulled off me at one point, undid my denims and my erection stood up. He touched it, rubbed it a little, then still kneeling on the bed, unzipped himself. He squirted more glue into the paper bag, put it over my face, sniffed some himself and said in that same tone of voice he'd used the first time I'd come to his room, "Like it?"

Before I could answer he'd begun massaging both me and himself. "Well?" he asked again looking at me, then leaned over and began to kiss me at the same time. By now I was floating and burning, soaring and sore with the friction of his hand. I murmured yes, I did like it. A minute later I was surprised that I was feeling so congested, hot and uncomfortable from his hand; I asked him to stop. For an answer, he thrust the bag of glue at me again and continued explaining, "It's going to make, watch!" I was off floating once more and though I felt what he was doing, it was as though his hand and my lower body were far away, except when the pain shot like hot coffee through my groin and at the same time Ricky leaned over me again to French kiss me, breathing his freshly inhaled glue fumes directly down my throat. I felt as though I was on a jet spinning out of control, plummeting into the open flaming lava cone of a volcano. I held onto Ricky's back and shoulders as though that would stabilize me. It was no help. I felt myself hit ground zero and explode into smithereens as though by the treacherously activated grenade in the footlocker under the bed. If his mouth weren't so tight over mine I would have shouted out. Instead I arched my back, kept holding him, finally slumped back half fainting.

When I opened my eyes, Ricky had moved away a bit on the bed. He was kneeling over me, jerking himself into orgasm. I was astonished to see his cock so red and hard, even more amazed to see something come out of it—a whitish fluid that hit the paper bag and my bare legs and tummy. I realized the same thing had just happened to me; for a second I wondered if it had happened the first time we had sniffed glue and kissed and if that had stained my underwear.

When I asked him, Ricky said, "pre-come, probably. This," rubbing the goo into a circle that quickly dried on my skin, "is the real stuff. You sure don't know much, do you?"

I admitted I didn't. I told him I'd seen one other "boner" before—Edward Young's. I didn't tell him about Susan Flaherty and that afternoon when her Aunt Selma had caught us and ran upstairs to commit suicide by drinking laundry bleach. I wondered now if I had "come" inside Susan that time. Then thought, no, I couldn't have. This was the first time I'd seen anything but urine emerge. The earlier sensation had been similar—if different in intensity—from this. With Susan it had been gentle, melting, soft. This experience had been much more forceful, sharp, incredibly painful, bone-clattering and had lasted a much longer time.

I tried to explain this to Ricky without in any way mentioning my time with Susan. Without much comprehension from him, I thought.

"You sure have a lot to learn," Ricky said without any presumption. "I do this every day. Sometimes twice, three times each day. Didn't it feel good? It always feels good if you do it yourself, but it feels even better if someone else does it, and . . ." He paused a minute staring at me and, I was certain, wondering whether to go on. He must have decided I was ready to hear more. "This feels even better!" Ricky said and picked up the second envelope of snapshots he'd earlier opened to show me his father's nude picture and laid out about ten more photos on the bed. Three were of his father in the same position as before, only this time he had his hand in the hair of a man whose head was in his lap. Ricky's dad's erection was in the man's month. As I stared, Ricky spread out the last two photos from the envelope. Both showed the two men stretched out on the sofa, Tony on top, Hersch on the bottom, erections in each other's mouths. "That's what a bj buddy is," Ricky said. "If you think jerking is good, wait until you try that."

So began a new and different kind of life for me, similar in some regards to what had occurred the year before with the Flaherty girls, but unlike those experiences, everything Ricky and I did together was defined, discussed in advance and afterward; every act given a name, and practiced until perfect. Sometimes Ricky and I would go up to his room for these almost daily activities. At other, rarer times when I was certain no one was at home, we'd go to my bedroom. Saturdays and Sundays we'd take long bike rides to secret places he knew of, to hidden little parklets, to abandoned houses and unused garages where we would sniff glue and kiss and make love until we were stoned and sore all over. Talk, too, because that was part of it. Ricky would tell me how he had found the cache of photos which even Tony hadn't known still existed; and then how he'd told Tony about them in a letter, and how Tony had come to visit and said how much he missed Tom Hersch and how those were the best times he'd ever had, and how he wished he had died along with Ricky's dad in that firestorm outside of Pusan instead of having to live and come back home and get married and go into the insurance business—which he hated. He told Ricky to keep the photos and to try to find a friend as good as Tom Hersch had been to him, and to teach that friend everything in the photos, as he had taught Ricky's father—and of course to never show the photos to anyone else.

What made our friendship different than my relationship with the Flaherty girls was although at core it was secret, in all other aspects it remained completely open and acceptable. Within weeks, all of Ricky's and all my friends recognized that somehow, while they weren't noticing, that all-important bond between two twelve-year-old boys that can forge one of the strongest life relationships had occurred. All bowed before its existence, it's power. It helped that we admired and respected each other. Ricky was the only boy I hadn't soundly defeated in a bicycle race. I the only boy who'd managed to give him such a licking in a fight that his mother and sisters had to separate us. He was handsome, dashing, adventurous, more knowledgeable about how the world worked than anyone I'd ever met, good at sports, popular among other kids, a whiz at building model airplanes. I was well-read, smart in school, well-liked, ready to take up any challenge offered, still the fastest bike racer and runner in a ten-mile-square area, and a quick study. Sexually we were completely matched in passion and, after some practice, in technique.

About two weeks after our first sexual contact, I discovered that I could get airplane glue too. Ricky's birthday was coming up in early February and I wanted to make a model of a Russian MIG-2—the only fighter not in his collection—as a surprise for him. I'd found a picture of the plane in a newspaper my father was reading, then went to the local library where I found an issue of Popular Science that had more detailed color photos and plans. I copied the illustrations and photos and went to our local hobby shop to buy balsa wood and decals. "Do you have glue?" the middle-aged shop clerk asked. "No," I replied innocently; a minute later, when he came back with a small tube, I asked for a larger one.

I began to sniff on my own, without Ricky. Work went slowly on the MIG-2, after all it was the first model I'd-ever built and I wasn't all that handy with files and handsaws and the other tools in my father's carpentry kit. After dinner, instead of watching *I Love Lucy* or *The Ed Sullivan Show*, I would go up to my room and work on the model, sniffing glue, masturbating, all the time thinking about Ricky and how much he'd like my gift. No one in my family seemed to miss me, to mind my defection from television. In fact, my father applauded my new avocation; he even offered tips in planning and varnishing the balsa wood. As soon as I'd finished the MIG-2, I decided to build an earlier model—a Piper Cub—for my younger brother's birthday.

Meanwhile the other members of the gang had begun to miss me. When one of them called with plans for the four of us to go somewhere together, I accepted half of the time; progressively declining until I was spending virtually all my time with Ricky, hardly any with them. It was easy: I wanted to work on the model or I had too much homework or I'd promised to run errands for my mother. I guess all of them eventually discovered where I was spending most of my time when I said I was raking or playing Lincoln Logs with my brother. Of course, Gregory knew exactly where I was most of the time and though he would sometimes stare at me accusingly with his big sad watery eyes, he never gave us away. But after a while those sad stares got to me and I made excuses to my friends at school doing chores for a teacher instead of walking home with my friends, or I would bicycle from the school building with Ricky to one of our hideouts. Once Martin began to make sarcastic remarks about our relationship, but I wouldn't let him continue—I simply walked away. James Kallas was content to have my company whenever he could; he made no demands on me. But all this made me more aware of the nature of my friendship with Ricky—its everyday intensity so qualitatively different from my other, more casual, friendships. One time, I asked Ricky if he'd ever jerked and blown with his cousin Gregory. He looked at me with disbelief. "That's only for best buddies, for my bj buddy," he declared. Then I wanted to know if he'd ever had that kind of buddy before me. He almost lied, then changed his mind and said he had; someone older. He wouldn't say who.

I began to think of Ricky at times when we weren't together. Once during math lesson, I wondered what he was doing at that very moment in his class on the same floor, around the U of the school building. I got myself excused to go to the boy's room and walked until I passed the open back door to his classroom. There he sat in profile to me, third row over, next to the last desk from the back of the room, doodling, obviously not paying attention to the teacher. I thought how lucky I was that he was my friend.

I was about to walk away when he suddenly turned as though he'd intuited my presence and stared right at me. I was so startled I moved out of view, against the corridor wall. Ricky put his thumb in his mouth and questioningly raised one eyebrow. I wasn't sure what he was gesturing about but I stayed where I was, watching as he raised his hand and asked to be excused from class. When he got to the door, he didn't join me but looked around to be sure no one else was nearby—the hallway was otherwise vacant. He signaled me to walk ahead. When I reached the boy's room, Ricky walked inside past me. A third grader was at the urinal, just buttoning up. Ricky told him to hurry up, then pushed me into a booth. Before I could say anything, he began to French kiss me and feel me up. When I was erect, he sat on the toilet seat and began to blow me. After I'd come but before I'd caught my breath, he stood up and whispered, "Now catch me," and I did. Later on, in the schoolyard, Ricky came up to me. "That was great! You were really smart to come by my class like that. I was so bored I was ready to go to sleep. Tomorrow I'll bring glue and we can sniff too."

After that, Ricky contrived other ways for us to be together at school. Boys had to have a sponsor to become members of the Visual Arts Squad. Ricky asked me to sponsor him. It was a great way to get him out of study hall and to get us together more often. Despite its name, this wasn't a group of artists but merely boys in charge of slide and film projectors. We would deliver the large, ungainly machines to a classroom and set them up as the teacher stood in the front of the room explaining what the students were seeing—highlighting with a pointer. We stood in the back of the darkened classroom, ready in case the film reels had to be changed or if some mishap occurred.

When Ricky joined the squad he became my partner through the simple expedient of our sharing recess and study periods. We would go into the classes like everyone else on the squad, roll down the window and door shades, shut off the lights and begin the projector. Then we would lean against the back cabinets of the classroom, waiting. Ricky added a new twist to this boring occupation—I mean how many times can you remain interested in "Our Furred and Feathered Friends: Ages 6-9"? Once the film was running, Ricky would grope me. As soon as I was hard, he'd take it out and jerk me off. If the film was long enough, or in two sections. I would do the same to him. We even managed to finagle our way into the wardrobes—where the electrical outlets were—on some pretense or other, and there sniff glue. We became so adept, so casual about these carryings-on that once, when I was working on Ricky, the teacher suddenly rushed to turn on the lights. She didn't catch us, of course. Ricky quickly turned around and I stood in front of him blocking her view. The projector was fixed, the lights shut off again, and I finished Ricky off.

Who knows what the night janitor thought cleaning our dried semen off the floors of various classrooms—we usually wiped any splatters that landed on the equipment. Like Hansel and Gretel's breadcrumbs, anyone could have followed our trail day by day from class to class, through these splashes.

In return for getting him on the Visual Arts Squad, Ricky managed to get me into his swimming class Saturday mornings at the local YMCA where we became "teammates." I had mastered swimming the summer before after being afraid of the water all my life, and next to Ricky—a born swimmer—I breasted, crawled, and stroked fearlessly and well. We soon took the lead among our age mates in tests and races and were given all sorts of leeway by the coach. We could arrive later than the others, and remain practicing later if we wanted. Naturally, we wanted exactly this as it gave us time alone in the shower rooms abutting the pool—time enough for a fast handjob or blowjob. One time we thought we'd been caught by an older guy (he couldn't have been more than nineteen) and we immediately stopped, pretending we hadn't been doing anything at all. He went to the far end of the big multi-nozzled shower and began to wash himself, ignoring us. We lingered on, waiting for him to leave. Finally, he said "Go on! Do what you were doing when I came in. I won't tell. I'll watch out." Ricky and I looked at each other. I was about to say no, but the guy was already at the doorway, so Ricky immediately knelt in front of me to continue. As the man watched, he masturbated, coming all over Ricky's shoulder.

Afterward, Ricky and I laughed remembering the man. Ricky said the guy must have been a weirdo to get himself off watching us. Several weekends later he showed up again. He told us he lived in a room on an upper floor of the Y and invited us up there if we wanted to have more privacy. He promised not to touch us. We never did go with him, he seemed so eager he wrote his room number in soap on the tile shower wall, twice.

The more time I spent in Ricky's company, the more I persuaded myself that I was right to give up my three closest friends for him. He was as smart as Martin; sweeter, when I got to know him, than Gregory; more loyal than James Kallas. Above all, he was desirable and I was by no means the only person charmed by Ricky. At the local soda shop we always got free chocolate chip cookies. If at the movies he went to the manager and said he'd dropped money, an usher would always arrive to hunt with a flashlight until we'd collected enough change under several rows of seats to pay for two more admissions. Ricky's mother and older sisters doted on him. The Taylor boys respected him and his privacy. Even the generally paranoid Grandma Taylor loved him and gave him money. Ricky always seemed to have money although I never figured out how: his chores around the Taylor place were few, and poorly paid. Even other children seemed to like Ricky, and why not? He didn't care whether they did or not, which he claimed was the only way to "Win Friends and Influence People," quoting the title of a then famous self-help bestseller.

To an outsider Ricky might have appeared to be an ideal child: handsome, polite, well-mannered, always well groomed, never caught misbehaving. But I knew his secret side: his addiction to glue and fellatio, his sudden impulses invariably filled with risks for us. In the light of this greater knowledge, his decision to race me under the Hillside Mall wasn't an aberration, but typical. For Ricky, the test had been not who would win the race, but whether I would race at all. Ricky said he knew we would be friends when I got up from the accident and left the parking lot. "Most kids would have stayed on the ground, crying. You could have really been hurt," he reasoned.

Later on, I would remember how proud and yet saddened I had become watching Ricky in class before he had become aware of me; living his life as though I didn't exist. That was the first time I realized that the closest friends couldn't be with each other all the time. No two people could. And yet, when we were together, Ricky and I weren't two, but one. A lover's paradox. I couldn't sort it out. It confused me and I tried putting the thought out of my mind. It wouldn't completely vanish.

One Sunday, I rode by the Taylor house to see if Ricky were home. He was there all right, all dressed up on the front porch. Evidently, he had just returned home from church, gone there with his mother and sisters and another woman I didn't know. They were all standing around talking. Ricky's mother's arm was around her son's shoulder. He stood quietly. Not the restless Ricky I knew, but as though he was actually interested in what they were saying. His posture was upright, his fine, longish hair was neatly combed, his tie was on straight, his dark suit and his black shoes were clean, shined, pressed, neat. A minute later they all got into someone's car and drove off.

I rode off too, shattered. I hadn't waved at him, hadn't tried to get his attention. Perhaps I'd expected Ricky to intuit my presence as he had in school, and when he hadn't, he showed me how apart our two lives really were. I wished we were brothers and could live together.

At these times I would think about the future: not such a good idea, for unless something drastic happened, we would be separated as early as summer. I was to go to Hyannis with my family, Ricky to remain here. Another, even worse, threat loomed. About a week after I'd seen Ricky with his family, I began mentioning the local junior high that we would be going to. I almost fell over when Ricky said he wouldn't. For years he'd planned to attend the Glen Fawn Academy after elementary school. It was the surest way to enter other, more advanced military schools, and eventually the Armed Forces as an officer, he told me—that was his real dream. He had already passed the entrance exam into Glen Fawn. Now he was waiting to see if he would win a scholarship or if Tony Warner would help pay the tuition. He seemed determined on this matter. The news plunged me into an instant and near total grief that all Ricky's soothing words and kisses couldn't completely assuage. Were we to be driven apart so soon?

The holidays arrived and not too long afterward, on February 2nd, Ricky's birthday. I stayed up until past midnight finishing the MIG-2 model for him, working by flashlight after my brother had gone to sleep.

Ricky loved the gift and told me so, hugged me in front of his family and friends at his birthday party and declared that I was his best friend ever, which made me terrifically proud. In private he promised that he would do something special for me. When the next day my mother asked if I would like to sleep over at the Taylor's, I was certain Ricky had arranged it through his mother—that was his gift. Only partly, he admitted when I arrived there Friday night with my little overnight bag. His mother had asked if Ricky would like me to stay over. We made love most of that night, not getting to sleep until after dawn—we had to shade the eastern window with a coat. Saturday morning we were awakened by the odors of French toast and ham rising up the stairway to his little aerie. I telephoned home and got my mother's permission to remain a second night. I even went to the Methodist services with Ricky and his family, a new experience for me, which helped somewhat to mollify my fears. For now, I wasn't a stranger but in that group standing on the porch as I had witnessed them do a week before, and felt so excluded.

Ambidextrous: A Valentine

When I arrived in school the following Monday morning, it was clear that in the ecstasy of the weekend I'd forgotten something very important—the half-term book report.

This was not just any old report, and I was well aware of the fact. When I'd first come into Mrs. Campanella's class the previous year, she had stressed the importance she placed on students' reading outside of class. We were to read two books each school year—one fiction, one nonfiction—and our reports were supposed to be lengthy and detailed, displaying not only how closely we had read the book but also our ability to convey that particular experience to others. The five best reports were read to the class, so all could share. Because I'd arrived late in the school year, I'd only had one report to write, for which I had selected the only book I'd read out of class that year: a history of Grand Tour bicycle racing. While my report had received a better than passing grade, Mrs. Campanella hadn't thought as much of the subject as I had. In her notes on the front page she had written "Your enthusiasm gets across the excitement of these races well," but she hadn't chosen to read my report aloud, concentrating on the essays of those students who had reported on the lives of Lincoln and Helen Keller, and other, more "ennobling" subjects.

This year Mrs. Campanella had us tell her in advance the two books we planned to read and report on, and in what order. Somehow or other, I'd picked up a paperback my father had been reading, which for some reason interested me at the time, Clarence Darrow For the Defense, a biography by Irving Stone of the famous lawyer who'd defended evolutionary theory at the Scopes Trial. Mrs. Campanella had repeatedly asked me to be certain the book wasn't one of Stone's fictionalized biographies like *Lust For Life*. I'd become so put off by her questions I'd finally brought the book to class to show her it was a legitimate biography. I hadn't yet decided on the second book I would read; that could wait until later as the second report wasn't due in until a week before the end of classes in June. I read about half of the Darrow book, slowly I have to admit, losing interest as I went along. The book was far less fascinating than had been promised by its jacket copy. Then Ricky sailed into my life and we became friends, glue sniffers, lovers. After which, I never again touched the Stone biography; I didn't remember where I'd put it.

The day we were to hand in our book reports, I went up to Mrs. Campanella's desk and made an excuse: I'd read a book, had written a report, but hadn't been able to finish it over the weekend as planned because of my Grandfather's sudden visit from Rhode Island and the subsequent confusion in our house. She didn't believe a word but her kind large brown eyes said she wanted to believe me. She reminded me how much trust she'd placed in me after my difficulties with Mr. Hargrave. She asked if I really was going to pay back her belief or let her down. I let her talk me into handing the book report in the next day.

I was disconsolate. I called Ricky and told him to forget about me that evening: I had to do something about a book report. At the same time I hesitated, wavered. I knew I could probably write some sort of report about *Clarence Darrow For the Defense* based on what I'd read so far. If I played my cards right, I could concentrate 'on the first half, on Darrow's tribulations in becoming a lawyer, rather than on his most famous cases, which I hadn't yet reached. But did I really remember what I'd read? It had been months ago. And wouldn't that make for a merely passable report? What about the report Mrs. Campanella (after last year's fiasco) expected of me? I felt doomed if I wrote it; doomed if I didn't.

I faced the five (five!) blank sheets of paper I was supposed to fill with a superb essay and all I could see was disaster. I would fail English (one of my three best subjects) this semester. My parents wouldn't let me out of the house at night any more. Indoors studying all the time I would hardly be able to see Ricky. My model airplanes would be taken away, and with them the glue I loved to sniff, the boy whose kisses I craved. I stared at those five sheets of lined paper for an hour and was so gloomy at dinner that my mother jokingly asked who died. The thought came into my mind that she knew all that had happened, all that was about to happen, and she was mocking me, or worse suggesting the only honorable way out of this impasse—suicide. This upset me so much I asked to leave the table, before dessert.

Honor was the problem, or rather honor in conflict with desire. I couldn't let Mrs. Campanella think I really was a rotten, ungrateful child. After the malicious nemesis of Hargrave, her class had been delicious as fresh air to a dungeon-trapped prisoner. I couldn't fail my parents or myself. I couldn't let all of us down, partly because I would lose what I now had—Ricky, affection, a sense of belonging to someone terrific, of sharing everything (even our bodily fluids) with each other. Thinking all" ' this, I found it vaguely familiar. Someone I knew had once been in the same—or a similar—predicament. Who? What had he done to get out of it?

I remembered who. It wasn't anyone I'd known, but someone I'd read about so often I'd felt I'd known him. His name was Achilles. His inner conflict was the basis of the story of *The Iliad* and had led to the temporary disarray of the Greek armies on the plains outside of the city of Troy—and nearly led to the destruction of their war effort. The problem had come about because King Agamemnon had demanded a girl named Briseis out of Achilles' fairly won war booty: a girl Achilles wanted to restore to her father, a priest.

In that moment of recollection I knew that I was saved.

Here was a book I knew inside out: the characters, the setting, every detail of the story.

In the fifth grade, Mrs. Campanella had given us a mimeographed sheet on the elements of writing a book report. It was simple, clear, to the point, complete. It demanded of the writer the following in this order:

1) Title, author and date of first publication, as well as background of the author and/or book.

2) The setting—temporally and geographically—of the book, with any interesting details about how the author had or had not used the known facts to help his story.

3) The main characters and their relationships.

4) The main themes or subjects of the book.

5) The plot line, as simplified as possible.

6) What initially attracted you, the reader, to this particular book over all others and whether those anticipations had been met or not.

7) Whether or not you liked the book, despite your answer to #6, and why.

This was an excellent tool to have when facing the enormous variety of thoughts and emotions garnered from reading any book, and it answered all the questions another potential reader might ask. I continued to hold onto this mimeo sheet through Junior and High School, and although I'd lost it by the time I went to college, I used its basic structure for more elaborately developed literary papers there. I still use it in one way or another whenever I'm professionally reviewing a book. I wish every book reviewer had had Mrs. Campanella for a teacher, or her mimeo sheet as a guide. Especially as she only allowed an individual's opinion after the main material of the book had been first presented, a point all too many reviewers—off on some tangent that they are creative artists—seem to have missed completely, leaving us with many clever, craftily written, self-serving essay/sermons of no use to someone who wants to know what the book is about, and if, for example, there are lots of camels in it or not.

With this solution I only faced one problem—it was a different book than the one Mrs. Campanella had approved.

I couldn't believe she would fail me for that: Homer had to be an acceptable author. I knew I could present his work so wonderfully all criticism would be disarmed in advance. Yet I faced a second problem: *The Iliad* was so superior to my ability to report on it. Look at the poor impression I'd made on my father when I'd tried to tell him about it. All he'd come away with was illustrations of disheveled people. I couldn't review or even report on *The Iliad*, the best I could hope to do was—well, sort of introduce it.

Filled with respect for the book, fear for my future, but also a sense that I might accomplish something high and fine, I turned to my first blank sheet of paper and listed the essentials of the book, then wrote a first line: "Homer's two epics *The Iliad* and *The Odyssey* are the earliest books that are still widely read today—and for a very good reason. They are among the best books ever written. Although the customs and beliefs of the ancient Greeks are very different than ours, Homer's characters faced problems we also face today, situations similar to our own. War and peace, love and duty, honor and treachery, foolishness and cunning are his themes, subjects which define how people think and feel in nineteen hundred and fifty-six A.D. as they did in eight hundred B.C."

Writing those few lines of introduction was like rubbing Aladdin's lamp, from there on it was easy sailing. For the first time, I felt inspired, as though all my ideas about Homer had somehow crystallized within a tiny section of my mind without my being aware of it, now they were being drawn out in a fine, glittering thread of words and phrases, clauses and punctuation, spun out in comprehensible sentences, sentences that coalesced to form perfect paragraphs. Once in a while I stopped to ponder the choice of a word, to choose a stronger, apter, more precise term than the first. When I read over other sentences I knew they were awkward, had to be rephrased. But the fact that I knew that and even sometimes" knew how to alter them was most encouraging.

I didn't hear my brother come up to our room, change into his pajamas, go brush his teeth, come back and get into bed. I didn't hear him click off his light (though I did immediately turn on my own small model, building light to work on). Nor did I hear my parents come upstairs a few hours later. I simply wrote, at one with the paper and ballpoint pen, filled with Homer, filled with the excitement of putting into words what I'd been thinking, thrilled to be writing. Then I reread my five and a half pages, amended it here and there, then began to write out a clean draft fresh paper in what I trusted was my best penmanship.

When I'd finished it was two o'clock in the morning. I read my paper over once more, then read certain sentences and paragraphs I liked best once again, and I knew that I'd solved my problem: it was good. More important at that moment however was the odd, extremely delicious experience I'd had just gone through for the past six hours—of suddenly being mentally transported to another place where I could look down and make something happen, using pen and paper; using words. I felt as though I'd been flying, but it was a calmer, more controlled high than sniffing glue while Ricky brought me to a teeth-gripping orgasm. I almost felt as though I were one of Homer's gods and goddesses: Apollo shooting quivers-full of plague-infested arrows into the Greek camp, Hera commanding the sun to set an hour early so her champion, Diomedes, would not tire and fall in the day long duel with Sarpedon. Hadn't I commanded words like armies? Won a major battle?

I was so excited I had to get out of my stuffy bedroom,

to creep down to the living room where I might feel some of the vast space I felt I needed at this moment to help defray my delirious sensation of power, of achievement.

I must have been there a half hour, pacing, looking at the still, lovely moon-bathed street through the curtains, when I heard my mother's footsteps on the stairs. "Bobby?" she whispered, thinking I was my somnambulist brother, "Is that you?"

To curb her fears, I whispered back that it wasn't Bobby, but me.

"What are you doing here? Don't tell me you've started sleepwalking too?"

"Of course not. I couldn't sleep. Couldn't stay in bed. It was . . . too warm up there."

She came all the way down the stairs, pulling closed her rose-patterned, deep magenta nightgown, noiselessly coming to where I stood by the windows. "Aren't you feeling well?" Her hand rose, caressed my forehead, fell away after assessing its coolness. "Why are you looking outside? Did you see someone? Did you hear someone?"

"No. Look how beautiful it is. The street. The Doria's front porch. The trees. All silver in the moonlight."

She kept a hand on my shoulder, let it slide down as she settled into a nearby chair. "Did you finish your book report?"

I turned to her. "Yes." But I had to tell her more. "Mom? Something . . . wonderful . . . happened to me tonight." In the moonlight I could see her familiar face, even the sparkle in her eyes, a silver blush on her cheeks like expensive facial powder, the soft glitter of her teeth in her partly open mouth.

She picked up the excitement in my voice, "Yes?"

"I wrote my report," I began. "I didn't write about the book I said I would, but about Homer. And it was . . ." Expectant as she looked, I didn't know how to tell her. I tried again: "It was better than . . ." and paused again. I couldn't very well say it was better than being blown while on drugs. "It was . . ." I tried yet again and suddenly realized I would never be able to explain it to someone who hadn't also experienced it. For a moment I felt the aloneness of my situation, the gulf that swept open like the Hellespont between me and my mother. I knew then that even Ricky wouldn't be able to share the experience with me, much as he might try, since he too hadn't experienced it. No one I knew had. And I felt betrayed by what had happened upstairs at my desk—alienated, different—still superior somehow, still accomplished; but utterly frustrated.

"Shhh. I'm sure it's a very good report. You're just overtired. That's why you couldn't sleep, why you can't find the right words."

What irony. I had found the right words before. Why not now? I looked out the windows, felt my mother's hand on me, and wondered if from then on my life would be one where I would be able to write down anything, everything I saw and felt and read and thought—no matter how complex, subtle, or difficult—yet I would never be able to speak those feelings, thoughts, and ideas to even those closest to me. For the briefest of moments, I prophesized that for myself, understood it would be true, and was chilled to the bone by the unshakeable loneliness it portended, worse than the teeth-shattering shivers I'd been sent into by the bicycle accident.

"You're getting cold," my mother said, grateful to be able to understand something of what was happening to me. "Let's go upstairs." We went up to bed, where I shivered myself to sleep and tried not to think about the frozen abyss of the future.

Near morning I had the dream again. I felt it coming on, tried to keep it from happening, then powerless, had to allow all its elements to come together into its preordained,

Ambidextrous: A Valentine

horribly familiar pattern. It was a recurrent dream, and like all such dreams, a nightmare of astonishing bewilderment. I don't remember when I first had the dream: I might have been as young as four or five years old: because even later, when I was twelve, it began the same way, as though having accreted the concerns of a younger me as a jumping off point, it had never discovered any other more effective way to begin itself. The dream also ended the same way, with me waking into a sweat-stained terror, my heart thudding in my small chest, the hotness of a scream stifled in my throat, the slow, growing realization that I was no longer asleep, but awake; and with that another terrifying realization that I had to urinate.

Terrifying because that was how the dream always began. I would awaken in my bed, in my bedroom—not a single detail changed—and have to urinate. I would get out of bed, put on my slippers, walk to the bedroom door, open it. But as I tottered, about to step over the lintel, there was no diamond-patterned wallpapered corridor faintly glowing from the tiny amber night light, no white, regularly slatted staircase fence, no adjoining bedroom doors, as usual. Instead, there was a void, an enormous black empty void studded with stars, patternless star clusters, nebulae in spirals, indistinguishable clouds, swirls of stars. It stretched ahead on either side of me, into an infinity that was not so much cold as it was undeniably there. Behind me was my bedroom, my brother's form, his light snoring; in front of me—nothing but stars.

In the dream I would begin to teeter in shock, but manage to grab onto the side walls, and I would remain standing there as long as I could, utterly terrified, certain I would urinate. So terrified I would finally awaken, find myself in bed, aching to urinate, in terror of going up to that door and opening it, fearing the dream wasn't ended, that the abyss would be there again, and no matter how many times I awakened, it would always be the same: a need to urinate, walking to the door, opening it, the abyss. . . .

I hadn't had the dream in perhaps four years. So when I had it that night, somewhere within my subconscious mind I remarked to myself, "This is the same old dream," as I got out of bed to open the door. Sure enough, there was the emptiness, the stars. And of course, once more I was terrified, even as I teetered on the lintel and peered into the depths of the blackness. Only this time it wasn't really so empty. Those stars seemed bright, individuated; not hostile as I'd always assumed them, but in some curious manner friendly; and while incredibly distant, they were somehow reachable—if I leapt toward them. Leapt toward them? This new twist was too much for my poor nightmare-programmed psyche and instantly brought on the cold-perspiration terror that led to a real (or was it? for a moment I couldn't be certain) awakening. Only this time I didn't have to urinate—had done so only a few hours ago on my mother's suggestion when coming back upstairs.

I lay in bed, fully, truly awake, uninterested in going to the door, peering out. Wondering why the dream—gone for so many years that I'd all but forgotten it—should suddenly return, wondering what those bright clumps of stars really were, and why this time I hadn't been afraid of them, but had felt, well, almost welcome.

Because I wasn't impelled to, I got out of bed and walked to the door, opened it—and was almost disappointed to see merely the top floor corridor of our house.

Fifteen years later, I experienced the dream again. Not as a dream but as a vision. And I was able to make some sense out of it, to comprehend a little why the dream might have returned when I was twelve, and possibly why I had the dream so often in the first place. At least I managed to come up with a rationalization—which is almost as good as a real explanation.

Ambidextrous: A Valentine

It was a Halloween weekend at a friend's house in the Berkshire Mountains. The rambling two-story house had been built on a gently sloping lower ridge of one of the tallest mountains in the range. Most of the land was grass and meadow, dry and crackling with iced dew in the lateness of the year, the fruit-killing frosts, the still hot afternoons. Ten of us, part of a loose commune that lived in Greenwich Village and shared similar tastes in men, drugs, rock music, parties, and ultra-liberal politics had come up to the little Western Massachusetts town in two cars earlier that day. Our shopping trips for records and food in nearby Pittsfield were observed by many young teens who surrounded us wherever we went, certain from our weird apparel and stoned-cool attitude that we were some rock group unknown to them. This was 1970, and by then even small towns in New England had been media saturated to the Counterculture which we represented so effortlessly.

After dinner Saturday night, we all dropped some excellent black Microdot Acid and went off in twos and threes. One group climbed the mountain behind the house. Another couple baked bread in the kitchen. Margaret and Arnie took an endlessly long and luxurious hot bath in the huge circular wooden tub set in the middle of a huge, earthy bathroom. The balsam attar of the Vitabath gelée they used seeped into the other olfactory sensations of hot buttered bread, incense, marijuana and cigarette smoke. Others among us listened to music in the living room or went off to their own rooms to talk or make love.

Tall, quiet Matthew, new to the commune, decided to go out into the moonless clear night and I went with him. Margaret loaned him her large bearskin fur coat. We trod out past the lights of the house into a sunken meadow which ended at a cliff that dropped sheer several hundred feet onto a horse pasture used by the adjoining stables, desolate past midnight. It was a cold, dark, star-dotted night, and once we lay down on the blanket I'd brought, only an occasional gust of wind carried the music playing in the living room to where we lay, the complicated harmonics of Love's *Forever Changes* album broken into three-quarter bars of silence then four-fifth bars of music, ever-changing, so that while we were intimately familiar with the music, it sounded new, different, as though it had become transformed into some mysterious Raga we were hearing for the first time. When I became chilled, Matthew took off the fur coat and placed it atop the two of us. We'd never really talked before, and now we lay on a slight angle to the immense black sky and just looked up, our bodies barely touching along one side with warmth, our heads angled in, feeling the peaceful freshness of the night.

Suddenly I felt as though I was angled up more than before, a moment later I could no longer tell whether I was flat down and the sky up, or I was leaning over forward and the sky was shallowly angled beneath me. I wasn't frightened, attributing this new perception—as we did almost all new or disturbing perceptions under the influence—to the hallucinogen. Yet because of this odd perceptual shift, this sudden perspicacity, I felt less at odds with the "up-thereness" of the stars than ever before, found them more approachable, almost touchable. looking at the sky, I felt clearly that some stars, some constellations and nebulae, were closer, while others were as clearly farther away. I knew that, was able to see their distances not only from me, but from each other. For the first time I was able to relate to the heavens in a three-dimensional manner and somehow I was also able to convey this knowledge, these sensations, to Matthew. I let myself go and "fell" into the stars, buzzing past the nearer ones, zooming along fearless toward the farther stars, checking their relationships as I now saw them.

It was then that I recalled what an old German astrologer had told me: all eleven points on the horoscope that he'd drawn up for my time and date of birth were extremely, unusually, close to the positions of fixed stars of the first and second magnitude: all of them. And one fixed star, Formalhaut—only twenty-three light years from earth, and thus a near neighbor—directly conjoined the location of the Sun at the moment of my birth. I was a star child, he'd told me, destiny's darling, and I would lead a more fated life than most people. So I had nothing to fear from the stars. Indeed, they were more closely linked to me, personally connected, than I'd ever imagined. True, that connection might bring evil as well as good into my life. But even then it would signify a specialness about me I'd intuited for decades. That childhood dream had never been hostile. I'd simply been unable to understand it.

I laughed with comprehension and joy, laughed and only stopped laughing when I felt Matthew's surprisingly warm lips nibbling my cheek, and I turned to him and exploding like stars gone nova, we made love.

The book report was accepted, but it required four more days for Mrs. Campanella to read it, more time than she'd needed for the other student's reports, and I was asked to bring my own copy of *The Iliad* to class. I suppose so she could check that I hadn't cribbed from someone else's preface. I later learned that she also called my mother who confirmed that 1) I'd read the book at least three times. 2) I'd written the report myself and thought it was good. 3) I'd been touched or changed in some inexplicable manner by writing the report.

My grade for the essay was the highest in the class, and Mrs. Campanella read it aloud. At lunchtime afterward, my friends looked at me oddly, but they didn't say a word about the report. Mrs. Campanella had written only one comment beneath the grade on the title sheet, "Nobly done."

A few days later, when I was at her desk, having just

collected some spelling quizzes for the class, she asked, "Do you write poetry?" I stammered back, "I don't think so. Why?" She looked at me, a strange expression on her face, then said, "At first when you came into my class, I thought you were foreign born, because you use words and phrases differently than they're usually used. After reading several of your essays, I decided it was deliberate usage on your part, your own style."

At that, I wasn't even able to stammer. I hadn't done anything stylistically different with words in my reports; or at least I hadn't tried to. When I finally found my voice enough to tell her that, she said, "Well, then it must be a natural gift. An original manner of expression is a gift. You ought to try your hand at poetry."

Now I was confused. I wanted to become an artist—like Van Gogh or Leonardo—not a poet. I scarcely knew any poetry except Joyce Kilmer's *Trees* which I thought was a stupid poem anyway.

"Would you like to read some good poetry?" she asked. I had to say yes, although I was embarrassed and wanted to back out of the conversation as quickly as possible.

A few days later, Mrs. Campanella handed me a small paperback anthology, Immortal Poems of the English Language, which she had inscribed to me on the title page. She advised me to dip in and around toward the end of the book where the language was more contemporary and work my way to the front, and the earlier poems. I was so surprised by the gift—it couldn't have cost her more than thirty-five cents—that I did actually read the book. I kept it on my bed table and whenever I couldn't get to sleep right away, I would read one or two poems, most of which I didn't understand. Later that summer, I would find that I'd packed the paperback inside a pair of favorite jeans, and would read it at odd hours on lighted screened-in porches at Petaquamsquatt where we vacationed that year, and where I began to slowly but surely fall in love with poetry.

I never mentioned the book report to Ricky except to apologize for not seeing him that night, and saying that it had succeeded, which—practical boy as he was—satisfied him that our sacrifice had not been in vain. School and schoolwork were our one taboo subject—because too boring and ordinary. But one day when he was in my bedroom, he spotted my anthology and began to pore through it. Surprised by this unusual activity, I asked questions. It seems that his teacher had asked each student in the class to memorize a poem, and he was looking for one he might like. We spent hours reading mostly opening lines to decide if Ricky would memorize a given poem. He had a million excuses for not liking them. Even my own favorites—Yeats' "A Coat" and Keats' "To Sleep" were too complicated for him. Then he happened upon Emily Dickinson's poem, "A Narrow Fellow in the Grass," and read it aloud to me. When he reached the last line, "and zero at the bone," he read eerily, as though he were Boris Karloff or Lon Chaney, and I almost jumped.

"See!" he laughed. "It's about a snake! She goes out for a walk and meets a snake!" He read it aloud again and was so delighted with the poem's unusualness and mischief potential in class, that he decided to memorize it. He thought he might even find a little grass snake and carry it to school in his pocket and draw it out during his recitation.

A few days after, I recited as much of the poem as I recalled while masturbating him on his bed. After he reached orgasm, Ricky asked, "Do you want to see a really big one?"

"Sure," I answered, waiting for him to pull out yet another hidden manila envelope full of pornographic photos. But Ricky jumped off the bed, got dressed and instructed me to do the same. We went out the window, slid down the Hickory tree and hiked off: destination unknown.

We rode about ten blocks out of our neighborhood into an area of older larger houses, similar in size and build (if not in dilapidation) to the Taylor house. At one driveway, Ricky swerved up the sidewalk and along a paved path behind an unfamiliar house. I followed and saw him circle the freestanding garage and disappear into a stand of trees. I biked after him and stopped only after I'd gone about five hundred feet into what looked to be several empty lots, where Ricky was stopped, astride his bike, talking to John Bayley. Beyond Bayley, I made out a sort of plank lean-to, roofed over with tar paper. This was Junior Cook's gang hideout. It was the last place in the world I wanted to be. And John Bayley was the last person—next to Junior Cook himself—I wanted to see.

Three years before while walking the block and a half to our local store to buy some groceries for my mother, I'd been accosted by Bayley and another boy. Although I didn't know this second boy, I'd seen John Bayley around a great deal; he only lived a block away and was in my older brother's sixth-grade class at the time. So I was naturally off guard that day when the two boys pulled their bikes up onto the sidewalk and blocked my way. Bayley asked what I was doing. I answered, surprised by his hard, nasty tone of voice. He said I was a liar and asked to see my mother's note and money. When I pulled it out of my pocket, he threw the note away and pocketed the cash. When I protested and tried to get the dollar and a halfback, Bayley slapped my face hard, twice, and told me to get lost. When I didn't go immediately, they got off their bikes and began pushing me, until pummeled and chased by two older boys, I ran off.

Having had my trusting nature so harshly repaid, I'd arrived home so upset that my mother not only didn't punish me for coming home without money or groceries, but comforted me. I wasn't the only child to suffer from Bayley and his cohorts. When their pre-teen terrorism continued with other small victims, our mothers stopped sending all but older children to the store alone, or opened up charge accounts, thus breaking off an important source of income for the Cook gang members, who had a far less easy time terrorizing kids out of their lunch money at school.

That incident was the last time I'd faced Bayley without being on my bike and going thirty miles an hour. But he seemed to have forgotten it, and in fact seemed not unhappy to "meet any friend of Ricky's." He let us into the gang house and I was finally face to face with Junior Cook.

I think that in everyone's early life there exists one neighborhood boy who stands out from all others by sheer dint of his troublemaking capacity; the boy whom children only mention with awe and fear and parents with anger and annoyance. Such a boy was Junior Cook. He came from an otherwise unexceptional Irish-American middle class family which boasted several other children of perfect mediocrity. But—as Mendel showed in the last century with his sweet pea experiments—sometimes out of four offspring, one gets all the dominant genes, leaving little to the others, and that might explain the phenomenon of Junior Cook. He was a third child (like myself) and a first son (unlike myself) which could have meant he was overly pampered as an infant and young child; or conversely that he was saddled with expectations he could never live up to.

That might explain his psychology, it didn't really account for Junior Cook's charisma or his natural talent for meanness and mischief. He wore his butterscotch hair in a tough year-round flat-top crew cut. Already at fifteen, he had a tattoo on his left shoulder. He had been in fights with boys two and three years older than himself and, rumor had it, once with an adult. He swore, smoked cigarettes, had been in reform school six month! for a particularly loathsome store robbery where a clerk had been nicked with a switchblade knife, and he remained unchastened by the experience—indeed, he was proud of it.

Not much taller than I, Junior Cook was slender, but wiry and already as well-muscled as a grown man. He could have become a superb athlete—runner, wrestler, boxer, decathlon star—with his strength and agility. But it was clear that he would never get beyond the ninth grade or his seventeenth birthday, whichever came first. He openly, actively hated school, parents, authority of any kind. Apart from his unexpected shortness, he was physically compelling; enough so to attract and mistreat many teenage girls. He had a squarish face, accented by a set jaw, long lips, eyebrows like horizontal brackets, a short almost snub nose with wide nostrils, all of it topped by the closed lid of his crew cut, with a small widow's peak that gave the only hint of angularity to his features. His eyes were long, but half shut most of the time as though clamped down to deliberately keep out the good things of life. Yet, when open, they were a startling Caribbean blue, specked with tiny yellow and white dots that made them look filled with stars. He dressed "tough": black body-fitting t-shirts with one short sleeve rolled up to hold his ubiquitous package of Camels, tight fitting blue denims (the first I'd seen on someone who wasn't a workman), a wide, black garrison belt with a large buckle depicting a charging bull and black motorcycle boots.

I quailed upon entering the hideout, despite Ricky shoving me forward with a whispered assurance that it was "okay."

Inside, the gang house wasn't much to look at, but as it had the aura of a fabled, forbidden place, I observed as much as I could without appearing to be nosy. A green metal shaded lamp hung from the ceiling illuminating a cramped single room with more or less vertical walls, but an oddly-angled ceiling. Loose planks of differing sizes and varieties of wood had been hammered together as a floor, but one could still make out the dirt ground below through a few large knots and ill-fitting joins. The furniture was sparse and worn—three old Windsor chairs with torn upholstery and cracked springs had their legs sawn off so they sat almost flat. Two black painted milk boxes held a variety of objects I couldn't quite make out as they were in the darkest part of the room. In another corner, on the floor, was a tattered, half-rolled up sleeping bag. Most fascinating was their primitive alarm system, devised of tin cans on a string, that wound from inside the hideout to outside and would be set clanking—and warning—if one didn't know exactly where the strings attaching them crossed.

Junior Cook was sitting in one chair, his feet almost straight out in front of him, as we entered. He was reading Argosy magazine; on its cover, lurid illustration of a bloody-chested adventurer beating to death a ferociously snarling Bengal tiger with blows of his huge rifle butt. Slightly behind them, a blood-spattered, breasty blond shrunk back into the jungle foliage. When Junior Cook deigned to look up, be greeted Ricky offhandedly, looked at me for an instant, and seemingly unable to place who I was ignored me. He popped open a Rheingold, told Ricky to share it with me, gave an unopened can of beer to Bayley, who perched onone of the milk boxes and began chugging. Junior Cook drank beer and told Ricky and I to "take a load off your feet." We sat in the two remaining chairs, while Junior Cook continued to read whatever article or story had captured his attention. When he was done with it, he rolled up the magazine as though about to use it as a weapon, but threw it harmlessly over his shoulder. Still ignoring me, he asked Ricky how he'd been.

If I had been astonished by our destination that afternoon, I was even more amazed that Ricky knew Junior Cook; that they had friends somehow in common seemed so unlikely. I hadn't lost a jot of my nervousness or defensiveness, even though I did share the beer with Ricky and tried to seem as relaxed as he was. Only when, out of nowhere, Junior Cook asked, "Who's this?" and Ricky answered back, "My buddy. He's okay," and Junior Cook stared me up and down for a very long two minutes, did I begin to feel uncomfortable again.

"He sniff?" Junior Cook asked and when Ricky said I did, Junior pulled out the biggest tube of airplane glue I'd ever seen, squirted a large gob of it into a plastic bag and handed it to me. I inhaled deeply, passed it on, and quickly realized that they were going to act as though nothing unusual was happening. I too would have to act "cool", even if I was already reeling from a single deep inhalation. Junior even pulled out a cigarette, offered the pack around and he and Bayley smoked between sniffs.

"So what brings you here?" Junior Cook asked Ricky and reached forward to put a hand on my friend's upper thigh. "You getting any?" he asked, before Ricky had a chance to answer his first question. Ricky nodded at me, and Junior Cook again looked me up and down, then said, "Yeah, but it ain't the same, is it?" When Ricky didn't respond, Junior Cook Went on, "I thought you said your uncle promised to whip you good if you ever saw me again?" Ricky said that didn't bother him, no one would tell. "Oh, yeah?" Cook asked. "Not even this little boy?" and he reached over and took my upper thigh in his strong grip.

In addition to my fear and nervousness and surprise, I now had to deal with a new fact not all that subtly revealed through their exchange: Junior Cook and Ricky had once been buddies, perhaps as intimate as Ricky and I, and somehow or other had been forced apart by Ricky's family. I felt if not exactly jealous then very much like it—and confused. I wished we would leave and turned to get Ricky's attention.

He was leaning forward, grasping Junior Cook's leg back, and he said in that slightly slurred voice I knew so well from our glue-sniffing sessions, "Got another cigarette?" When Junior Cook shook out a Camel, Ricky said, "Put it in, will ya?" When that had been done, Ricky made Junior Cook light it, and made a big show of blowing out the match. For a minute I thought they would kiss, their faces were so close, the air between them so thick with beer and cigarette and glue fumes, and I felt really uncomfortable. But Bayley began to laugh, and Junior Cook leaned back and turned to Bayley to bark out, "Shut it, or I'll shut it for you." Bayley got quiet really fast, and Junior Cook repeated his first question, "So what brings you back here today?"

Ricky puffed on his cigarette then slowly said, "I told him about Bayley's big dick, but he didn't believe me. Wants to see it for himself."

Now I'd seen Ricky Hersch in many situations in the months of our friendship: as a child among schoolchildren, with his family, with his friends, with grown-ups; I'd seen him compassionate, angry, merry; I'd seen him with my come dripping out of the sides of his mouth he was so sensual. But I'd never seen him like this: cool, hard, manipulative, challenging, playful yet dangerous too. Evidently he considered himself at least Junior Cook's equal—probably his superior—to toy with him as he was doing. It calmed me a bit, not much.

"Yeah? Is that *all* you came here for?" Junior Cook said back and took Ricky's cigarette out of his mouth, puffed on it, handed it back.

"Why else would I come here?" Ricky answered, and stamped the cigarette on the floor without putting it to his lips again.

Annoyed, Junior Cook said, "You heard him, Bayley. Whip out your meat for pretty boy here."

Bayley jumped down from the milk boxes to stand right between us. He unzipped his pants, reached into his slightly yellow-stained jockey shorts and extracted an almost erect monster of length, girth, and redness.

"You like that?" Junior Cook asked me. "Go on touch it, see for yourself. Go on. It won't bite. Though it may spit at ya. Go on," he prompted. I looked at Ricky to see what I should do, but he wasn't paying us any mind. He was slumped back in his chair, sniffing glue again.

I touched Bayley's cock and it got stone hard, veins quivering all over its length.

"Go on," Junior Cook insisted, "jerk it," and I did, although not much as I couldn't get a purchase on its smooth thickness. "Use two hands," Junior Cook instructed, and I did. "Ain't nothing Bayley likes better than having a pretty boy jerk his meat," he added, "unless it's having someone with a ten dollar bill jerk it. Ain't that right Bayley? Or even better, having a pretty boy suck on it. Go on. Put it in your mouth. Go on." I wouldn't. I let go of it, embarrassed, frightened, not by Bayley's cock, but by Junior Cook's words, his insidious tone of voice—and the situation altogether. Ricky was now slumped even more deeply in his chair, the glue sniffing bag over his face. I felt alone.

It could be dangerous. I remembered hearing about people—children mostly—who'd smothered to death with plastic bags over their faces. I reached for the bag, pretending I wanted to sniff more, and Ricky came to a bit, looking at me, at us, as though from far away.

Junior Cook had leaned forward again, and begun caressing Bayley's cock, still erect between our faces. He began going "ooh" and "aah" as he jerked it, then made a big show of licking its length, then offering it to me, and when I shook no, of taking the big red tip of it in his mouth, and slurping a lot as though it were a lollipop, taking it out again and rubbing it all over his face, lifting his eyebrows

Ambidextrous: A Valentine

and following his eyes whenever he put it in or took it out of his mouth, continually offering it to me, once even saying, "Mmmm. Better than a lollipop, dontcha' think?" until I couldn't take my eyes off him.

He must have seen it was as fascinating as it was repulsive to me, but that I would not give in to his blandishments, because suddenly Junior Cook said, "Hey, Ricky baby. Why don't you show this little boy here how to do it. You was always an ace cocksucker." He pulled Ricky up from the cushions of the chair, at which Ricky became more aware of what was going on, although not by a hell of a lot. Bayley began moaning and groaning, and Junior Cook, still jerking him, said, "C'mon boys. Get ready for your freshly made egg creams when this fucker shoots." He almost didn't finish. Bayley groaned once more and splattered against the wall two, three, four, five, six times! before almost falling over, trying to get Junior Cook's pumping hand off him. When Junior Cook did release him, Bayley stumbled back a few steps and fell onto the sleeping bag. Junior was already on his feet. He unzipped himself and grabbing Ricky's head, pushed his cock into Ricky's mouth, where Ricky sucked him to a quick, noisy orgasm. Junior Cook fell back into his chair, his still hard cock sticking out of his fly, saying "You always was the best head, Ricky. Never got any better, even at the Home. I really miss it, you know."

Nothing much happened after that. Bayley went back to drinking his beer. Junior Cook lit another cigarette, but still didn't put his cock back inside his pants, and Ricky looked sort of sheepish and very stoned. So I finally said in a small voice that I had to get going, and when I nudged Ricky, he sort of shook himself and stood up. Since no one stopped us, we left the gang house. Before we closed the hideout door behind us, Junior Cook said in his most insinuating tone, "Now don't be such a stranger, Rick. And you too, pretty boy. You both come visit any time you want to chew on Bayley's flank steak."

We didn't answer back but got on our bikes and rode back home. As we passed through the now chilled, dank streets, I began to get more and more angry and upset over what had happened. Without my meaning to, tears started to my eyes and began to flow so copiously they began to blind me. I had to stop the bike and wipe them away, hoping Ricky wouldn't notice.

"What's got into you?" Ricky asked. He'd circled back to where I'd stopped.

"I don't know," I said, then I blurted out, "I wish you hadn't taken me there."

"C'mon. It wasn't that bad. You crying?"

"No." But it was evident I had been. "I don't like what he did to you. And you let him!"

"C'mon. Don't be like that. It wasn't anything special." Ricky took my shoulder, trying to comfort me. "It didn't mean anything, you know," he insisted.

"I know." I dried my eyes. "But he made it seem so nasty, so dirty. Both of them did. I don't see how you could have ever let him be your buddy. "

"Well, I'm not now. I'm *your* buddy. I got smart, see?" He hugged me and I was beginning to feel that what I'd intuited, felt, behind all of Junior Cook's carryings-on had been exaggerated, when Ricky added, "I don't mind, see, because, well, because it's not true that my uncle said I had to stop being his friend."

"It's not?"

"Nah! I told Junior that because I didn't want to see him any more."

"You didn't?" My hopes soared.

"Nah. I mean, he acts all tough and everything, but I got sick and tired of him. I only went there today because of you. I wanted to show you off to him. Swear on it!" he declared. "He's a tough act with his beer and his cigarettes, but he's just a jerk like all the rest of them!" Ricky went on as though talking to himself. "I mean, you know, I like sucking and jerking as much as the next guy. But the real reason I stopped seeing him was that he began to get all mushy and huffy about my other friends. Acted like I *belonged* to him, for Chrissakesl Can you believe it?"

In the dark, he couldn't see the look on my face that would have told him to stop right there, to not go on. But he didn't, and what he said next stunned me at the time and would come back to haunt me.

"I don't belong to anyone!" Ricky said, as though I were arguing the point. "Not to Junior Cook. Not to anyone! And I never will. I'm my own person. I belong to me, myself and I."

I didn't know what to say, which gave Ricky the time to add, "Hell! You're just a kid compared to Junior Cook, and even you know that. Right? Right?" he insisted when I didn't immediately respond.

"Right," I finally said, less than enthusiastically, hating to have to say it at all. Then I slid out from under his hand on my shoulder, got on my bike and rode off, so fast Ricky had to call out twice for me to wait up for him.

At the time, even though I'd clearly heard Ricky's declaration that he didn't belong to anyone and never would, and even though I realized that it was a warning as much as a statement of self, it didn't really sink in. After all, we were still buddies, weren't we? Ricky had affirmed that at the same time he'd declared his independence, hadn't he?

Perhaps so, but after the clubhouse incident I began to feel a new uneasiness whenever Ricky and I were together. I knew that keeping that uneasiness from him was the worst thing I could to our friendship, but I couldn't bring myself to mention it to him, couldn't bear to hear him say, "And I don't belong to you, either. Never did. Never will." Which I was sure would happen if I pressed him.

That wedge so lightly hammered in, I would stare at Ricky whenever we were together and I was certain he wasn't noticing me looking at him, and I would attempt to see what other personalities I'd never seen in him before would emerge: as awful as the one Junior Cook had elicited. No more did, and I'd almost forgotten the gang house and its implicit warning to me, almost relaxed back into the old security of our friendship—the most important thing in my life at the time—when another, altogether unrelated incident occurred in my class at school which showed me how in love I really was with Ricky Hersch, how little real reciprocation I might expect from him, and most important, what a dreadful thing love could be.

I guess we'd been making and giving Valentines in school since the first or second grade, usually devoting at least one and usually two art periods in the week previous to the holiday to making the cards. So, when Mrs. Campanella suggested we make Valentines, all the boys in the class murmured a disappointed "Aww" and all the girls said "Yay!"

Mrs. Campanella was in no way dictatorial so she set out to persuade us boys to consent to making Valentines by telling us about the history off" the custom. According to her, it came from Roman-Christian times, and somehow or other was connected with a Saint Valentine who used to send gifts to his close friends on that day. "So you see, boys and girls," she summed up, "although the date has come in our time to have romantic associations, it really means that you are offering someone a proof of friendship when you give them a Valentine. And to show how good your intentions are, you really ought to present them with a handmade token of friendship."

She never did quite convince the boys in the class that we should give each other Valentines just to show we were friends—we already knew we were friends without the need for any "tokens". But her little talk defused the romantic connotations of the day a bit, and since most of us felt we ought to give our mothers, grandmothers, Godmothers or favorite aunt a card, we figured we could waste at least one art period on such otherwise useless trash.

We set to work with red and white construction paper, pen, scissors, and glue. Mrs. Campanella showed us how to fold our paper in half and using only one half of a heart, how to make a completely symmetrical entire one. She showed us how to fold lighter weight paper into fourths and how to cut out tiny patterns within to make a plain sheet of paper into a rather authentic looking lace doily. By the end of the period, we'd each made at least one Valentine and envelope. But the girls had been long prepared with ideas and designs and some of them managed three or four Valentines in the two-hour class.

Evidently they also spent time at home making them because the following day, the Fourteenth, some came into class with loose-leafs bulging with cards. Mrs. Campanella waited until our last hour of the day, a free period, before letting us hand out our cards. Then it began: a shower of Valentines descended upon us. Some boys in the class had been more convinced by our teacher than it had first appeared. They also decided to make cards at home to give them to some girls in class (but not to any boys) and to sign them "Anonymous" and "Your Secret Friend" or even "From You Know Who", although some didn't even bother with those ruses and boldly signed their own names, which became fuel for minor scandals and much giggling.

To accommodate such an amplitude of friendship tokens, our teacher had all the cards piled on one of the back cabinets, then sorted out by the name of the receiver, to be handed out row by row by the first person in each row. This not only solved the logistics of getting all the cards to the right students without everyone running about willy nilly in the room, it also cut down the embarrassment factor of having to actually hand your Valentine to someone, complete with blushing, stammering, the possibility of rejection and/or reception only with hesitation or giggles. Once distributed, the cards could be opened and the receiver could then get up and go over to thank the donor.

The girls in six-one had been "socialized" beyond credibility so every single person in the class received at least one Valentine; even smelly Billy Kraus, even frog-faced Myron Goldblum. I received two cards, one from "Someone who likes you more than you like Her!" obviously Carolyn Tree whom I pointedly ignored every conceivable moment of my class life, and one from my friend, Nancy. Some students received heaps of Valentines. Among the boys, Edward Young led; among the girls, naturally, Lynne-Anne Fribourg—neither any real surprise to the rest of us as they were both class favorites. After the cards were handed out, the boys more or less opened theirs. Leaving them on their desks and taking advantage of the ability to visit each other, we gathered in twos and threes to talk about other, more interesting matters. The girls also grouped themselves, but to slowly open each card with the maximum amount of suspense, with little whoops of triumph and delight, with exaggerated thanks to each other, and with even more exaggerated wonder at whomever could have anonymously signed a particular card. All very boring and predictable until Lynne-Anne opened one large, rather nicely made card decorated with all sorts of lace and ribbons. Out of it dropped a thin gold neck chain with a gold charm pendant. This was largesse indeed. The jewelry must have setback someone at least twenty-five dollars, a lot of cash for a twelve-year-old. An explosion of wonder swept through the girls at this extraordinary, this magnificent Valentine.

It wasn't easy to keep word of the gift from spreading.

Soon, every girl in every group in the classroom was butting into the fluttering mass of pre-teen females surrounding Lynne-Anne trying to get a look at the chain and charm. This sudden surge of students attracted even Mrs. Campanella, who broke through, took one look at the gift, another at the card, and said, "It really seems you do have a secret admirer, Lynne-Anne. A very generous one. Perhaps too generous for a mere classroom Valentine." It wasn't hard to follow the meaning behind our teacher's kind though pointed words. Lynne-Anne, who had been blushing with confusion and who knows what other emotions since the moment Nancy had spotted the chain, caught on quickly. Handing the gift to Mrs. Campanella, she said, "It's lovely. But I couldn't possibly accept it."

During all this activity I'd moved my seat over a row or two to sit and talk with Martin O'Connor, so both of us had a select view of the gift's opening and the various reactions to it. We both noticed that Lynne-Anne had never left her seat, and neither had Myron Goldblum, who sat directly behind her, even though this meant he had been surrounded by girls. We'd also noticed his more than usual interest in Lynne-Anne's opening of her cards, poorly as he tried to pretend to be indifferent to it. And how, when the gold chain and charm had fallen out, Myron had flushed with pleasure and almost swooned when Lynne-Anne held it up to-her pearly neck to see if it would fit. During the melee surrounding the gift, Martin had made a deft, unnoticed snatch at the card accompanying the gift. One glance at the handwriting confirmed our opinion: the Beast had given Beauty the magnificent Valentine.

"Children," Mrs. Campanella called us to attention. "Lynne-Anne has received a gift that she naturally cannot accept. She wishes to return it to the person who gave it to her with her heartfelt thanks. We all realize of course the affection such a wonderful gift symbolizes, but we also all agree that it is the thought behind the Valentine, not its value, which really matters. Now will whomever gave the anonymous card and gift raise his hand and allow Lynne-Anne to thank him and return the gift."

It was a good try, but no dice. Every boy in the class immediately fell silent. Many looked at Edward Young as the most likely perpetrator, but when he was asked point blank, he said he'd made only one Valentine, which he planned to give to his mother. Where would he get the money for such an expensive gift anyway? Edward's unflinching honesty ended all speculation about him. Mrs. Campanella said that left her with no choice. She would have to ask every boy in the class, one by one. The next boy she asked was my friend Martin, who sneered: "Are you kidding? I wouldn't spend money on a girl if she was dying."

It became instantly apparent to Mrs. Campanella that the spirit of amity that she had been hoping to foster would be completely destroyed if she received another answer like that. On the other hand she knew she had to act somehow to settle the matter of the chain. "I've made my decision," she declared. "I won't ask any more. I'm going to keep the chain at my desk, and after class the person who gave it anonymously to Lynne-Anne, may as anonymously claim it. It must be returned."

"*Why?*" the bellowing call came from Myron. "Why does it have to be given back? Why can't she keep it?"

All but Martin and I were startled by the outburst. We'd been watching him contort in agony as Mrs. Campanella began her speech and interrogation.

"Why?" she answered his question as though it were purely rhetorical. "Because young ladies don't accept expensive gifts from young men not related to them. That's why it has to be given back."

"*Why?*" he asked again. "Why? If the person who gave it to her wanted her to have it."

"Did you give it to her?" Mrs. Campanella asked, unable to hide her astonishment.

"How do you know anyway," Mryon went on, unheeding, "that the quality of the affection shown isn't greater with a gift than with any old Valentine card?" To demonstrate he picked up the single, small card he had received in class. "How can you possibly know what someone feels, what someone values, how someone loves?"

The class, naturally enough, was aghast at this eloquent, if stricken, outburst, and by the agonized look on Myron's face which made him appear even more Quasimodo-ish than before.

For once, even Mrs. Campanella had a situation which she didn't know how to control. Her composure gone, she stared at the boy, then at Lynne-Anne who had almost fallen out of her seat in her effort to get distance between herself and her unlikely suitor. Without a word, our teacher merely moved forward a few steps and held out the chain to Myron.

"I don't want it back," he moaned. "It's for her! Her!"

"She can't accept it. You have to take it back.'

"I *can't* take it back!"

Mrs. Campanella stepped up to his desk, placed the chain and charm on his desk top and started toward the front of the room. Myron stood up, picked up the chain and held it out to Lynne-Anne, who was now cowering flat against the classroom wall. "Take it!" he said fiercely. "Take it. I saved up my allowance all year for it."

Mrs. Campanella spun around and sharply said, "Myron! Sit down and be quiet or I'll . . ."

"Take it *please*?" Myron begged Lynne-Anne and went on, oblivious to Mrs. Campanella or the other two dozen students in the room. "I'll throw it away in a trash can if you don't take it. And then I'll kill myself," Myron said. "I will," he groaned. "I'll kill myself if you don't take it. I know how to and it will be your fault. My death will be on your head, because you wouldn't take a measly little gift."

Lynne-Anne burst into tears at this little speech, but though Myron, pressed the chain at her, she clenched her fists tight.

"Damn you!" Myron shouted. Then my blood is on *your* hands!" He rushed around the row of seats toward the back of the classroom toward the windows.

"Stop him!" Mrs. Campanella screamed and three or four he jumped after Myron, who was now yelling something incomprehensible at the top of his voice from on top the long radiator housing. He'd managed to open one large window and was holding his ground, kicking out at any boy who got near.

The clamor brought other teachers into the room. including Mr. Miller, who taught six-seven down the hall. Between the three teachers and the four boys they managed to grab Myron by the belt and cuffs just as he turned to leap out of the fifth story window. Kicking and flailing and yelling at the top of his lungs, he was dragged back inside the classroom and onto the floor. Trapped and thwarted as well as thoroughly humiliated, Myron twisted around to bite Mr. Miller's hand. The teacher repaid this with a smart punch to the boy's jaw knocking him out. Without waiting for him to regain consciousness, Mr. Miller threw Myron over his shoulder, shouting that he would be in the gym teacher's office. If Myron woke up kicking and screaming, Mr. Miller and "Mac" the gym teacher ought to be able to keep him down.

Mrs. Campanella told us to all sit back down. She assigned us something to read, and left Suzanne in charge before she got Lynne-Anne, who'd fainted onto Nancy's desktop, out of class and down to the nurse's office.

Suzanne Friedman didn't have much to do while the others were gone. Even the cleverest among us had been

Ambidextrous: A Valentine

shocked to silence by the unexpected strength of the passions acted out in front of us: adoration, revulsion, suicidal mania. It was as though some terrible accident had occurred. We spent the final ten minutes of class eagerly avoiding it by following Suzanne's instructions to quietly read and not talk.

Although I too opened my reader, I couldn't concentrate enough to make out more than a word or two at a time. I was as stunned as anyone in the class by what had happened. But—and I was certain I was alone among them in this—all the while that Myron was pleading with Lynne-Anne, demanding she accept his gift, screaming, kicking out at everyone and trying to throw himself out the window, I was sympathizing completely with him. I'd seen what he was doing not as unnatural, not as perverse, but as exactly what I would do if I were in his position. The object of my passion wouldn't be Lynne-Anne Fribourg, but Ricky Hersch. And Ricky wouldn't shrink back and cry and clench his fists at my expensive offering. He would sneer at me and say, "jerk! You're like all the rest. First you get mushy, then you get huffy, then you think I belong to you! Well I don't! I don't and I never will! I belong to me, myself and I!" And when he said those words, I knew I would do exactly what Myron had tried to do. I would jump to the window and leap to my death. And it wouldn't be from a classroom window, but from Ricky's bedroom window, and there wouldn't be any children and teachers to stop me. I imagined the scene so completely that I had to lay my head on the desk. I stayed there until Mrs. Campanella arrived back to pry the chain out of the side molding of the wardrobe where Mryon had thrown it so violently it had become imbedded.

At the school bell, I put on my street clothes along with the other students and walked out of class with Martin and Gregory. When they began to talk of what had happened, I didn't say a word. I scarcely knew where we were walking.

It was as though my imagined death had in some way been real—my spirit had gone out that window, while the shell of my body remained. My friends couldn't help but notice my silence and were friends enough not to tease me or in any way bother me about it.

About halfway home, Ricky caught up with us. He was full of energy and curiosity. His teacher had been one of the half dozen who had eventually wound up in our class and he wanted to know what it had all been about. He listened as Martin told him the sequence of events (totally objectively; hand it to Martin) and I watched Ricky's reaction. When Martin was done, Ricky whistled and asked, "Do you think he really would've jumped?"

We had arrived at Martin's house and he went in. The three of us walked on, Ricky talking about something else, and every once in a while looking at me. When we reached the Taylor property, Gregory went in, and I started to walk on.

"Hey," Ricky said, grabbing my shoulder. "Want to come up to my room?"

I looked up at the dormer window opening onto the branch of the Hickory tree and shook my head. Thinking fast, I lied, "My father's coming home early today. I have to be there right away."

Once home, I went straight up to my room where I lay down on my bed as though exhausted or ill. I wasn't sick of course, except with the realization that I was in love, and that it was a horrible sensation. Scenes of my past months with Ricky flashed into my mind: how we'd fought over Gregory's ditches; how he'd covered me with his father's bomber jacket while I lay shivering from the bike accident; how he'd shown me how to sniff glue and asked, "Do you like it?" so eagerly; the photos in the metal footlocker, and how we'd kissed an hour at a time; how he'd held me down on the bed, my hands in a tight grip as he sucked me for the first time, exulting over his control and my pleasure; how he'd just slumped in that broken Windsor chair not paying any attention to me and Bayley and} Junior Cook; and—returning again and again, a leitmotif through it all how he'd circled back to me on Springfield Blvd. after our first visit to clubhouse and the exact intonation and accentuation of his words as he' said, "I belong to me, myself, and I." It was all so vivid, that I found my wondering if this was what drowning men experienced going down for the third time.

Naturally my mother thought I was sick. She even found a slight fever when she took my temperature. She put me to bed and pampered me and kept me from seeing and having to deal with anyone else, which I needed the most. She even kept me home from school the following day.

At three-thirty the next afternoon, Ricky phoned, as I thought he might. I knew I had to take the call. During that day I'd calmed down a bit and come to a decision: I was being a fool to condemn Ricky without even giving him a chance to defend himself. Since I couldn't bring myself to declare my passion for him and risk the total rejection as I envisaged, I'd struck on another, less desperate, yet equally risky way by which to test the depth of his affection for me.

"I'm okay now," I said when he asked how I was feeling. Then added the words that I knew would either end or confirm my pain. "Listen, Ricky, something's happening here. My mother caught me sniffing glue. She threw the tube away and made me promise not to use it anymore."

Silence on his end. Then, "Did you tell her I got you to sniff?"

"No. I didn't say a word. But I'm sure she guessed we sniffed it together."

Silence from him again.

"Don't worry," I said, "She won't tell your mother anything. I told her I discovered it while making models. I told her that I got you to try it once, and that you got sick."

He was still silent. I continued to hold back my trump card.

"What did she say?" he asked.

"She said I can't see you anymore."

A moan from his end.

"I mean, we can still see each other in school and all . . . You know, maybe away from our houses . . . But, like, not as much as we used to . . ."

I waited for a response. What I wanted was for Ricky to immediately begin to plan ways for he and I to get together, places we could meet, schemes by which we might get around this imaginary ban. If he did that, I would know he really cared for me. Perhaps as much as I cared for him.

He was silent for a very long time. Then he said, "Well, if that's the way it has to be . . ."

"Yeah," I said, the blood draining out of my body, out of my frozen heart, "that's the way it has to be." I hung up the phone, wrapped my bathrobe around myself, slowly went up to my bedroom, and cursing myself for my cleverness, wishing I were too stupid to understand human nature, wishing I had been wrong about Ricky, hating myself, I cried myself to sleep.

Myron Goldblum was transferred to another class for the rest of the term. Whenever he noticed one of his former classmates in assembly or in the hallways, he would turn his head, his entire body away. His family moved during the summer and none of us ever saw him again. Lynne-Anne returned to class where she continued to be as well treated as before, pitied at times for her unwilling role in the hideous occurrence on Valentine's Day. But she had been deeply touched in some ineffable way by the event. Five years later, in high school, when she was going steady with Billy Soscia, the star quarterback of the varsity football team, the two of them the beautiful couple of the year,

Ambidextrous: A Valentine

tragedy struck. Billy went to help two small boys who'd fallen through the ice at Cunningham Pond. The children were saved but he drowned, with Lynne-Anne looking helplessly on. She had a nervous breakdown and didn't return to school until the following term. I never saw Lynne-Anne again after that, but I heard from schoolmates who said that her troubles had continued. She'd lost one husband in an auto accident several years later and when she remarried, she lost her second husband to a rare form of bone cancer. Then she disappeared. If I were superstitious, I might think that like some magic working gremlin in a Grimm *Maerchen*, twelve-year-old spurned Myron had put a curse on her love life.

I too had been touched—horribly—by that Valentine's Day. The rest of that school term I kept to myself. I started going to the library every other day, reading widely in Greek, Roman, and Egyptian history. I put my model airplanes away and then stowed them in our garage: they never l surfaced again. Every once in a while I would go to the movies or on a bike trip out of our neighborhood with my old friends, Martin, Gregory and James Kallas. But I was no longer the bubbly, active, aggressive, outgoing boy who'd been their leader: so it wasn't really the same. Ricky called a few times and tried to work up some enthusiasm in me for doing things with him that we'd previously enjoyed, but when he saw how little shared his interests he gave up trying to please me, stopped calling me. Within months, we pretended to scarcely notice each other when we accidentally encountered each other in school, or in our neighborhoods.

One Saturday, as Martin, Gregory, James Kallas, and I were riding home from a long trip to Great Neck, we passed an oddly familiar street in the next neighborhood. Passing large old frame houses on well-kept properties, I spotted a familiar looking one. On an impulse I told the others to go ahead, I would catch up with them. I biked up the driveway ramp, skirted the garage, got off the bike and crept up through the trees to where I could get a good look at the clubhouse. I shouldn't have been as surprised as I was to see Ricky's bicycle parked there. I turned and biked off as quickly as I could.

And Ricky Hersch? Well, when he returned to school after summer vacation he did attend the military school he'd always wanted to go to and which his father's buddy Tony Warner got him admitted to and paid for. And Ricky did go on to West Point to become a professional soldier, as he'd always wanted. You can find his name among fifty-seven thousand others, chiseled in gold onto black marble on a long, low, shallow V opposite the Washington Monument in the District of Columbia. I found it immediately and without looking for it—Richard Victor Hersch—and I stood in front of it for maybe a half hour, among the scores of grown men who can be seen there every day and night of the year, openly weeping for their first, or their best, long lost buddies.

The Effect of "Mirrors"

"Don't look now, but disaster is on its way."

It was fourth period math class, Geometry mostly, which I had already succeeded in mastering, despite Mr. Thirrel's anxieties. Mr. Thirrel's anxiety was his one recognizable human trait. Otherwise, he was a man of appalling beigeness, from his lank hair the color of dry corn silk to his unwashed looking, unclocked socks. A disaster in Mr. Thirrel's class was as unexpected as it was hoped for.

Better yet, the whisperer of the surprising statement was Denny Tobin, a handsome sly-faced boy, instinctively distrusted by all, but unfailingly reliable whenever trouble of any ilk was to be sniffed out. Hadn't Denny been the one on the school bus trip to the Museum of Natural History to point out Mrs. Andersen's Nile-green pallor, just before the young teacher's assistant began to retch like a madwoman over the driver, who swerved us close to annihilation for ten hair-raising minutes before tearing onto and grounding us on an island in the middle of the Belt Parkway? Hadn't Denny been the boy who stood up without permission in science class and only when he'd reached the doorway yelled, "It's going to blow!" before running out of the room, leaving us with a retort filled with a midnight blue solution fizzing and gurgling at its open end like a Roman Candle?

Hadn't Denny . . . ? But why go on? Denny promised and Denny delivered.

Still, I saw nothing to back up his latest promise. The classroom appeared unchanged in any way. The twenty-four students were ringed in a wide, irregular rectangle of double seat table desks, unaltered in their postures an iota as I observed; unchanged except perhaps in the deepness of their boredom as Mr. Thirrel went on and on about how to measure with unfailing accuracy the sides and angles of trapezoids—as though any of us ever would.

"What?" I whispered to Denny. "Where?"

He had been looking down at his desk. He now looked up, directly across the room, and half-laughed, half-whispered, "Carolyn McClintlock."

I looked at the students facing us. At first I still saw nothing. There sat Carolyn pulling herself up on her elbows out of her lethargy for the tenth time in five minutes attempting, however momentarily, to seem alert and attentive—one of the least convincing acts this pretty but moonfaced girl was able to pull off. Carolyn's long straight chestnut hair in the stupidest of pony tails was not—as I expected—on fire. The number two pencil tapping her buck front teeth was not dripping blood. She was not unconsciously drooling out of her overlarge, unlipsticked mouth. A long and disgusting booger was not hanging out of the nostrils of her pug nose. It was just Carolyn McClintlock, in her pale blue fluffy short sleeve sweater, her high shoulders, bare arms, biggish breasts even in a class full of well-developed girls—Ruby, Rita, Ellen, Charlotte.

And then I saw. One of Carolyn's big breasts was where it was supposed to be. But the other was somewhere around her left midriff.

Unable to hold it in or to whisper my amazement, I said very much out loud, "Falsies!"

I might as well have cried out "Fire!" in that classroom

for the revolution of time, space, and action that instantly ensued. Twelve pairs of female eyes swerved to land on Carolyn's torso. Mr. Thirrel spun around from dissecting rhomboids on the forest-green blackboard to shush us up. Six boys looked up from their ill-starred attempts at secret doodling. Carolyn looked down at herself and turned every hue in the red spectrum of the chromatic scale before settling on a particularly unattractive shade of magenta. Then she stood up and fell back against the classroom wall as though trying to escape from the horrible truth. As she did, she missed the wall and struck the tall, narrow, open-door storage cabinet dislodging an entire shelf of test papers Mr. Thirrel had placed on top. The tests skittered off into the room like bleached, overlarge Autumn leaves suddenly caught in a gust. Everyone jumped up to grab them, except for those students who burst out laughing, with much pointing up at the papers and over at Carolyn. Mr. Thirrel saw the girl was beginning to slump in a faint and shouted, "Rita, Edith, get her to the lounge!" which caused even more confusion as he pointed out not those two girls but Franny and Elaine to help their classmate. This was followed by more laughter, as four girls jumped out of their scats to help Carolyn, bumping into each other and saying, "Me! He called my name." "No, me! He pointed to me!" before they managed to get to her and to drag her out of the classroom door, amidst chaos of boys under the desks and in the middle of the room with hands full of test papers, one or two students—August, sleeping, Martin, uncaring?—just now realizing what had happened belatedly burst out laughing which started up the rest of us, who thought we were all laughed out. Mr. Thirrel shouted for us to sit down and be quiet. The period bell rang.

    We flew out of the room and exploded into full-throated hilarity in the corridor; we flooded down the hallway in a river of laughter and punching and slapping and shouting, jibes, animal roars, and bird cry imitations, wisecracks and more laughter.

Luckily we were off to lunch period instead of to another class. No teacher ever born could have been able to calm down such an adolescent storm. In the large, modernized cafeteria, along with five other classes—including 7 SP3, who for some reason we wouldn't associate with—and 7 SP 1—who for some equally arcane reason we always associated with—our hilarity in recounting the incident was dissipated a bit.

Not completely. It came up again all the rest of the school day, a sort of quiet recurring hilarity which broke out onto the surface with the merest provocation, a word, a sigh, a glance at one's own chest. Carolyn of course refused to return to class and went home "sick." Franny and Elaine, who'd seen her to the third floor teacher's lounge, came back during lunch period, but didn't say a word more than that. But even they couldn't hold it in. It was Elaine who began it in Science class after lunch. Our teacher, the "beautiful Jerry Strauss," was bewildered about our sudden, inexplicable, prolonged laughter, but was wise enough or spaced out enough to let us get it our of our systems before going back to his valence charts. Our rotund, tortured, bespectacled English teacher, Mr. Collins, was far less tolerant. Stuck with us for a two period "bloc," Collins sensed mutiny brewing with every tiny titter that he heard half-stifled around the room. He confirmed Toby Ross's belief that he was a secret child molester—if not worse—when, after the seventh period bell, he dropped all pretense of teaching us how to parse adverbial clauses and had the window shades pulled down and all the lights shut off. Mr. Collins lit a candle he kept hidden in his desk. He held it under his shadowed face, and began to intensely and horrifyingly read aloud Poe's tale, "The Pit and the Pendulum," complete with shrieks, moans and other sound effects, until our high spirits were considerably dampened. After which, he blew out the candle, had the shades opened, the lights put back on, and said, "Ladies and Gentlemen, the adverbial clause!"

Such was a typical seventh grade day in school.

As different from the sixth grade as I could have imagined. Not that I hadn't received my share of hints and intimations about how Junior High School differed from elementary school. I had. If only I had listened. My older sister had already been there a year, my older brother two years. Still, as I've already mentioned, we no longer had the contact we used to have, except during the summer months, away from home, when we were forced into each other's company by the lack of playmates our own age; and even that coerced communication lasted only until one of us made a new friend at one of the summer resorts we stayed at. Nor did it help that I was completely preoccupied those two years that I might have been closely listening to my sibling's talk about their new school—first with Mr. Hargrave and the Flaherty sisters, later with Ricky Hersch.

I did have an idea of the structure of the new school: three grades, seventh through ninth, all the students between twelve or thirteen and sixteen years old (with exceptions like "Smitty," who at eighteen remained unpassed in the ninth grade). I also knew that one had a homeroom teacher who usually also taught the entire class one subject, and that, unlike high school, where each student had more or less individual schedules, here the entire class traveled to other rooms and other teachers for the remainder of the curriculum. Sometimes two or more classes came together in larger groupings, art, music, gym, cafeteria, and study period. Our junior high took students from five elementary schools in a fifteen-mile-wide area; yet both my brother and sister continued to travel with friends they'd made in primary grades even as they made new friends.

That continuity factor was missing for me. As was temporal continuity. Because there were several thousand students but only a limited amount of space in the building, we had to go to school in shifts: my brother's grade at eight a.m., my sister's at nine and mine at ten. We came home in shifts too, at two, three and four in the afternoon.

Why, if both my siblings had old friends in their classes, didn't I?

Because I had been placed in a special class: 7 SP 2, one of five such special classes in the school, a group of twenty-four students per class, geared to learn the standard three years program in two years. Seventy-two (and later, after the dullards had been weeded out for the ninth grade, forty-eight) such students existed out of over four hundred and fifty freshmen: or about one in eight, for a ratio of one special class student out of twenty-four in the entire grade. Sure enough, I was one of three students I'd known from my own sixth grade to be in such a class, along with my friend Martin O'Connor in 7 SP 1 and the always problematic Suzanne Friedman, in 7 SP 3. Being special, I discovered, meant being alone—at least in the beginning.

To explain how I ascended in a mere year and a half of school from near-suspension in Hargrave's class to this tiny elite for the gifted is perhaps more difficult. I suspect it had little to do with anything but the Board of Education's dogmatic reliance upon the I.Q. tests it gave to all elementary school students and to the scores they received.

In the middle of the sixth grade, one entire day was given over to this test, which was administered not by our teacher (although Mrs. Campanella did look in on us from time to time) but by a City Regent and his assistant.

Since none of us students knew what these tests were about, and as we had not been forewarned about them or told to study for them, they came and went in our school life without leaving a trace for most of us. However, about a month later, just when I'd broken off relations with Ricky, I was among four children called to the assistant principal's office and told by Mrs. Strang that we were to be retested. She wouldn't tell us why, but she did tell us not to worry about it. The four of us tried to figure out why we had been selected out of a classful, but there seemed to be no common thread. Besides myself, the others were my friend Nancy, Edward Young and Billy Masters. Three days later, we four joined some twenty other sixth graders to be retested in a seldom-used classroom located at the farthest ell of the fifth floor of the school building. By now, I was somewhat familiar with the test and worked on more confidently, actually coming to enjoy the often silly similarity and disparity questions which seemed for the most part incredibly simple. Two weeks later I was retested again! This time not in a classroom at our school, but at our local junior high. With me were five other students from my school's sixth grade, and a group of students none of us knew.

I later discovered what all this testing was about when, two weeks before the end of the school year, my parents received a letter from the school principal notifying them that I had been accepted into the gifted student program the city education board had instituted a few years before. Even later, in college, as I sat on a high, hard bleacher during orientation in that school's vast gymnasium, I realized that the bulging manila folder I was holding contained my school records from kindergarten on. Naturally, I looked through it, and naturally I came across those sixth grade test scores and saw why I had been tested three times. My first score had been 149, which everyone who knew me was certain was a fluke. The second score, however, was even higher, 170, and that had required a third testing, for a score of 162. The average of the three was 160.33, which I discovered in my college Psychology course was considered genius level. In a more advanced psychology course I took, as part of a project with four other students, I helped dismantle and critique the very Stanford-Binet tome on which I had tested so well, and attempted to devise an I.Q. test of our own which would not be culturally determined. When I then took that new test, I was amazed that I still scored at genius level, and have since wondered how I could harness all that supposed intelligence, which I clearly still haven't succeeded in doing.

And Edward and Nancy and Billy? Well, the first two had scored much lower on the tests than their six years of school grades would indicate, and Billy a great deal higher. On the second test, the expected lower I.Q.s of the two popular students were confirmed; Billy's luck also ran out and he tested only average.

So there I was, in a class that no one but those students and teachers already involved in the program knew anything about. My siblings were certainly in the dark about it, although they immediately began to call me "the Professor." Nor were my parents very knowledgeable about it, even after a long talk with my primary school principal. They asked me if I wanted to enter the program. Ask a twelve-year-old if he wants one less year of school in his life, and unless he's downright retarded, he'll say yes. I did. And that was that. There would come moments in the following two years when I might rue this decision. We were kept a lot busier than other junior high students, not only stuffing three years work into two but also having to take enriched courses—two foreign languages, not just the required one; a literature course in addition to English; art and music history. Add the fact that we were expected—pushed—into becoming involved in as many extracurricular activities, sports, clubs, etc., as the school offered, and it sometimes seemed that I was in the school building from eight in the morning until eight at night. Hell, some days my father got home from work long before I did from school.

But there were compensatory factors. First, status. There was no question that the SP classes led their grades in all matters. We actually led them into assemblies. The two assistant principals of the junior high, especially the devilishly handsome Mr. Wolff, were constantly in and out of our classrooms, selected us as monitors, messengers, liaisons of one sort or another, as we were deemed capable of and motivated enough to make up any time we lost of a particular lesson. We were the class from which the school newspaper and magazine staffs, the political organization representatives, the sports teams and clubs first chose their members. By the ninth grade, after ferocious weeding out when we'd been reduced down to two classes, we were even more in demand. The student government was officered entirely by our members. Nor did this sense of privilege end when we left junior high: it went on long after. When we moved on to various high schools we were automatically placed in that school's top echelon, which if one didn't screw up too badly, also put one in line for the best colleges, and eventually for the top post-grad schools. What had begun as an experiment in the finest tradition of ultraliberal education ended in an extremely useful Old Boy network, beginning at age twelve.

The second compensating factor after status was freedom. While we were carefully watched by a few teachers and by those in the administration with an interest in our program, it was spotty and erratic. We were treated as grown ups—a foolish concept, except that in many ways we were more mature than others our own age. There were other freedoms: moving about from class to class, getting excused from class on flimsy, if bona fide, excuses to take care of some pressing need in some extra activity. We moved about the school as though we owned it: quite differently than those students who walked in tight-knit groups, amazed to find themselves in a new corridor on a new floor or wing of the building.

The third factor was personalities. Whatever the state Regents were doing with their IQ testing, they certainly managed to hit on a group of corkers. My own class seemed the worst of the three. There wasn't an ordinary child in the lot, and several were downright eccentric. Our teachers were also a madcap bunch, I suppose chosen to teach us because they possessed a bit more imagination or panache themselves. The Poe reading stunt of Mr. Collins was not really that surprising. We soon drove even the placid Mr. Strauss to extremes of temperament, and our homeroom teacher, the blowsy economics teacher Mrs. Childs, more than once walked out of the room in tears, humiliated by the girls' haughty and deadly accurate fashion critiques of her garb.

Not only were the students (or most of them) in our class smart, they were also *smart*. Many came from two elementary schools just north of Alley Pond and Cunningham Parks, where evidently they were in closer contact with the world (for which read Manhattan) than we benighted kids living in the "valley" south of Hillside Avenue. The girls dressed themselves carefully, in some cases expensively. They wore makeup, dated eighth and ninth grade boys—but some their classmates too—and seemed utterly sophisticated to me. Unlike my earlier friends from primary school, the boys I met in this class paid little attention to baseball, preferring tennis, squash and golf. Several were already quite accomplished in these sports, and it was through them that I learned how to golf and became a member of the Douglaston Country Club. Still, for these new colleagues of mine, sports were to be played, not talked about; discussions were filled with politics, science, social events—and sex.

Where I had been in the sexual vanguard of my age group for the past two years, I suddenly found myself if anything a bit backward. Both Toby Ross and Michael Regenstreif, the boys I admired and wanted as friends, seemed completely blasé when I confessed (with much hesitation and emendation) to my own sexual experiences. They both admitted to having had similar intense relationships with other boys that they now termed "juvenile stuff," although it was evident to me that Toby's affection for David Manetti continued to be both strong and physical. Their experiences with girls seemed even more intense. Both had been "laid" more than once, and spoke of it almost offhandedly. As for glue-sniffing, they had done it and found it interesting if ultimately wanting. "It rots your mind," Michael once airily declared. "After a few years of that stuff, your brain is honeycombed with pockets of air," a statement he remained unable to definitely prove to me, even if his father was a surgeon. Still, they—and Thom Meserole and Barry Schoenwald and David Manetti—formed a cohesive and fascinating clique, and I was soon included, although I seldom saw them every day after school, as they lived a considerable distance from me, even by bicycle. Toby and Barry later admitted that one reason for my inclusion among them, even though I clearly didn't possess their already high level of civility, was that I possessed what they considered valuable individual qualities: 1) I was "weird," capable of almost anything: *viz* my "Falsies!" shout in Geometry class; and 2) I was universally considered "cute" among those girls they were most interested in getting to know better, and so bait for them on any social occasions.

If we five boys soon formed a loose elite within the elite of 7 SP 2, the girls did too. The four prettiest, most intelligent, and most sophisticated girls in the class were Ellen Schock, Charlotte Lipton, Rita Tacchino, and Karen Kristopher. But there were other girls, like the smoldering pale blonde Janette Muir (distantly related to the famous poet) and Franny Solomon, who weren't part of the four, but were also highly desirable, perhaps more desirable since they were more mysterious. By the end of the first term of the seventh grade, we five boys had all kissed, necked with, petted, and in general "had" those four friends. But Denny's one attempt at feeling up Janette Muir had ended in his being punched off a sofa and repeatedly socked until he'd made his escape. And none of us had even come close to the petite, dark-haired Semitic beauty Franny, who, even with her smallish breasts, was considered by my group of male friends to be the *ne plus ultra* of our entire grade.

Picture a girl of thirteen with the poise and bearing of a diplomat's wife; a girl with such aplomb she was left in front of classrooms while teachers ran out to check on emergencies or to smoke half a cigarette, whom no one sneered at; a girl so carefully dressed in her gray flannel jumpers and pale pink and lilac blouses that grown up women asked where she shopped (she didn't; she and her mother made all her clothing). Her hair was pitch black, lustrous, long, but usually pinned up or back in some currently fashionable manner. Her skin was porcelain blushed with a rose and as soft as the satin on an old Valentine. Her lips were the color of coral and as perfectly shaped as that golden fragment from ancient Egypt on display at the Metropolitan Museum of Art. Her eyes were honest-to-god amethyst: the only pair outside of Elizabeth Taylor's I've ever seen. Any boy who stared at them too long usually got the full treatment, for they could be as flat as a mirror one minute, or as deep and fascinating as a whirlpool.

Franny was unfailingly cordial to all, useful, clever— and totally untouchable. She was known to not date at all (her mother thought it vulgar), and she seldom joined any out-of-class activities, chaperoned or not. She didn't carry around movie magazines in her fat ringed loose-leaf. She didn't have pinups of Ricky Nelson and Tab Hunter in her locker. She was never heard gossiping with the other girls. Yet they all sought her out, and selected her as their best. Denny Tobin had once been to her address but claimed Franny had never come out of the house, or even acknowledged his bell ringing, but had peeked out at him from a window. She certainly never went to the movies, or to the park, or roller skating with other kids her own age, although she was always asked to be part of such outings. She was like a princess under some bizarre enchantment, so subtle yet powerful a spell that it seemed to bar anyone else from getting near her, as invisible as an electrified fence.

Franny was one of a kind and she was to become the third lover of my life; how or why I only found out later. Of the three—Susan Flaherty, Ricky Hersch, and her—Franny was the one most responsible for causing me to grow up and ultimately, and despite myself and the world, to become a writer.

You might think, following my *success d'estime* with the essay on Homer in Mrs. Campanella's sixth grade class, that I had found my milieu and was a true budding author. You would be wrong.

Doubtless it had been a wonderful experience, having that almost professional piece virtually write itself out of my passion and knowledge. But it was clearly a one-shot deal. The next paper that I'd written for the class had been on the promised subject of Irving Stone's *Clarence Darrow for the Defense*, and while it was a successful effort, it was very much an effort, and had far less effect on my teacher and the other students, not to mention being sheer drudgery for me to write.

So I learned the first lesson that any writer needs to know: your first successful piece of writing is your best piece of writing—until you finally out achieve it with another piece of writing, terrifically new and phenomenally well done. At which point, that piece of writing becomes the new criterion by which all your new work is denigrated—until you do even better. Even then I recognized this vicious circle and how it could ruin my life. Whereas in the visual arts you had an oeuvre: a series of pieces in different forms all of which were considered worthwhile. Of course you might paint a brilliant oil, but you would also be able to do pen and ink sketches, pastel drawings, lithographs, sculpture, watercolors, either as studies before or after your painting, or as references to it. While art connoisseurs would always have their "masterpieces," they were more than willing to see these sketches and studies as important steps leading up to and away from the *chef d'oeuvre* as part of the *process of art*.

As I was a lazy child, not terribly interested in pushing myself forward, this more relaxed and experimental sort of career seemed far more congenial than the hectic celeritous chasms and arêtes of a writer's life. This decision was quietly seconded by my father, who had once possessed some (unsubstantiated) drafting talent and had thought my scrawlings good enough to be encouraged. There was even talk, briefly, of sending me to art school. My older brother had gone a year, and his heavily pigmented oil of a particularly loathsome emerald green vase filled with inexplicable blooms hung with some honor in our playroom. But I demurred about art classes the one time I was asked, being too busy with schoolwork; then summer arrived; then I began the seventh grade with its unexpectedly heavy workload. The subject of formal art classes was never revived.

Meanwhile, I had discovered other books as interesting as *The Iliad* and *The Odyssey*. Thanks to the unsubtle promptings of my next door neighbor's older sons, the Caruso twins, I began my reading program with an odd and somewhat inappropriate next step: Aldous Huxley's *Brave New World*. Joe Caruso handed me the book one day as I visited their house to help them build a one-hundredth size scale model of a building they'd designed for their classes in the Pratt Institute's School of Architecture. Actually I did little more than paint the small twigs they'd collected and glue green excelsior to the tops, and sometimes lay out the green matting that became the lawns and greensward plazas of their various models of hospitals, schools, and suburban home offices of giant corporations. Frankly, while I was interested in architecture and forced the Caruso twins to teach me how to read floor plans and scale drawings and cross sections, I could have cared less about Huxley's book. Every time I would go to the Carusos' large finished basement to help them, Joe or Vic would give me an impromptu lecture on why I should read it and why it was important, which I felt was worse than Mrs. Campanella's lectures. But soon enough it was "charette" for them, and they had to finish their models by a deadline, so they forgot about me and my reading.

Not until the sixth grade had ended and Summer began did I finally make another stab at reading the incomprehensible opening of Huxley's book. It still happens to me. Some friend will recommend a book, give it to me, thrust it at me, demanding not only that I read it, but also adore it as much as he, and every resistance I possess rises and clamps into place. For weeks the volume lays about as I make yet another doomed effort to read the first paragraph with interest in what the second paragraph may contain. Because I feel some obligation to the person who made the recommendation, I will try and try again, keeping the book handy—on the coffee table near my reading chair, on my desk, at my bedside table. After weeks, months, the book will slowly sift to the bottom of a pile of occasional debris—magazines, greeting cards, boxes of tissue, ashtrays, invitations to parties, letters from friends abroad, cups of cold coffee—which slowly accumulated like the nine cities Wilhelm Schliemann first had to uncover above the sought-for ruins of Homeric Troy. With luck, the book will finally disappear altogether in some burst of sudden cleaning into another, more distant, less visible pile of effluvia, still near enough for me to infrequently see and wonder about it. Until it finally ends up in a boxful of other hardcovers and paperbacks, read and unread, given to the Salvation Army, to a needy local library, to a block sale committee, or picked over by friends before I toss out the contents. And I'll never think of it again, except perhaps whenever I see that friend (by now so fed up with me as a reader he'll never think to give me another book) when I'll vaguely remember the novel and rue that I have friends who so little understand me.

    Such might have been the fate of Mr. Huxley's book in my life if I hadn't suddenly developed yet another weird childhood illness: an early summer allergy known as Rose Fever, which is actually tree pollen fever. This allergy, which has affected me to this day with varying degrees of discomfort, broke over me for the first time early that June with such explosive force that I began sneezing at the breakfast table and went on to sneeze seventy-two more times—my siblings counting out loud in wonder, dread, and admiration—before I passed out from lack of oxygen. Which undoubtedly saved my life. Within two days I was tested, the problem pinpointed, and I suddenly found myself once more an invalid. I was alone, weakened (especially after a long sneezing jag), and in a distinctly irritated frame of mind. My siblings were off at school or out playing in the warm sunshiny early summer weather, and there I was once more cooped up in my bedroom, staying as still as I could so as to not conjure up that insidious first sneeze that would lead to another and another, *ad infi-*

nitum. Of course by then I also had a variably effective medicine, a potion so rich in Benadryl that I would fall asleep twenty times a day.

What else was there to do but curse (not too loudly or violently lest a sneeze be evoked), lay back looking regretfully at the beautiful wasted summer day, and read. I picked up the Caruso's book, thinking "all right, you win!" and began to read. Amazed that I now understood what a few months ago I couldn't for the life of me make out, I went on reading. I finished the book in two days. At dinner that night, I mentioned the book to my father, asking him if Huxley had been thinking of the U.S.S.R. (then very much in the news) when he'd written the novel. My father only half answered me, looking toward my mother and asking, "Is he old enough to be reading that?" To which she responded a plaintive, "Phil! Let's not start that again. It's too late. He's already read the book." After dinner, I went over to the Caruso's house and began asking them a thousand questions. So many, they suggested I reread the book; they were certain most of my questions would be answered by a closer reading. It was in one of these conversations, however, that they happened to mention two other books similar to the Huxley, George Orwell's *Animal Farm* and *1984*.

Much as I'd admired Homer two years before, all my questions about the world depicted in those epics were decipherable in indexes, footnotes and glosses, such as Edith Hamilton's *Greek Mythology*. Not so with Huxley or the two Orwell books. I could think about, talk about these books for hours, and still not be any closer to answers. More interesting, no one else, not even college seniors like the Caruso brothers, had the answers. How could they? What I was asking for was no less than the answer to the future.

The future. I'd thought about it at times, naturally, but

only in connection with myself or my family. Would I be thrown out of school after what I'd done in Mr. Hargrave's class, and end up a criminal? Would our family go back to the North Shore mansion this summer, or up to Hyannis, or to some spot on the southern coast of Rhode Island as my aunt Lucy and Uncle Billy had suggested? Would I like being in the SP class or hate it? For the first time I understood that there was a larger future, that I was just a small part of it, no matter how much importance I gave my life and the lives of those around me. I now saw that while in the twenty-second or so century which Huxley pictured I might—by dint of my acknowledged higher intelligence—be a desired Alpha, others would be Deltas, even Gammas. Poor James Kallas, for example; or my older brother, who seemed to be failing out of school. Would I like that? Would I even know these people in the society of New Ford? It seemed unlikely. In fact, the world as I knew it might be as unreal as tenuous as those Orwell and Huxley so convincingly depicted. How would I like a world in which there were no families, no mothers, no little brothers? Would I even miss them if the possibility didn't exist in the first place? And what of love? True, I'd suffered with Ricky, but in a sense that had been something I could live around, past. I couldn't think of world as Orwell had devised without the possibility of love.

This might have led to a profound case of early existentialism or anomie and, who knows, perhaps even a sort of catalepsy or autism. Sensitive thirteen-year-olds have gone into complete psychosis over love. But while I was sensitive enough, I was also in some larger and more protective manner, pig-headed. I felt certain that answers for everything were obtainable. If people didn't have the answers, well then another book would. Since two of the three books that had perplexed me had been taken off the Science Fiction shelf of our local library, where I had also seen *Brave*

New World, I went back to that section and began to take out other titles. Looking for a short cut, I began with collections, foolishly thinking that among twenty-five stories by twenty-five different authors, I would obtain a consensus or at least a prevailing opinion about the future.

I know now that this was what I have come to call a Major Wrong Move. Instead of anything approaching an answer, I received twenty-five new views, with hundreds more questions. All the stories took place in the future, but in different futures than Orwell's or Huxley's, wildly different from each other. In one, World War Three had destroyed all earthly life but insects. In another, mankind had populated the galaxy but had moved out so far that it had forgotten the home planet. In yet another, people had so much leisure, they gambled and joined in wild, prepaid and preprogrammed adventures. In still another, two genders had been replaced by six (to me) unclear ones. In another, robots had been integrated closely into the population with mixed and often hilarious social and economic results.

If there were so many possible futures, I childishly reasoned, it was because the future hadn't yet occurred, and thus was open to anyone's speculation. Answers therefore had to lie in the past, which, since everyone agreed that it had definitely occurred, should possess some of the answers I was seeking. So I went back to some of the history books that I'd been reading the previous year, rereading them with a purpose rather than merely to find out how people had lived and what my heroes were really like. And here I found the problems were as bad. Bury's *History of Greece* presented one theory about who the ancient Greeks were, where they had come from, and why they declined. H.G. Wells' *Outline of History* presented another, completely contrary one. So, although I'd shot back from galactic empires 28,000 years in the future to the Nile Valley peoples in 5,000 B.C., where people walked sideways, adored deities with bird and dog heads and wrote in pictures on walls, the result was more confusion, more farfetched speculation.

By this point it was the end of the summer, and I was in a better state of physical health, but definitely in a state of mental confusion. I decided that history was as bad as Science Fiction, and in fact, that my first instinct had been the right one: all books were made up and thus not to be trusted, not to be looked into for answers of any reliability. End of my reading career, stage two.

Cut to: my first date with Franny Solomon.

I'm still not certain precisely how this came about. All I know is that one evening about two months into my seventh grade, a social was held in the school cafeteria for the parents and teachers of the three SP classes. My mother surprised me by attending, astonished me afterward by telling me that Franny's mother and she had become friendly, and that Mrs. Solomon had asked if her daughter could join us that coming Sunday on our annual trip to Manhattan's Lower East Side—or, in my mother's innocuous if frank New England parlance, "Jewtown."

This was a trip we children associated with the coming of the holidays and it was as much a tradition with us as Thanksgiving turkey or trimming the tall, blue spruce tree my father always bought to put up in our living room for Christmas. I don't know how this tradition had begun, but it had started years before. My parents were involved in some sort of community charity which each year provided inexpensive toys for underprivileged children somewhere or other in the county. Over the years, the number of children to be gifted had grown and my parents had found themselves purchasing gifts for a hundred or more. Several seasons before, a business crony of my father's had connected him up to a toy manufacturer on Eldridge Street on

Manhattan's Lower East Side who, by the last days of November, had already shipped all the toys he was going to sell that season, and who had overstock he was willing to sell my parents cheaply by the cardboard box-full if my parents wanted to bother going to the trouble of picking over the dolls and trucks and games and construction sets for what they wanted.

This required several hours work, but with children along to help went much faster, barely an hour. The task was presented to us not so much as a duty but as a right we well-fed, well-clothed, middle-class children could use to boost our self-esteem. We believed it and eagerly joined in selecting the plastic wrapped presents from enormous piles thrown on vast trestle-top tables in a sooty, dingy, sky-lighted factory inventory room, thinking how happy we were making some unknown poor children less lucky than we. And, it was fun.

Other attractions came to be connected with these trips. On clear, cold sunny Sunday afternoons, we could roam through Eldridge and Rivington and Broome and Grand Streets, fascinated by the old world atmosphere and outrageously old-fashioned costumes and foreign languages, and believe that we were in medieval Cracow or Prague. On an earlier trip, my father had discovered a large delicatessen in the area, and we stopped there to eat potato knishes, cheese and fruit blintzes, *kasha varnishkes*, kosher frankfurters, and rich, nut-soaked cakes—food we wouldn't elsewhere be able to eat became *de rigueur* for all future trips. We were just another family among many in the restaurant, and more than once, some wizened Reb would grab one of us children onto his lap and feed us some tidbit and kiss us and compliment us in guttural Yiddish to my uncomprehending parents' pleasure. I suppose they assumed we were Sephardic and not Italian-American. I clearly remember one man who fell for me on one of these excursions and who pulled a brown satin yarmulke "just bought, never worn" out of his pocket and insisted on placing it on my head and keeping it there. Looking at my even-then longish straight nose, he said, "He'll never starve. A nose this sharp always points to money."

We also discovered in this part of town hidden away cloth shops with their phalanxes of bolts of cloth, and tailors who seemed miraculously able to cut and sew a suit for any size or shape in less than an hour (while we ate lunch at the deli). My mother had worked briefly as a runway model for Filene's, a large department store in Boston, and she knew good material when she saw it. After one visit to several of these mercers, she insisted that every future excursion include stops for buying clothes for parents and children alike, made out of the inexpensive, superb materials she would uncover at these marts.

Thus, our annual trip had become an all-day affair, often ending with us taking in a movie at the Roxy or Radio City Music Hall, and so, perfect days. Real family days too, which was rare and which was why I was so surprised that Franny Solomon, whom we barely knew, was to be included that year. My mother's only explanation was that she had somehow told Mrs. Solomon of our trip, and Franny had been empowered to go along with us to help us with our toy selection, and also to buy material she would be making into clothing for herself and her family.

So I quickly learned two facts about Franny which no one else in class knew. 1) Mrs. Solomon was a "working mother" who supported the family, employed as some sort of advertising agency account executive in Manhattan. And 2) Franny's father was an invalid; had been for some years following his return home from the Pacific Theater in World War Two. This somewhat explained Franny's lack of sociability with her peers.

She not only made her own clothing, but (my mother

explained) she had to cook and keep house for her mother and father. It also explained their unexpectedly meager living circumstances. The one time I'd ridden by their house on a bicycle, I was surprised to see it was the bottom floor of what was then called a Garden Apartment, a series of small, two-story attached homes which were tiny by the suburban standards of the time.

That afternoon, all went as expected, up to a point. Franny sat between me and my sister in the back-facing third seat of our Pontiac station wagon, and they soon became friendly. I joined in their conversation a little, but mostly felt out-of-sorts I have to admit by this forced joining of what I wished to retain as two different axes of my life: school and family. Once inside the toy factory room, my mother, sister, and Franny went to one end of the trestle tables to choose toys for girls, while my father, brothers, and I picked through the mounds of plastic ray guns, Parcheesi sets, and Lincoln Logs for the boys. It required three trips down the huge freight elevator to get the unwieldy if rather lightweight cardboard boxes into the car. They took up so much room we had to fold up the middle seat. Going home, my elder brother wound up in the front seat between my parents, my younger brother—then six years old and skinny—back with us. After we'd packed up and locked the station wagon and headed toward the mercers and tailor shops, my mother took me aside on the pretense of wanting to wipe a speck of dirt off my cheek with her lilac-scented handkerchief to whisper to me, "I like your schoolmate very much."

At the tailor shops we split up again, as was our custom, and while usually my mother often came by to add her taste to our sartorial decision-making, this time she remained with Franny and my sister the whole time, barely visible as she moved through the dusty, hazy late afternoon distance of the huge room, her head over the high bolts of cloth, inclined slightly. I was certain she was in constant conversation with Franny.

My embarrassment began when we arrived at the delicatessen. The place was unusually crowded, and there seemed to be no possible way get seven chairs around a table in the remaining space although I have to hand it to the waiters who tried to for five minutes. Finally, my mother said to me, "Look! There's a table for two. Why don't you and Franny sit there. You haven't been alone together all afternoon."

The table she'd pointed out was on the far side of the room, within sight of where my family would be sitting, hemmed in by several family-filled tables. Franny and I moved there and into the ambient especially festive gathering of middle-aged couples, who immediately leaned over to begin recommending dishes to us.

"It's my Dad's treat," I told Franny, once our cream sodas had arrived along with vast, somewhat food-stained, fox-edged menus almost as big as we were, an entire dinner plate stacked high with rolls, bagels, pumpernickel, and bialys, what appeared to be a soup bowl filled with swirls of sweet butter, and another heaped with pickles of all sizes, shapes, and vegetable origins.

"My mother gave me lunch money," Franny said demurely,

I could just imagine how little that would be. "It's part of the trip," I insisted, "For helping with the toys. My Dad pays."

This disconcerted her a bit, but when the waiter finally got through schmoozing with the women at the adjacent table, Franny was ready with her order. And it was a solid enough meal she ordered: more, I decided, than her mother's money would have paid for.

We attempted to chat and it all came out halting, hesitant, Fanny said my family was very nice, especially my mother.

She said she wished had a large family. I asked if she'd found the material she'd wanted. She said no, but that she'd found other materials she could use. We talked about school a bit, mostly about upcoming papers and tests and about our teachers (she found all of them "nice," which hardly surprised me). Not a word about other students. Then we lapsed into silence again, a silence more deadly for all the noise around us in our central location (waiters sailed around us like ketches, their overflowing trays like awry wind-filled jibs), and not a window to stare out of.

Our food arrived and grateful for the distraction we began to eat

"Such a little lady! Such a little gentleman!" one of the women at the table nearest us said. "Look, Rose. I wish my Richie was like that. What's your name, dear?" she asked, leaning over the tiny space between our tables. "I'm Netty. This is Rose. Look, Rose, how polite! And how pretty she is! So well-mannered. Like grown-ups!"

Franny and I exchanged a look of "Oh-my-God-what-do-we-do-now?" at the women. Netty, in a periwinkle blue dress with hair tinted like tiger lilies, had a once-handsome, now paunchy face in which two pale blue eyes shone out like escaped criminals only partly camouflaged by generalized swipes of eye shadow. Rose, brunette and thin, had bangles on her wrists and neck as richly detailed and numerous as a Bantu bride, lipstick the shade of dry blood and warm brown eyes set in a puckered, over-dieted face.

"Is he your boyfriend?" Rose asked.

"We're school friends," Franny answered, unperturbed.

"Are you sure?" Rose asked.

"What school? On Essex street?" Netty asked.

"Oh, no. In Queens," Franny answered, and went on to give details. "That's a ritzy neighborhood," Netty said, knowingly. "Remember, Rose? Your nephew, Harold the Stinker, moved there with that *shiksa* wife?"

"If he isn't your boyfriend," Rose went on, undaunted by her friend, "How is it you're having a lunch date together?" She made it seem as though a Sunday afternoon lunch date was a Roman orgy.

Franny attempted to explain, and I helped her out. Rose seemed unconvinced.

Then: "So? What's wrong with this one?" Rose asked Franny. "Or do you have so many other boyfriends?"

Once again we tried to explain, but Rose cut us short.

"He's good-looking and he seems healthy and his father is rich enough to buy for charity. What else do you want?" she prodded Franny.

"They're only kids," Netty put in.

"Only kids," she scoffed. "Have you been bar-mitzvahed?" Rose asked me.

"I'm thirteen," I answered, knowing her question really was, "Are you a man?" Then added, "But I'm not Jewish."

"So then what are you?"

I barely got out the words, "Italian-American," before Rose turned to Franny. "What could be better? Italian men make the best husbands after Jewish men, take my word. Sometimes better husbands. If I hadn't met Nate, I was going to marry an Italian. Tell them, Netty. They're good family men, steady, take care of children, and they know how to make love to a woman."

Netty was laughing out loud.

"It's true," Rose insisted. "Even at his age." She leaned over to Franny, who by now was turning a mild shade of rose, and whispered something into her ear, of which I only caught the words, "thick like a derma."

Franny blushed beet red, and the two women began laughing and hitting at each other's arms, talking in Yiddish, turning to their relatives to say something. All of them looked at us, and laughed.

By now Franny was mortified. After a few sips of water,

Fanny's color settled to its normal porcelain glow, but two high spots of paprika on either cheek remained, and she avoided my eyes. Luckily, our table neighbors had long finished eating, and were getting up to leave. Rose stopped and said, "Don't wait until you're old and dried up, little darlings. Promise me that."

A few minutes after they'd left and Franny and I were drinking milky tea and eating walnut pound cake, I broke the silence by talking about an upcoming project for our Social Studies class, which I thought would make a great stir at the school's Science and Art Fair. I managed to keep it interesting enough for Franny to respond and even to look at me in the eye. I smiled to see her coming around and said, "You know you have really pretty eyes. Everyone thinks so. Denny, Barry, Michael, especially Michael. He really likes you a lot. He thinks you're stuck up, which is why you won't talk to him. But I'll tell him how nice you really are when I see him tomorrow.

"No," she said. "Don't."

"Why not?"

"I don't know. Just don't. Please."

"All right. Don't you like Michael? All the other girls in the class do."

I couldn't conceive of her not liking Michael. Only thirteen, he already had the tall wiry body of a junior executive, eagle-like ice blue eyes, a handsome, strong Teutonic face, and a shock of ash blond hair. In fact he was the image of Hitler Youth, despite being Jewish on both sides of his family.

"Not that way," Franny said.

"What about Barry?" If Michael was Teutonic and striking, Barry was cute, with large, soft, luxuriantly lashed brown eyes, ringlets of hair the color of maple syrup, and the most perfectly modeled body of ant boy in our school; along with that special grace and easy sociability of a child who'd been told he was beautiful from infancy.

"Yes. But not in that way. Besides," she lamely added, "my mother is very strict about boys."

And that would have ended our date, and any future date, except that Franny blushed again, saved only by the sudden appearance of my sister joining us at the little table. But with that blush Franny had revealed an important fact: not only didn't she like Michael or Barry, she liked me. I was sure of it, intuitively certain, even if I didn't know what to do about it quite yet.

Weeks went by before I found an opportunity. But when you're thirteen years old, weeks can seem to contain a year's worth of incidents, even with an exactly defined goal in mind, never mind the ambiguous challenge that Franny Solomon seemed to offer.

The first event to enliven our by then routine seventh grade days was a poem titled "The Strawberry Patch," which Denny Tobin somehow or other got hold of and brought into school. When the affair finally blew apart, he admitted the poem had come from his older brother's private drawer, stolen without the elder Tobin's knowledge. But the poem might have come from a number of places.

You've no doubt seen or read such things. In certain places of the country they're called "pocket books," in others, "hand books." In one classy private girl's school they're called "wets" because that's their most apparent effect on impressionable, well brought up young ladies. They came in a variety of sizes from stapled mimeograph sheets to perfect bound booklets. Their titles are by now infamous, if not exactly classic: "Behind the Green Door," "Modern Affection," "Preferred Choice," "Her Master's Voice"—and "In the Strawberry Patch." Their literary genre varies from wordless cartoons featuring ripped-off Disney characters to flip photos of stripteases to simple prose tales. Our own little booklet was physically unprepossessing yet was an ambitious piece of writing: a poem written in iambic pentameter, Spenserian Rhyme Royal (more or less) of over a dozen cantos, for a total of about 120 lines. The rhymes available for such a form had declined since the freer usage of the Elizabethans, and the author could not keep the whole from falling into a sort of dogtrot meter at times. But no one thought to criticize the poetics of "In The Strawberry Patch." It was the subject we were interested in: a detailed, if bucolic, representation of heterosexual intercourse with all the action spelled right out for anyone to read themselves.

If there were four boys in our class out of thirteen who actually had a sexual experience with a female as claimed, we certainly didn't let that stop us from savoring Denny's poem. He charged a dime a read, usually in the gym locker room; and everyone (except slow August, who was mathematically brilliant but virtually dyslexic) plunked down their money to read. Of course other boys also tried to read over your shoulder, But, as Denny guaranteed, you had to sit holding the mimeographed sheets of the poem yourself to receive the fullest effect, which consisted a rock hard erection and a sense of true liberation. Someone had actually *written* those forbidden words down on *paper*. That's what astonished me so much. Someone had written them in a conscious (and quite successful) attempt to describe what I'd always thought so amorphous a complex sensations and emotions. And it worked! Not a single boy who sat down on the hard wood bench in front of Denny Tobin's locker to read "In Strawberry Patch" stood up again unaffected. Some were shocked, some were flushed. A few laughed nervously and looked seasick. Two went to the john immediately with no explanations needed or offered.

After school four of us, Michael, Barry, Denny and I, discussed how we could make money out of this, in the true entrepreneurial spirit of our time and place. Denny argued that it was his poem to do with as he wanted; he had no intention of sharing profits. Michael counter argued that Denny had a pretty lousy reputation, whereas he, Michael, could actually get the poem to other seventh grade classes. Barry had the use of a mimeograph machine. We would run off copies and sell them for more than the dime reading price. All four of us would be salesmen with an equal cut in the loot. It didn't take too long for Denny to see the sense in this. He'd already used up his contacts in our class. He saw how much more money he could make off the poem by making us partners.

We wavered over how much to charge for the poem, A dollar seemed awfully high. A quarter divided up four ways seemed too little. After more discussion we settled on fifty cents. We envisaged a large profit, especially when we managed to get our business past the seventh grade and into the eighth and ninth grades of our school. We even made plans for our earnings. I wanted a new bicycle—a real English three-speed model just introduced that year, with full hydraulic hand brakes and handlebar gearshift. Denny said he would reinvest his money in real (i.e., photographic) pornography—he thought he knew where he could get his hands on some Swedish magazines. Barry wanted to put up a new basketball hoop on his garage, and to buy a season's pass for the Knicks, his favorite team. Although Barry had the short, close-muscled body of a wrestler, he dreamed of being six-foot four and the first white member of the Globetrotters. Michael would put his earnings into rocket parts and fuel for the small but powerful remote controlled missiles he built and repeatedly crashed at so much expense.

The plan worked. The poem was mimeographed and stapled, the boys in nearby classes were approached during cafeteria and gym and study periods in assembly hall, and soon we four were raking in ten to fifteen dollars a week. At one point, every third boy in our grade owned a copy of "In the Strawberry Patch," as well as about a quarter of the eighth grade and a fifth of the ninth. We became bold. Denny would carry a hundred or so copies at a time into home room class in the morning and distribute them to us for sale during the school day. Suddenly we were all very popular, suddenly quite respected. One afternoon two boys from 9 SP 1 walked into our lunch period on passes—ninth graders always seemed to have passes to go wherever they wanted—and came directly to our table to congratulate us on our "good business sense and enterprise." They also told us they would recommend us for the audio-visual squad, the elite club of the school.

I imagine that Samidzat literature in the U.S.S.R. and other Eastern Bloc nations is the closest one could come to describing the secretiveness, the complicity and yet the all-pervasiveness of our anonymous, omnipresent poem in junior high school. After a few months, eighth graders we'd never met could be heard shouting key phrases from "In the Strawberry Patch"—"the berries were very ripe!"—across the aisles of school buses. Some boys gave the poem to girlfriends, using it to excite and thus help seduce them. Barry calculated that one out of every ten girls in the school either had read or owned a copy, including the girls in our class, although none of them every said a word about it to us.

After netting us about five hundred dollars, our business collapsed suddenly one day when I was absent from school with the flu. I returned two days later and attempted to figure out what exactly had happened, piecing together the sequence of events from a suddenly quite somber group of friends and classmates. All the boys and a few of the girls had spent the previous day being interrogated in one or another of the dean's offices, but so far none of them had cracked under pressure. The day I showed up I was just in time for the entire class to be lectured by Mr. Wolff on civic responsibility and how unity may be commendable but how because of a few of us, pornography had riddled the school like a cancer, etc. We still didn't tell him who was responsible for the poem, and 1 when it was my turn to go into Mr. Wolff's office alone, I simply said that I had been out sick for several days and had no idea of what was going on, which he only partly believed.

It turned out that Denny had dropped some of the mimeo sheets out his loose-leaf folder while leaving our homeroom one morning. Mrs. Childs, our homeroom teacher, had picked them up. If it had been our English teacher, Mr. Collins, instead, he might have given us a talk on the poor influence doggerel had on our own writing, and that would have been the end of it. Mr. Strauss also might have been more tolerant; he later proved to terrifically understanding of the adolescent psyche, at least in my case. But Mabel Childs panicked. She was probably truly shocked. Since the papers had fallen out of Denny's looseleaf, Denny bore the brunt of the blame. I'm not sure how the rest of us were implicated—possibly our own blasé attitude to what was for us by now a passé sensation—but our corruption was assured: our jadedness damned us all.

That night, Michael, Barry and I brought all the remaining copies of the poem to a central spot and burned them. We also discussed whether or not we ought to threaten Denny if he "squealed" on us. Or if that mightn't be exactly the wrong thing to do. Denny had already been suspended from school, but we expected him back soon.

"No sudden spending of money," I suggested. "People get careless when they're scared." It was a line from an Audie Murphy gangster movie I'd recently seen.

Phlegmatic, Barry said, "If we're quiet, it will all blow over. G.O. elections are beginning next week. Everyone will get involved in the campaign."

"As long as the money part of it doesn't get out," Michael worried. "That will really make trouble for us. As it is, they think he was just carrying them around, maybe giving them out, not selling them to anyone for fifty cents."

We all moaned at the horrible possibilities.

The next day in home room class, when Mrs. Childs put Eileen charge of the class so she could step out, Michael stood up. He'd awaiting exactly this moment for several days and he said in most persuasive public speaking voice, "Listen up, guys. We all have to stick together on this. No matter what happens. They can't really do anything to us anyway. You all know that. But if they ever get an idea of the size of this operation, we're all out of the SP. Not just the people who were involved. You're all silent accomplices. Got it?"

Some girls complained. Some boys said, "No fair!" But the room was silent the minute Mrs. Childs stepped back in, and everyone must have decided that Michael was right— no one ever ratted on us.

Interrogations continued for weeks. In the middle of French or Social Studies or even Gym, one sometimes two students would be called to the dean's offices. We all kept to our story: Yes, the boys said, we'd seen Denny with the poem, somewhere in the school, and had read it, and didn't think it was all that important. The girls said they didn't know anything about it. Period.

When it was my turn for an in-depth interview, I said the same thing all the others did, admitting I'd seen the poem. I added, "I couldn't be bothered with it. It wasn't very good poetry, you know."

Mr. Wolff's mouth dropped open at my effrontery. "And what would you consider to be good poetry?"

"All sorts of things," I hedged.

"Such as?"

"You know, sonnets and epic verse."

"For example."

"Well, Homer to start off with, naturally, then Virgil and Dante."

"You've read them?"

"Sure. I read Homer in the fifth grade."

"And Dante too?"

"Sure. My father has the Carey translation of the *Inferno* in a huge old folio edition. With the Doré etchings," I said, laying it on thick.

"Not the original edition?" Mr. Wolff asked, interested despite himself.

"I wish. No. It says, 'New Edition, 1885' on the title page. I've only read the *Inferno*, so I guess that makes me pretty ignorant for a seventh grader," I pushed.

Undaunted, he went on. "And what sonnets would you recommend? Say, to someone just beginning to read poetry."

Here I could have blessed Mrs. Campanella for her gift of *Immortal Poems of the English Language*. "Well," I began hesitatingly as though he really had me, "Wordsworth, 'It's a beautiful evening, quiet as a nun,' and Keats's 'Oh, bright star, would that I were steadfast as thou' and Shakespeare, of course."

"Of course," he murmured.

"'Shall I compare thee to a summer's day?'"

"You know something, young man," he suddenly interrupted me, looking very tired. "I knew that we would encounter some really smart kids in these special classes and I also knew that putting you together in classes would make you even smarter than before. But being smart isn't always the same thing as being in the right."

"And then there's Tennyson's 'Break, Break, Break ... '"

"Get out of here," he said without emotion in his voice. "Go back to your class."

Despite various mutinous rumblings from some of the girls in the class in the following days, we never broke our silence or our unity, and as Barry had predicted, the furor over "In the Strawberry Patch" died down the day that the General Organization listed its nominees for school government officers. A cloud remained over our class as the source of the poem, even though Denny Tobin was placed in 7-7 for the rest of the year, where he found other friends and even a few large, stupid henchmen to protect him, and by that Spring he had his porno sales going quite well.

The rest of us waited cautiously before spending our ill-gotten gains. But we did all eventually get what we wanted: I, my new bike, Michael his rocket parts, Barry his basketball hoop and season pass. And, of course, the incident had drawn all three of us closer together. If Barry and David and Michael's houses were still too far away for daily afternoon visits, we'd gotten into the habit of telephoning each other a great deal during our crisis, with almost hour by hour updates. This habit remained throughout our junior high years, and when I think back on my friends from that period, it is the young pornographers who come to mind first.

No sooner had the results of our business enterprise begun to subside than our second distraction arose, in a rather disguised form.

Mr. Collins, our English teacher, was given to strange enthusiasms and equally unexpected depressions. These latter some in the class attributed to his feelings of guilt, frustration and fear of retribution that we assumed any self-respecting child molester must on occasion suffer. We had no proof of this tendency, of course—he'd certainly never touched any of us—but weren't we, after all, too old for his depraved tastes? His enthusiasms, on the other hand, were less easy to account for as many of them were, to our thirteen-year-old minds, odd in the extreme. I mentioned earlier his reading aloud of a Poe tale to dampen our high spirits one afternoon. It was partly that, partly also to raise his own spirits. Mr. Collins liked nothing better than reading aloud—either from text or from memory—a story, paragraph, a poem. Usually the more exotic the better, and always at the most inappropriate times. Once, in a class earlier in the term, on one those sultry early October days that are more summer than mid-August and, because of their lateness and fleetingness, all the more stultifyingly distracting, he stopped in the middle of a lesson where clearly not one of the students were able to pay attention for longer than two minutes at time, to suddenly dash for the nearest window. There he intoned in a surprisingly basso voice, "I caught this morning morning's minion, king- / dom of daylight's dauphin, dapple-dawn-drawn Falcon in his riding / of the rolling level," and so on, accenting the sprung rhythms, the clashing sounds, the wildly irregular meter and disturbingly similar words of what I (alone, I suspect and only because of Mrs. Campanella's gift years before) knew to be Gerard Manley Hopkin's poem, "The Windhover." Then, Mr. Collins turned around to us, his round face almost gleaming with spirituality—or some other ineffable emotion—and said, "Lovely, no? Now, Elaine, perhaps you can tell me what the rhyme scheme of a Shakespearean sonnet is?"

This particular lesson, Mr. Collins waited until the period bell had rung before shouting out in his best Drill Instructor's voice, "Stay in your seats! I have an announcement to make." Disregarding the general *"Awwww!"* that burst from twenty-three throats all at once—it was our last class of the day, and we still had to get to our home room to get our jackets—he waited until the bells were rung, then held up a sheet of paper, tantalizing us.

"This, children, could be your passport to fame and riches," he began melodramatically. "What is it, you ask?" None of us had, of course. We were posed in our seats like Olympic sprinters, one foot out, one dug into the floor for instant total release. "It is a contest. A contest for the entire school system of the city of New York. Any student from grades seven to twelve may enter. There are two categories, junior high and senior high. There are three prizes in each category. Cash prizes up to five hundred dollars for the lucky winners."

By now, despite the lateness, he had managed to get our attention, although we remained suspicious, poised to flee the instant we heard the final syllable—or even the first syllable—of the word "dismissed."

"What kind of contest?" August asked, always the class straight man.

"A writing contest, of course," Mr. Collins said. "A short story writing contest."

The boos and hisses that greeted this were inaudible, but still there.

"In most classes in this school," Collins went on, "this contest is extra, voluntary, simply one way to receive a higher term grade. But not in this class. In all SP classes in this school, by fiat of Mr. Wolff, our dear dean, entering this contest is required."

"*Awwww!*" sounded from about half of the class, disappointment too deep to be restrained.

"Quiet!" Collins shouted. "I told you it was a chance for fame and riches. It's also a chance to prove to me that your supposedly brilliant minds are capable of some imaginative writing. That clearly has yet to be demonstrated in your woeful essays and despicable book reports. A sad lot those have been," he said, attempting to form his brows into a frown, of which he was physically incapable and so ending up looking like a large, red-faced, pouting boy with two small wireframe glasses and a pasted-on (although it was real) moustache. "You will all write me a short story. You will all enter the contest. You will do so by the time we return from Easter vacation. That gives you almost four months. Surely you can find time among your many social obligations and sports activities to do this."

"How long does it have to be?" Franklin asked, the first and most natural question following any declaration of required work.

"No shorter than two thousand words. As long as you wish," Mr. Collins said, then began to read the rules off the paper.

"Can we write about cowboys?" August asked, typically.

"You can write on any subject you wish," Mr. Collins said. "But it must be fiction. You know what I mean by fiction, August? The excuses you give me for not handing in reports on time. Those are fiction."

"On any subject?" Ellen asked.

"Any subject," he repeated. "Any length over two thousand words. Any style. Any form. Any genre."

"Like a mystery?": Barry.

"A mystery story, yes. Or a love story. Or a moral story. Or—"

"How about outer space?": Dick Wygrand.

"Science Fiction is fine. All the topics are right here on this piece of paper. I've had copies mimeographed for you. Of course we won't enter all of the stories in the final contest. Only the best ones. We'll have the class select them. And I'll select them too. But all of you will write a short story or else—"

"Can I write about my grandmother? She came from Russia during the revolution," Ruby asked.

"Absolutely," Mr. Collins said, doubtless pleased by the possibilities offered by the students, which foretold at least a smidgen of interest in the project. "I would like all of you to think about the story you would like to write. And, in a month or so, I would like you to hand in a paragraph or so, a sort of précis." He had calmed a bit, realizing perhaps that Mr. Wolff's idea might not have been such a bad one after all, despite the initial resistance. "You know, students, writing stories can be a lot of fun. Stimulating and creative. And if any of you wish help with your stories, I'll be happy to help you out." What he didn't tell us, and what I only discovered years later, was that Mr. Collins was an amateur writer himself who'd had several rather shorter and more obscure than usual pieces printed in several extremely short-lived and obscure magazines.

For the next few weeks, the writing contest became a sort of *leitmotif* of our conversations in class and out, especially with the students of 7 SP-1. Walking home, in the cafeteria, even in the locker room, someone would suddenly say, "I think I'm going to write a funny story. About my first year at summer camp." We'd all listen to the kernel of this potential story, and then offer advice, characters, scenes, and someone else might offer his or her story idea.

My own ideas—after I'd gotten over the fact of it being required which definitely made the project ambivalently intriguing—were manifold. I thought I'd read enough Science Fiction to write a good story of that type. But I also wanted to write something different, say a historical tale, perhaps set in the Eighteenth Dynasty of Ancient Egypt and making use of all of the knowledge of the place and period that I'd gathered.

By the time the needed paragraph précis had to be handed in, I'd settled on Science Fiction. Not aliens and monsters, of course, but what was known as "hard" science. I'd read about the narrow temperate band between the subpolar cold of the "nightside" of Mercury, the innermost planet of our solar system, and its hellishly hot "dayside." It was obvious to me that any landing and colonization of the planet that man achieved would have to be done in this narrow band between night and day. I envisioned an emergency, a multi-national space mission set up by the United Nations to monitor some sudden perilous sun spot activity

Ambidextrous: The Effect of "Mirrors"

that threatened our own planet in some as yet unspecified manner. There would be dangers, risk taken, lives lost and saved, a daring last chance rescue—say involving the launching of missiles with thermonuclear warheads into the sun. It would be about twenty typed pages long, and so completely realized that I would win first prize.

My presentation—four paragraphs, not one—was well done, and Mr. Collins accepted it, muttering only a bit about how he would have preferred that I'd written on a subject "closer to home." But I was persuasive. So the day before the Christmas Holidays began, I sat down to write "Mission to Mercury."

I'd written about the first half of the story when I was distracted by a more important series of events in my life—not the first time this has happened to me or to a chosen piece of writing. As it turned out, both my decision to accept the distraction, and the distraction itself changed the story I would write. The distraction was Franny Solomon.

"Would you mind walking me home?"

The speaker was Franny, the person addressed myself. The place was directly outside our Social Studies class, which we'd just left. The time 4:45 p.m., in mid-December.

Six students had been working on large projects in the Social Studies classroom after hours. Franklin Alt, Thom Meserole, and Franny at one table; Ellen, Barry and myself at another. The room was almost twice as long as the regular classrooms in our school, so there was space left for the two large work areas. Our project was an eight-foot-square topographical model of the eastern half of New York State, from the Canadian border and Lake Champlain's elegant meanderings, past the Adirondacks, through the long, at first twisting, then anchor-straight Hudson River Valley, to Lower New York Bay. At the other table they were doing the same for Western New York, from the Great Lakes down to Pennsylvania. When we were done, the map would be fitted together and be a major contribution to the school's upcoming Science and Art Fair, held eve February 25th.

My own part in this huge scheme was primarily that of initiator. From working on the Caruso brothers' architectural models, I'd learned how build up mountains from papier mache and creased cardboard. Forests and valleys were also a breeze for me, although more painstaking. Lakes were old mirrors. Rivers were Mylar strips painted blue. Little flags with differing symbols, explained in a table, signified natural resources, man-made resources (parks, dams, bridges, dairy farms, etc.), and other such information. Little had I known when I'd mentioned to Franny in that delicatessen on Rivington Street that I knew how to build such models that I would be drafted to oversee their construction. I still hadn't learned not to volunteer, but I knew it would help me to ace an already high grade subject for me and thus compensate for Spanish, where I was certain I couldn't get a good grade to save myself. Our teacher for that class, Mr. Sensale, remained convinced that I was Spanish-born and Spanish speaking, and couldn't be persuaded otherwise.

I guess I shouldn't have been surprised that Franny wanted someone to walk her home. At 4:45 pm, it was almost dark. And she'd already told me that she was afraid of some "tough boys" in her area. What surprised me was that she'd chosen me, and not Thom or Franklin, who lived near her.

"Sure," I said. Barry and Ellen were listening. What else could I say?

Our walk home through the icy early evening was uneventful. The air was frigid, filled with potential moisture, although the sky wasn't gray with a portending storm as much as it was alternately striated with starry blackness and cirrocumulus clouds, through which a nearly horizontal sliver of waning moon faintly shimmered like the edges of a huge light bulb about to go out. All I could really think about was the equally cold—and twice as long—walk back to my own house after I'd dropped her off. Arriving at the door to the Solomon house, I was surprised again. "Don't you think you'd better come inside to warm up a little? You can call your mother. She might be worried," Franny said, as though she had school friends walk her home and drop in daily.

The small kitchen was warm and bright; yellow lighting made it seem even toasty. As we got our street clothes off and I dialed home, Franny offered to make hot cocoa and I accepted. She did more than just that in the kitchen; she prepared an entire roast and slipped it into the oven by the time our cocoa was ready.

At first I thought we were alone. But a telltale click suggestive of someone picking up then quickly dropping the phone receiver on an extension in another room told me we weren't. As we sat at the little table to dunk Lorna Doone cookies into our cocoa, I heard a soft rattling noise.

"My father," Franny said.

He came into the room in a wheelchair, pulled up to peck her cheek, swerved smartly toward me to shake my hand. Mr. Solomon—I never found out his first name—was tall even sitting in the wheelchair, long and bony, with a high browed unhandsome face, short uncombed hair as blue-black as his daughter's, and large, kind, wide-set gray eyes. His most obvious facial feature was his extremely high hairline and the two large identical dents on either side of his forehead, as though he'd been pulled around by a pair of round-ended pliers. His lips too, thin and pale, stood out. As did tufts of blue-black frizzled hair and long ears that reminded me of a marmoset I'd once seen. He was wearing house slippers, loose, worn corduroy trousers, an overlarge, faded flannel shirt covered by an antique smoking jacket: burgundy with black satin lapels, cuffs, and embroidery. He dove right into the cookies, asked for and received a cup of tea. He seemed more like Franny's older brother than her father, a young thirty-five years old. He moved and spoke with the awkward vivacity of the young. I couldn't keep my eyes off a little tubular gleaming instrument hung on a chain around his neck, like bifocals older people often wore, I wondered if it was a jeweler's loupe.

He caught my eye, and held the little tool for me to inspect. It was a tiny microscope, not a loupe. He told me it was for optics. He studied optics, the science of light, as a hobby, he said, and had even written articles for *Nature* and *Scientific American* on the subject, as well as a highly regarded, if now out of print, book. He told me he'd become fascinated with optics while in the VA hospital recovering from "a lot of shrapnel" he'd received in the war. Someone had brought him a prism there, he explained. The rest he owed to his boredom with being laid up in between surgery to remove over four hundred shards of metal from his body.

Mr. Solomon seemed, as he spoke, a rather happy-go-lucky man despite his wheelchair. After our snack, he took me past the living room with its convertible sofa, which opened to become Franny's bed at night, into a third room, separated from the others by a wall that ended a few feet from the ceiling with a row of paneled windows that could be tilted open to catch summer breezes. In this room he and his wife slept; it was where he had his little "laboratory."

His lab consisted of a huge old desk like those one sees in 'twenties offices in old movies, but littered with books, tools and pamphlets. A small, cleared space was filled with tiny mirrors, shards of glass and lenses. He pointed out a chunk of Ruby glass, black until you held it to the light, when it suddenly became the color of sweet wine. He showed me true black glass, which remained ebony when held to the light but showed stellar pattern of refraction. He showed me milk glass which straight on was opaque, but could be a powerful enlarger when looked at sideways, and various tiny mirrors he had designed which enlarged, lengthened, thickened, or reduced images.

As I looked and he explained, Mr. Solomon also asked questions about myself, so subtly that only later would I realize how much he had learned. It was clear that Franny had spoken of me before. When I excused myself to allow him to go back to work ("my little obsession," he called it), he invited me back to their house.

I remained a few minutes more, dreading the weather that would face me outdoors. Franny closed the bedroom door, saying she didn't want to bother her father, sat me down on the convertible sofa, and thanked me walking her home. Then she astonished me by kissing me on the lips.

It wasn't just a peck; it was a long, although closed-mouth, kiss. I responded by enfolding her (awkwardly, given our angle) in my arms and kissing her until we broke away at the same time. Then I got up to put on my scarf, hat, gloves, and coat.

Walking home, I wondered what it all meant. I resolved to kiss her again as soon as I could.

My opportunity came a few days later, again after our New York State map project, when I asked if Franny would like me to see her home. We walked through another frosty evening: an overcast one, as the first winter snow was predicted. Once again Franny invited me inside to warm up. This time the door to her father's room was fully closed, and when she went to peek in, she returned to the kitchen to say he was sleeping. We were a bit more comfortable now, and we talked on a variety of subjects related to school as she moved around the small kitchen preparing dinner, and I wondered how I could get her to kiss me again. It didn't look very likely until she finally got a casserole put together and into the oven, washed her hands and said, "There!" She turned to me. "Would you like to sit in the living room?"

In truth, I was comfortable where I was. But if we sat on the sofa there seemed more possibility of our being near each other than at chairs catty-corner around the table, so I said sure.

We sat on the sofa, Franny warning that we had to be fairly quiet not to awaken her father. Then she pulled out a scrap book she said she'd put together over the past year. It was mostly filled with dried flowers and high score tests and school reports, and a letter from her pen-pal in Tokyo, a boy who, in the black and white photo, seemed to have the same coloring) as Franny. Among all this more or less expected stuff, I was surprised to come across three swatches of material with no identification other than a date.

"Recognize them?" she asked.

"Should I?"

"Those are the pieces of the material I bought that lovely Sunday that I joined your family in Manhattan. Remember?"

"Sure, I remember."

"They're my souvenirs of that day," she said a bit wistfully.

I looked at her amethyst eyes and was reminded of the Poe story called "The Maelstrom." I sank so deeply, so instantly into those eyes, looking for a single hue, a mote of iris to hold onto, finding nothing but fluidity and motion.

We were already holding hands. I leaned over and began to kiss her. Where the first time she had been tolerant, pliant, this time she seemed cagier. After a short while, I probed her lips open with my tongue, and we began to French kiss. Hands went up to necks and ears, roamed along chests, shoulders, arms and backs. In no time we were down on the sofa, my hands flickering all over her clothed body. We kissed like that for a very long time, rubbing and caressing until Franny's face became flushed and she began to pant, at which, remembering my past experiences with girls, I reached down, got one hand into her underpants, and quickly began massaging her to climax, never stopping kissing her. She came, grabbing me so hard around the back I thought I would need Ben-Gay ointment, but I kept massaging her, planning to bring her off a second time, while she lay back, sunk in the luxury of the sofa, my body, my lips and hand. Then the oven timer went off.

Franny leapt up, pushing me off her. She looked around the living room as though she had suddenly awakened on Mars. Regaining her wits, she ran to the kitchen to shut off the timer and check the casserole. When she returned, she had completely regained her composure. She wouldn't come back to the sofa, despite all my urging.

She did kiss me again at the door when I left her house.

My dealings with Ricky Hersch over the past year hadn't completely wiped out those months I'd played in the Flaherty girls' basement. This time was different. I had an only partly willing partner, one whom I could show what to do. I was as excited by that prospect as I was by the idea that Franny was what my mother would call a "good girl": someone she liked and could respect, take out with her family, like to see me with. Add that Franny's legendary status as the untouchable girl in our grade and you can understand why I became obsessed with wanting to fuck her. It was strong enough to eliminate the few qualms I felt remembering how my last two sensual relationships had ended, and my unspoken decision, after the affair with Ricky, to forget about sex for a while.

Each time I walked Franny home from school, I moved closer and deeper into a shared world of sensuality. As long as her father wasn't awake. That wasn't always the case. Sometimes he'd be waiting at the table for us, and would remain there until he chose to show me something new in his "laboratory," some new glass with bizarre and wonderful optical properties he'd received from a colleague abroad, or some new combination of mirrors that he had devised. He was the first person to use the word "laser beam" to me. This was in 1956, remember, and he called it "undifferentiated light" and showed me how a thin, directed beam of light could burn a hole in the already scarred edge of his desk. Usually, what he showed me in his lab almost compensated for the lack of sex with Franny. She seemed not to mind, and once, when her father appeared just after we'd had tea and I was about to ask her to move into the living room, she seemed almost relieved. At other times, Mr. Solomon would hear us talking and come out of his laboratory, remaining so long I would have to get back home.

But it was the times that he was in his room when we arrived at her house and remained there long enough for me to prod Franny into checking if he were asleep or not. If she peeked in and, inscrutable with the news, nodded yes, he was asleep, we made love. Once I wondered why he had such odd hours, and Franny explained it was because of the nature of his optical work: he preferred rainy afternoons or late at night when no distracting outside light interfered. She told me she would sometimes awaken at four a.m. and look up from the convertible sofa bed where she slept and see the dim glow from his desk lamp through the clear window panes separating the two rooms.

Meanwhile, slowly, step by step, I proceeded to strip away both her defenses and her clothing. Each time we ended upon her sofa, I would take another step. Once I unzipped my pants and made her hold my erection while I masturbated her. Another time I showed her with quiet precise instructions how to masturbate me. I kissed the surprisingly large areolas of her small firm breasts. I kissed and nibbled at her labia, gently bit her clitoris while fingering her inside until I thought she would scream. My memory of the Flaherty girls' genitalia had all fused together in my mind. What I saw with Franny was hardly a "gash" a "twat" as the boys in my class called it. It was more like a fleshy exotic flower, especially from some angles and in dimmer light. With her clitoris extended, her labia swelled, it sometimes looked like an orchid, a sort of Lady Slipper, speckled with light dew.

As her fears subsided into pleasure, my daring grew. One time I began to rub the head of my erection all over her genitals until I came. I rubbed it on top, on the bottom, all the while lightly fingering her until she became accustomed to the sensation. The next time we met she was relaxed enough for me to put it inside her, if only an inch. I lay above her, poised on my elbows, looking down, thinking that would be all I'd do that day, when I suddenly felt myself drawn in. I was so surprised I began to withdraw. But the look on her face—almost blank with pleasure—told me not to. It didn't take long for the two of us to reach orgasm, which, while not as sharp as those I enjoyed when masturbating or being fellated, was just fine.

Franny jumped up, rushed to the bathroom, ran out again into the kitchen where she frantically searched in various cabinets, grabbed up what seemed to be a bottle of white vinegar, then disappeared into the bathroom again: to douche, I suppose now, although at the time I didn't have a clue what she was doing. It was weeks before she let me come inside her again, and she never much did like the idea. Nor, when she told me the risks involved, did I. Neither of us wanted to be fourteen-year-old parents. So we made an agreement: I would enter her but withdraw before climaxing onto her thighs, or tummy, or breasts or sometimes into her hand. And, as our meetings went on and this became comfortable, I began to hint to her of yet another way she could bring me off with no danger of pregnancy. At first she was hesitant, but step by step I got her to suck me.

All these activities took place on the convertible sofa in

the living room while Mr. Solomon was sleeping, between four-thirty and six-fifteen, when Franny's mother arrived home from work. Only once did we almost not make the deadline. Luckily, we were both already dressed, with a borrowed library book in my hand, when Mrs. Solomon came home. I only remained another few minutes. I didn't think Franny's father mentioned the real frequency of my visits to his wife, perhaps because he slept through three-quarters of them.

In school things were quite different. There she was simply Franny Solomon, the same girl as before. One of the most intelligent girls in class, she continued to be polite, cordial, a bit stand-offish, useful, deferential to our teachers, well-liked by all.

We were now noticed to have a "special" relationship, although it was perceived quite differently and far more innocently than the lubricious reality. No wonder. Franny had laid down some cautions about our public behavior together, and I wasn't about to risk what we had, so I went along with them. We could never be alone together. We could sit together in the cafeteria or study hall or in special assemblies where films and occasional shows were put on. We could—but didn't always—walk together from class to class each day. We could—infrequently—hold hands, but we couldn't kiss or otherwise touch. This was to show that ours was quite different than the more obviously passionate relationships that had been formed in our class: several times Thom Meserole and Lolly Lipton were found staggering out of the Science Department office storage room (where Thom worked) flushed, their clothing in disarray. Rita and David King, from 9 SP 1, were known to have spent several weekends alone in David's house when his parents were out of town vacationing in the Caribbean. In fact, there was great deal of sex happening among the students by mid-term of our seventh grade, a fact that Franny was more aware of than I—from hearing, without appearing to listen to, class gossip, I suppose—which was why she was so prudent about us. But even I had heard about several unchaperoned parties that had taken place among students we knew where girls had been topless and where cigarettes and liquor had been consumed.

Naturally, I was invited to these parties. Naturally, I always declined. Shortly after Franny and I were recognized to be "going out together" by the canny, inquisitive girls in our class, the boys also found out, and I was suddenly the cynosure of a score of questions in the locker room changing for gym. Most of my friends were amazed that "Iron Tits" as they called Franny (with some admiration) had given me any encouragement.

"Did you kiss her?" Barry asked, his stylishly torn gym shorts revealing what Ellen called his "dreamy" thighs.

"Sure," I said, determined to seem innocent as possible.

"A lot?"

"Each time I walk her home."

"At the door?" Michael asked.

"Sometimes inside the house."

"French kiss too?" Thom asked.

"Sure."

"How many times?" Barry again.

"Come on!" I said. "What is this? Twenty questions?"

"He's embarrassed," Barry explained. "Did you ever cop a feel? Without her bra on?"

I tied my sneaker laces and said, "See you on the track."

"Look, he's blushing," said Thom.

"Of course he's blushing," Bill Klaum said. "He's in love."

"You wish Franny Solomon would kiss you," Barry defended me. "Or any other girl for that matter."

"Oh, yeah? Plenty of girls kissed me."

"Sure. On your ass."

"Oh, yeah?"

I ran out of the locker room and onto the track where I quickly ran off the erection I'd gotten during their interrogation from the briefest memory of Franny's face raised between my thighs the night before, her tongue flicking away at the sensitive inside skin. I wondered what they would have said if I'd told them what we really did, loving the secret life we shared.

Franny and I were soon considered a "sweet" couple, i.e., an unexpected, well-matched, "cute" and innocent twosome. Which was exactly the way Franny wanted it. Me too. Of course I also yearned to tell *someone* what our relationship was really like. I didn't dare. I was still at the point where once, when I'd had to hurriedly dress and leave the Solomon's house because Franny heard her father stirring in the next room, I got out the door and ran half of the mile long distance home. When I arrived inside my house, I encountered my mother in the kitchen. She was in a chipper mood, and without any warning, she grabbed me as I went by and kissed me. I immediately drew back, at the same time trying to be nonchalant about it so she wouldn't notice. Luckily she didn't notice and went back to rolling out dough for cookies she was baking and continued to chat with me. I was so distracted wondering whether my mother could smell or even taste the flavor of Franny's cunt on my unwashed mouth (it seemed impossible she couldn't; it filled the room for me) that I finally got away and ran up to my bedroom. In the bathroom looking at my sister's *Trite Confessions* magazine, with its small but beautifully illustrated ads for "bust crèmes," I masturbated twice.

In the following days, several large and small incidents happened to show me it wasn't mere lust I felt for Franny. The first time I realized this was about two weeks after I'd first penetrated her. We were in Math class and Mr. Thirrel was handing out test papers from the week before. When

Franny got hers, her neighbor Lolly let out a squeal. Franny didn't say anything, but I stared at her so hard that she finally held up the test so I could see her score—perfect! I blushed from head to toe with pleasure and pride in her.

After that, whenever a teacher complimented her in class or I overheard a student say something favorable about Franny, I would feel the same pleasure—feel the compliment was partly for me too. But having Franny right there was sometimes too much. Because our classes had more or less open seating plans compared to the rigidity of elementary school, some days I seated myself so I couldn't see her and thus be distracted from my studies. At other times, I arranged to be in her line of vision and kept my eyes on her. Then too, if in the middle of a class I was bored, I would remember our evenings together and lose my way completely.

I'd never been terribly self-conscious, but with Franny around all the time, and the other girls in the class aware of us—of me—I became more sensitive to the impression I made. I dressed with more care, even shopped for clothing at the shops in Kew Gardens and Forest Hills, where Barry and Michael bought their preppy wear—striped cotton button-down shirts, thin ties, white bucks, chinos with straps below the back waist. Even though this sometimes put a crimp in my allowance (when I couldn't get my parents to see that I needed new shoes *desperately*, even though the four other pairs in my closet were perfectly wearable), I thought it was worth having Franny be able to point me out to someone without shame. But there were difficult moments.

One occurred in Science. I can't remember exactly what Mr. Strauss was discussing, but by mid-period I finally managed to drag myself back enough in my seat so that I couldn't see Franny and tried to concentrate on the difference between an elemental mixture and a chemical compound. Science was one of the few classes with fixed seats, mounted in ascending rows: a sort of mini-theater so we could all view experiments on the immense basalt-topped lab table. Trying to appear attentive, I held my ball point pen lightly tapping my front teeth as I listened. Mr. Strauss stopped in mid-sentence.

"What's wrong with you?" he said, not unkindly.

I put my pen down, certain my cloud-walking was apparent, and said, "Nothing."

"Ohh! *Look* at him!" Carolyn McClintock screamed.

Her outburst was followed by stares and various kinds of expostulations from other students. I still didn't see anything wrong and foolishly sat there, wondering if they were all mad. Then I noticed my pen was leaking all over my desk. I looked down and my shirt front was covered in ink dribbles, as though a child had finger-painted it.

Mr. Strauss called me out of my seat. When I got to him, he said, "You've got ink all over your mouth. You'd better go wash it out."

I still didn't understand what he was saying. Then I did, and I was mortified in front of Franny. I turned, but she was looking down at her notes.

"Go on. Go!" Mr. Strauss said. "Here's a pass. Barry, go with him. Make sure he washes it all out. Some inks are toxic."

Barry grabbed me and half pulled me out of the classroom and into the boys' room a few doors away. Once I got a look at my ink-stained face and my blue mouth the mirror, I too panicked. With a lot of splashing water and gargling, I finally got my mouth flushed out, although my teeth would remain outlined with a pale blue tinge for another two days despite vigorous brushing.

Then I realized I couldn't possibly go back into the classroom and let Franny see me like this: my shirtfront streaked with ink and soaking wet, my lips and teeth still tinted blue. I sat on a closed toilet seat and refused to move, no matter how much Barry tried to persuade me.

He finally gave up and returned himself. A few minutes

later, Mr. Strauss charged into the boys' room. "Now what's all this about?"

"I can't go back," I said. "Look at me."

He did, and almost burst out laughing.

"See!" I said. "I can't go back to class. I don't care if you report me to the dean or have me thrown out of school, or . . . I can't."

"Why not? Everyone already knows you had an accident."

"I just can't."

"How did you do that, anyway? With the pen, I mean?"

"I don't know."

"No one will laugh at you. I promise."

"1 can't go back."

"What are you going to do? Stay here all afternoon?" he reasoned.

"I don't know. I want to die."

"Hey! It's not that bad. I know Science isn't all that interesting, but . . ."

"It has nothing to do with Science."

"Sure it does. You seemed to like the subject. Now you can scarcely keep your mind on it. I could almost believe what the girls in the front row said."

I panicked. "What? What did they say?"

"That you're . . ." He looked at me, then seemed to view me as though from an entirely different angle. "Is it possible?" he asked himself. "Could you be . . . at your age?"

"What? What?" I was terrified of the answer, but had to hear it.

"In love?" he tried.

I must have turned the color of Plaster of Paris. I felt the blood drain out of my head. I felt dizzy, ready to fall off the toilet seat.

I must have begun to fall. Mr. Strauss caught me. Kneeling, he held me, his large face close to mine. "I'll be damned," he said. "You are!" he said. "Or at least something like it." Then he laughed. "Well, congratulations. I won't ask the name of your lady. But don't worry. It isn't that terrible. And we can fix it up a little."

"You can?"

"At least the shirt. I think we have a spare in the Science office. boys have accidents all the time. It should fit. You can change there."

"I don't know," I wavered. The clean shirt would help but it would hardly remove the horrible memory.

"Don't worry. If she loves you too, then she won't be embarrassed, only concerned about you. She's probably worried you aren't coming back, afraid you're sick.

"Do you think so?

"I sure do."

"Okay." I said, trusting his judgment. I wouldn't have trusted any other teacher in the school.

We were about to leave the room. Mr. Strauss had stood up and taken my hand firmly his own large, freckled one when he suddenly turned around and knelt so he was at face level again. To my astonishment, grabbed me and held me so close against him that I could see the previously invisible weave in his brown and gray tweed jacket, see the red blond stubble on his check where he'd missed a spot shaving.

"I envy you," he said in a low voice. "To love so early, so well, means a life of love. Don't miss *any* of it."

Then he stood up and looked at me. "Blue Boy!" he said, and smiled.

I smiled too and went back to class.

Of course Franny had been embarrassed for me, but as Mr. Strauss had so wisely seen, she was more concerned. She didn't say a word about the incident when we met later that afternoon, and no one in the class (warned I suppose while I was changing my shirt) did either.

One upshot of the incident was that I began to understand that teachers were human beings. This was not an unimportant lesson. And although Mr. Strauss called me "Blue Boy" sometimes later on in the term, it was said affectionately, not mockingly.

The incident also revealed Franny's unfailingly good conduct in all situations, and thus led me to believe that she was perfect. I used my by then considerable artistic skills to draw her face and her torso, from life and memory in class, covering pages which ought to have been devoted to the geography of the Finger Lakes or to diagrams of paramecia.

After the incident, Mr. Strauss seldom called on me for answers, although to show him I was interested in his subject, I occasionally raised my hand. The other teachers hardly mattered. At times in the middle of class or in fact anywhere at all, I would fall into reveries that naturally included Franny and our lovemaking experiences, then quickly moved ahead to fantasies of us three years in the future as high school seniors leading the waltz at the graduation prom; or even further ahead, to college, the two of us living in a small house in Cambridge (I'd go to Harvard, she to Radcliffe); then to our college graduation, the two of us radiant in our caps and gowns, surrounded by admiring families and friends; and even further ahead to Franny holding our infant child as I received a prestigious award for a magnificent oil painting on some grand subject.

Everyone now noticed my inattentiveness in school and out. Even my normally blasé family. What was worse, now that I was having sex with Franny three or more times a week, I was suddenly horny all the time. I masturbated three times a day, rushing up to my room to do "homework" when my favorite programs were on television, just to unclog my now perpetually jazzed gonads.

All might have continued like that: Franny and I might have gone on to fulfill several of those naively banal thirteen-year-old daydreams. And why not? Others have, only stopping themselves after twenty years or more of marriage when their children have grown up and left home. One evening they turn to each other and realize they are fifty years old, their life a madness of complacency and illusion. The probability was high of such a life for me. And following the daring of my servicing of the Flaherty sisters and my deliciously perverted lust with Ricky Hersch, I was finally more or less back on a kind of conventional track again in my love life, feeling almost normal.

It couldn't last.

My first hint that something was wrong in our relationship was subtle, so fleeting I scarcely noticed it. I had spent twenty naked minutes sixty-inning with Franny on the convertible sofa in her parents' living room. She had already climaxed several times, and she now lay across my legs sucking me while I sat back and idly continued to finger her genitals, until she pushed my hand away. To not wake Mr. Solomon, sleeping only a few feet away on the other side of the wall, I gritted my teeth as the sweet fire tore through my lower torso and poured out of me. I threw my head back—and noticed something glinting from the ceiling. An evanescent tiny flash of yellow light, only a pinpoint in size. After a minute or so, I was able to correlate its flashing to the movement of the small gold ring I'd received from my parents as a birthday gift only a few days before. I wore it on my left hand, which had been gently combing the loose, blue-black hair of Franny's head deep in my lap. How odd, I remember thinking, and I wondered what was on the ceiling reflecting it.

Then Franny looked up, and we kissed passionately. The tiny refection was forgotten.

Two days later, I was standing up on the sofa, leaning against the wall, penetrating Franny from behind—another one of the dear girl's suggestions for new ways for us to enjoy ourselves—pumping along and playing with her breasts when I glanced up and once more caught the tiny golden glimmering reflection. Once again it came from my ring, but this time I was closer to the sailing, and I saw that the reflection was from a mirror: a thin, long pane of mirrored glass angled deeply inward, embedded somehow in the two-inch drop of the ceiling at that spot.

At the time I could make little sense of it. Perhaps I didn't want to look into it any further. For a minute, I had that very specific prickling sensation once gets trying to remember some important fact—a well-known by temporarily forgotten name—"on the tip of your tongue." The I let it go, relaxing back into what I was doing.

I didn't think Franny noticed me pause. If she did at the time, she didn't show it. Later, after we were dressed and I was ready to leave, she put a hand on my arm and asked if anything were wrong.

"No," I said, truthfully, my hesitation forgotten.

"What we're doing . . ." she began and modestly lowered her eyes so that once more she was the polite, demure Franny Solomon of my classroom experience. "Does it . . . bother you?" she finally said after hunting around for the words.

"*Bother* me? Are you kidding?" Then, trying to be sensitive to her, since I had no idea where she was leading the conversation, "Why? Does it bother you?"

"Oh no. Of course not." But she blushed, so I kissed her quickly and left.

The following day Franny told me I couldn't come inside, her father was sure to be awake. His hours had changed and he was expecting company: a colleague from Germany, also interested in optics. I still walked her home through an unusually warm, late February day which had followed a one-night snow melting into rain. The early darkened streets were still wet. We had to hop around puddles at street corners and climb up murky damp side-lawns to get around more substantial collections of rain water. The earth around us steamed from the warm rain and air hitting the frozen earth. The mist thickened as we walked, enfoldingly intimate yet frightening. I kept one arm protectively over Franny's shoulder all the way to her house.

She talked the entire distance about her father. How he'd come from a large immigrant family from somewhere in Swabia. How he, the youngest of six brothers who had all shared one bedroom in a Brooklyn tenement, had been the most promising, the most intelligent of them. While the others, like their parents, had to work hard at mostly menial jobs to survive, Franny's father had been spoiled, given things, allowed to complete his studies at Boys' High, and finally had even been accepted at City College. His future had seemed unlimited, Franny told me. He was at the top of his class. He'd received scholarships that would allow him to go to Columbia University Law School. He'd already met Franny's mother, and they had married with the stipulation that she would work to support him through his schooling. Franny's conception was an accident, if an understandable one, and neither parent ever regretted it. Her father's plans had been interrupted by World War II. He was conscripted in 1943. Franny believed she was the result of her parent's coupling that last night of panic and regret. Her father was on leave between basic training camp and his flight to a California airbase from which he was shipped out to some outpost on a northern Pacific island.

It was there he'd been so badly wounded. Several chunks of shrapnel had lodged in his spine. He'd lost the use of his legs, and with that his belief in a future.

Franny had never known her father except in a wheelchair. She told me she used to pore over photos (which her mother kept hidden} of her father before the war. Especially those taken on the beach or in summertime, showing him in shorts and bathing trunks. It was difficult for Franny to believe he'd been so tall, so straight, so active. Growing up, she'd never once glimpsed his legs. He kept them covered all the time, she believed because they were withered from disuse.

I had no real idea why Franny was telling me all this, except that part of "going steady" was to share such intimate details of each others' lives, and for her to show me why she loved her father. Although he might be a failure in his own and in the world's eyes—a cripple living off his wife's labor—to his daughter he was a brave man of great potential achievement in the prime of his life. His very existence, never mind his unfailing good spirits, love of life and of his avocation, was a daily miracle to Franny.

Naturally I agreed with her, and said I thought he was a "terrific guy." We kissed for a long time in the shadows of her deeply recessed front door and made a date for the following afternoon. It was just as well with me, Franny might not have to study, but there was a math exam the next day, and I did.

I'd been warned, and while I didn't know it exactly, I wasn't so dense to not know something was going on. The next time Franny and I were alone together in her living room, I was totally alert, ready for anything. Anything, that is, but what happened.

It would take almost twenty-five years for me to finally understand that intelligence and perceptiveness and alertness are not always a gift, often a curse. My teacher would be a man a few years younger than I was, admitted to possessing none of these qualities to any advanced degree: sweet, textbook-handsome Baird. I'd picked him up almost gratuitously one muggy September near dawn as I was walking the few blocks from a local discotheque which fronted the Hudson River. To my surprise, this vision in black leather sitting on the steps of the building in which

Alexander Hamilton had died (after being rowed across the river from the dueling ground in Weehawken, New Jersey) had not only deigned to talk to me when I ambled by, he had also quickly revealed to me what he was "into" that night: to wit, "servicing" me. I was not to even touch him. Ordinarily I would have found this an impossible condition: the man was *stone* handsome. But I had just left a group of some two thousand shirtless, sweating males any hundred of whom were about as attractive as Baird, and so I was somewhat jaded. I said okay.

Thus began one of the oddest and most satisfying "relationships" of my life. Unlike almost everyone I've met as an adult, Baird lived simply, had easily fulfilled desires and clear goals (he wanted to be a radio announcer in his hometown in northern Florida). He worked as a waiter in one of the many local West Village restaurants at night and by day he studied enunciation and voice training (he didn't have a trace of a Southern accent left, except when he was tired). Our relationship consisted of this: about the time he was getting off from work, two a.m. as a rule, and I was about to go to sleep, he would telephone, ask if I were having "trouble getting to sleep," and if I said yes, he would ring my bell five minutes later. I would put down the magazine or book I'd been reading in bed, let him in, and Baird would massage my feet, then my legs, take off my jockey briefs, sniff them, play with my genitals for a while, then blow me. We seldom spoke; not even obscenely during sex. There was no especial tenderness; neither was there dominance and submission, never mind S and M. Yet it was never mechanical. Baird fell so deeply, so completely into whatever fantasy it was that we accomplished together, that he managed to make it seem fresh and exciting, somehow exceptional, even though this happened scores of times over a two-year period.

Once Baird, for some unknown reason, slept over instead of getting up to go home. The next morning we were in the shower together and I began to ask if he were aware of the nature of the fantasy we were playing out, hoping he might share it with me. "You don't have to know," he said without any rancor. "You're doing just fine. Besides, you already know too much." When I tried to persuade him how helpful my knowing would be in helping me to play my role better, he said. "No. You'd just spoil it." Then he became my big brother. We were toweling off, and Baird put one arm around my shoulder and said, "You know, I feel sort of sorry for you. You think so much, you don't have time to enjoy your life. You always have to know what it signifies!" His Southern usage pleased me, if not his meaning. I laughed and said something like, "Show me how to enjoy myself," which he did. But as I lay there with Baird's handsome face looking up at me, I thought, he's right. And I remembered Franny Solomon and our last time together.

It began as ordinarily (if that's the right word) as any of our previous bouts of lovemaking, yet it was tinged from the onset by a sense of expectations, a hint that something extraordinary was about to happen. A sort of tickling sensation in the sternum, or that sharp momentary incising of the palm of your hand by another thread of line spelling out your destiny. Franny too had somehow intuited another level of awareness, and she made love with me almost frantically, as though determined to flood my mind with so much sensation that no thought could intrude. This was aided by my own wish: I'd made a bet with myself that I could pretend that all was as it had been before I'd spotted the mirror embedded in the drop ceiling. I gave in to her attentions, wondering how long I could hold out.

Almost to the end it turned out. But the temptation to do otherwise was too great. Even if I hadn't worn my ring—so as to not see those telltale reflections—Franny wore a metal barrette in her hair, and those fleeting reflections became almost blindingly obvious.

Finally I couldn't stand it any longer. I stood up on the sofa to get a closer look at the mirror. Franny began pulling me down, whimpering, "He'll see you." Nonsense, I thought. The windows were two inches above our heads. But Franny kept pulling at me, then stood upon the sofa herself and, I suppose realizing what she'd just blurted out, altered it to, "He'll hear us."

From this new height, I looked at the mirror and calculated its angle, all the while holding Franny in front of me, nibbling at her nape and playing with her breasts to distract her. That's when I saw the second mirror. It was just above the first down-angled one: I'd taken them for a single pane of glass. The second mirror was angled slightly up. This baffled me for a few seconds. Then I thought, there had to be a third mirror somewhere in the front of the two, i.e., over and in back of our heads.

I turned Franny around to face me, and then turned both of us sideways to the mirror. This allowed me to hide behind her head and to peek through the glass panes dividing the living room from the bedroom. All I saw at first was matte ceiling. Certain more had to be there, I moved up onto one of the thick sofa arms, and despite her protests that we were going fall, I managed to drag Franny up there too. Still using her to block what I was doing, I stretched myself until I could see into the dim bedroom, right to the far wall.

Dim but not dark. The vague incandescence of pewter against black must mean the gooseneck desk lamp Mr. Solomon used for his work was turned on, if at its lowest wattage. It gave enough light so that even in the murk where the far wall met the ceiling, I could see the glassy reflection of another slender mirror angled up, and another angled down, just as they were in the living room.

And there, flat on his desk, was the fifth mirror, into which Mr. Solomon peered so intently that he was completely undeterred by what must have been our oddly high and perilous position on the sofa. Or perhaps, from the quickening strokes of his hand up and down in his lap, it no longer mattered where we were or what we were doing, since he was unable to stop himself.

"What are you doing?" Franny asked. Then she too stretched up to within eye level of the glass panes between the two rooms, and I heard a gasp.

Her father pushed back from the desk in his wheelchair and arched his back so that we could both see his embroidered robe fall to either side of his stork-like legs and shrunken shanks, and spurting erection.

"Damn you!" Franny said. She pulled away from me, and grabbed me down onto the sofa. We fell in a tumble, and she began hitting my face with her fists, crying "Damn you! Damn you! Damn you!" Until I regained my balance and pushed her hard against the back of the sofa. I held onto her there until all energy seemed to drain out of her and she began to whimper.

When I had gotten dressed and let myself out the door, Franny was still huddled, naked, her knees up to her chin, weeping as though her heart would break. I don't remember even saying goodbye.

"Well! You seem to have a great capacity for surprise. I thought you were writing a story about lethal sunspots and the planet Mercury."

Mr. Collins looked at me with great curiosity, as though seeing me for the first time. We were sitting in a small annex to the English office on the third floor, his "cubbyhole," a room bare but for desk, chairs, and an ancient freestanding oak bookcase with glass doors. The only decoration was a reproduction of a famous if unverified portrait of John Keats in profile.

I squirmed in the seat, trying to figure out how annoyed

Collins actually was. It was difficult to determine any emotion from his bland, round face, his agate-like eyes.

"I meant to tell you that I decided to try a different idea," I began, then hesitated in the glare of his owl-like visage.

"Well, then, why didn't you tell me?"

He couldn't be too pleased, I assumed. After all, earlier that afternoon, when handing back our stories to the class, he'd held only mine of all twenty-three, asking only me to meet him in his office after class.

"It happened sort of fast," I said. I had wanted to find out what he thought of my story. Now I wasn't so sure.

"And your title, 'Mirrors,' did that just happen fast too?"

"It seemed like the right title,"

He had been leaning forward. Now he leaned back in his chair and took his time filling his pipe with tobacco, tamping it down, making me sweat.

"Isn't it a good title?" I asked.

He looked at me over his glasses, continued to tamp down the pipe and said, "It's perfect, of course. The story is perfect. Of its type. Reminiscent of Irwin Shaw or perhaps Scott Fitzgerald's early stuff." He emphasized the names as though I was supposed to know them. I didn't.

"Then you'll accept it?" I asked. That was all that mattered tome. Mr. Collins had made the short story one-third of our grade for the year.

"Yes, of course, I'll accept it. Your grade on it," he turned the top page. It had been blank except for the title and my name, but now it held a large penciled-in "100," which elicited a small gasp from me, along with some writing I couldn't make out, as the grade grew larger and larger, hovering in the air as though alive, filling up all the space between us.

"But that's not why I asked you here," Mr. Collins went on. "First, I want to enter it into the citywide contest. I think it has a good chance of winning. And second," he paused dramatically, and lit the pipe, puffing slowly, methodically so it would catch, "I want to know why you wrote this story."

I was thrilled he wanted to enter the story. Despite all his bluster months before while giving us the assignment, I had discovered that from the start the school had been limited to entering only three stories altogether, one from each grade.

But how could I answer his second question? I couldn't.

"It's quite adult, your story," he said, trying to get me to say something.

I made a face.

"Could it be based on actual experience?" he attempted. "Say, something you heard happening to someone older?" he added and I relaxed a little. "You have an older brother, don't you? How old is he?"

"Sixteen."

"Perhaps it happened to him? You intimate that the young people in the story are about that age, don't you?"

I shrugged.

"Well, I can see you're not going to tell me."

"I'd like to. But I can't." And when Mr. Collins stared at me, "I . . . promised someone."

"I see. Well, that's the author's prerogative, of course," he said grandly, convinced now that the story was, as he'd suspected, something that had happened to someone I knew, which I'd somehow learned about. "Now, if you don't mind, I would like to have this story retyped so it can formally be entered into the contest. That will take the weekend. If wish, you can take home the first page to show to your parents."

I thanked him, took the title page, and left the office.

I wouldn't show it to my parents, naturally, although if they asked, I'd tell them I'd gotten a high grade. I doubted they would ask to read it, but didn't want to take any chances. The title could refer to almost anything, couldn't it? I'd tell them the teacher kept it, and make up some other story to tell them.

Mr. Collins had kept me twenty minutes after school with our conversation. I walked home alone thinking, trying to resolve the conflict he'd brought to the surface and which had subconsciously bothered me since that moment, three weeks before, when I'd sat down at my bedroom desk, opened a notebook, and began to write this story instead of "Mission to Mercury" as I'd planned.

Why had I written "Mirrors?" Out of revenge, possibly. Out of a need to understand, probably. Out of the overwhelming need to exorcise the break-up of what had been (in retrospect) the strangest relationship of my young life, certainly.

The story was a thinly disguised retelling of my affair with Franny Solomon, with specific large lapses and major alterations. The narrative began not with our real "first date" in the Rivington Street deli, but with more a ordinary date at a local drive-in hamburger stand. Franny, of course, was physically changed to a willowy, ash blonde girl of Scots-English extraction named Patricia. Her apartment became a suburban split-level house. The sex was completely removed. The action centered upon languorous kisses given to the narrator by the otherwise icily attractive girl, which always happened in the very same spot in the house: a room no bigger than a closet off the foyer, adjoining the library. The eponymous mirrors were not the elaborate ceiling and wall fixtures of Mr. Solomon, but a simple arrangement of otherwise ordinary mirrors, including a small one hung on the wall with part of its silver backing removed. The father who watched the kissing from his vantage point in the library was a philologist, and quite different than Franny's father, except that he too was confined (through muscular dystrophy) to a wheelchair. The ages of the narrator and of Patricia were not stated; and indeed, I had added hints to suggest the milieu of high school juniors to make the story more acceptable as well as to disguise any autobiographical elements.

What I would not change and what I thought made it a real short story rather than merely an odd anecdote, were the basic personalities of the three characters: the naive, love-struck boy surprised with his luck; the coldly beautiful girl who becomes for him only a passionate wanton; and her pitiful and much admired father.

Even more crucial, I did not end "Mirrors" with the boy's discovery that the two of them were being watched, had been watched, indeed that the only reason for their relationship at all was so they could be watched by Patricia's father. No, I added a final scene, which actually happened, and which was probably the real reason I wrote the story: more important than revenge, exorcism and the need to understand.

When I left Franny Solomon's house following my discovery of her watching, masturbating father, I was too stunned to react. My getting out of the place was instinctive: every nerve in my body said "move it!" I got home, just managed to avoid an argument with my older brother over something trivial, took a phone call from Barry about homework, watched television, had dinner, then went up to bed.

I lay on the unmade bed almost blank with so many different emotions.

My brother came upstairs and tried to tease me into some sort of response. I undressed, shut off the light and lay awake hours more until past dawn, when I heard my father rise to leave for work.

On one level I simply didn't believe what had happened. To do so meant that I had to believe that: 1) Franny had never cared for me for myself, but because her father told her to. Somehow, I had been selected out for the role of physical lover. 2) Franny's father exerted so much control over her that he'd persuaded her to have unadulterated sex with me. And 3) Franny could do all this, and still retain her untouchable "good girl" facade without anyone—probably not even her mother—being any the wiser, or Franny cracking up under the pressure.

All this assumed that human nature was more gullible, malleable, manipulative, and perverse than I'd ever imagined. Nothing in my past—not Hargrave's enmity, not Ricky Hersch's desire to corrupt—had prepared me for this experience. Naturally I wondered what other dreadful secrets people I knew possessed, what kinks, what strange invisible holds over each other. Veils had been torn off my eyes about how people could use one another, and how they concentrated on those most vulnerable areas—nakedness, sex, love—as tools of coercion. Therefore, I would always look at members of my family, at friends, at teachers and adult friends and wonder what they were capable of, what they were hiding. I became cynical, unastonished by anything I read, wise-cracking, sarcastic. By the ninth grade, a year later, graduation photo showed the unmistakable physical evidence: lip curled in a scorn that I couldn't hide even when smiling, trying to appear "academically serious" as the yearbook required.

I dreaded having to face Franny the following day in class, I needn't have. She behaved as perfectly as ever: she completely ignored me. By the end of the school day, it was common knowledge that we had "broken up." After David Manetti's simple question to confirm the fact was met by my cold, bitter, "mind your own business" in the gym, my friends ever asked again: Within a few weeks it was almost as though nothing between me and Franny had happened.

My ego suffered terribly. Even though I had been the one

to do the rejecting, I couldn't for a minute forget how I'd been used by the Solomons, father and daughter. Despite my more or less uncaring public attitude about the affair, it took me a long time to recover. It was years before I would allow myself to become serious about another girl. Luckily, this turned out to be witty, fun-loving, critical Ruth, whose open, honest, distinctly unmysterious personality was worlds different from Franny's. But at the beginning of our separation, I would feel odd little stabs of pain in my chest just seeing Franny. I avoided looking at her, closed my ears to her voice whenever she spoke in class. It wasn't that difficult to avoid each other. I changed seats, we entered and left rooms by different doors. With the almost unconscious sensitivity that adolescent boys possess (although most would loudly deny it), my school buddies remained near me at all times in her presence, surrounding me like protective phalanx, until I asked them not to bother.

Another three weeks passed before all relations with the Solomons finally ended. It happened during Sunday dinner, one of the few times my entire family managed to gather. We were all on such wildly varied schedules, that this supposedly peaceful once a week meal more often resembled a three-ring circus or group therapy session than it did a mere repast. Each of us would attempt to get a week's worth of communication accomplished—complaints, demands, favors, bones to pick—in this one hour as fast and with as great an effect as possible, even if it meant arguing. My poor mother was interested only in making sure we all ate (she no longer had any real control over our nutrition) and kept urging us to try a little more chicken, or have another potato, or "For God's sake eat some salad, who knows the last green thing that entered your body."

It was in the midst of one of these general conversational melees that the phone rang. And rang, oblivious to all but my sister who those days always seemed to be expecting a phone call of such earthshaking importance that she would closet herself for hours with her callers, leave any meal, visitors, the shower, food burning on the stove to take the phone. This time, however, she returned to the table to say the call was for me: "Some man" was the extent of her explanation. She did nothing to hide her obvious disappointment, and before sitting down warned me not to take too long.

I had no idea who could be calling me. For a second I thought it might be Mr. Collins to tell me either that my story had won the contest (it was far too early) or that he'd changed his mind about its worth and wasn't entering it. When the caller identified himself as Mr. Solomon, I almost dropped the phone. I had to sit down on the chair next to the phone table.

"Yes?"

"Well, how are you?" he asked, his voice sounding even younger over the phone than in person. I wondered at my sister's astuteness in guessing that he was a grown-up.

"Fine, I guess."

"Haven't seen you in a while. I thought you might be sick."

"No. I'm not sick."

"That's good. You never visit anymore. Did you and Franny have a falling out?"

He didn't know! She hadn't told him. Yet.

"I got busy with school work." I lied, not without an effort. I told him my parents had complained that I spent too much time away from home, and not enough studying.

"I guess I can understand that."

"My mother thinks I ought to spend less time with . . . girls, and more with boys my own age."

"That makes sense. So you didn't have a falling out?" he asked.

"Not really. I thought Franny already told you all this. Didn't she say anything?"

"Not a word. So, you can't study all the time. When are we going to see you again? A colleague from Germany visited and brought me all sorts of interesting optical materials I'm certain you'd like to see."

Now I really felt deep in it. "I don't know. I'll have to ask my parents. They've become pretty strict lately," I lied.

"Surely they can't have anything against your coming here, can they? Not if you told them it's educational."

"I guess." I said, thinking it had been educational all right.

"Didn't you like coming here?" he asked.

"Sure, I did."

I didn't have to lie about that.

"So, when are you going to come again?"

Faced with a direct question, all I could do was say, "I don't know."

"Do you want me to talk to your mother? To ask her myself?"

"No!" I said quickly. "I don't think that's a good idea. She might feel pressured."

"Next week?" he asked.

"I don't think so."

"How about the week after?" he asked, and while he didn't sound it, I knew it had to be humiliating for him to plead.

"I'm really not sure."

He was silent, as though putting all my answers together. "If you really did like coming here and want to come again, you'd give me an answer, or let me try to convince your parents," he said, not sounding too happy. "So, I guess you don't want to come here after all. Is that right?"

"I can't."

"Well, I'm disappointed in you," he said, and now he really did sound like a kid. "I guess it's good-bye."

I put down the receiver, relieved. I'd no sooner gotten out of the chair and halfway to the dining room when the phone rang again.

Sure it was Franny's father with some new idea, I ran to pick it up. It was Mr. Solomon. After checking to make sure of my identity he said, "Listen? You know a lot of people at school, don't you? How about getting one of your friends to come spend some time here? Someone nice. For Franny. You know? Someone good looking and nice—"

I didn't let him finish. I hung up the phone and slumped against the wall, then reached forward slowly, and took the receiver off the hook.

My sister found it that way an hour later and screamed at me for my carelessness. Mr. Solomon never called again.

That scene, written verbatim in "Mirrors," had been its best stroke I was certain, and would win the contest for my story.

Life after Franny Solomon wasn't a complete loss. Children are resilient even if they have far longer, deeper memories than most adults believe, and I had already learned through my experiences the two previous years that I could survive what at first seemed to be a major catastrophe. One support of those earlier years was gone. I'd grown so far apart from my parents that our conversations nowadays consisted of questions and demands on their side, of answers and evasions on mine. Partly this was due to changes in their own lives. Since the sudden death of her fifth child, my mother had lost a great deal of her sparkle and humor. I would come upon her sitting alone in the twilight-dim living room, unresponsive until directly spoken to, when she would be vague, her voice strangely deep. Shortly after that she began menopause, which proved both physically and emotionally difficult for her. My father also had problems. He'd bought out his partner and while his business was flourishing, it seemed to require most of his time. He would often have dinner in his office; not come home until we were in bed, or asleep; and he got up so early we only crossed paths on weekends, when he usually wanted to be left alone. After midday dinner on Sunday, he lay down on the couch to watch baseball and football games and fell asleep in a few minutes, even after drinking coffee.

My siblings were involved in their own lives to the seeming exclusion of all else. We would have perhaps one more summer together as a family until we began to drift inexorably apart forever. My brother now had a driver's license and lived, breathed, ate, and drank cars. My sister, after being too tall for years, at fifteen-and-a-half and finally the right size for her age, was away from home with her girlfriends or out dating boys. Only my younger brother, now seven, ever wanted my company. Those Saturdays and holidays when my mother wasn't feeling well—i.e., was depressed—I would take my younger brother to parks and movies and sometimes, riding on the handlebars of my bike, to friend's houses, where he played with their younger siblings.

Most importantly, my private, personal life had not only outstripped my family's simple rather conventional life, but I was certain it had outgrown all their combined experiences too. After all, I'd already been fornicator and petty criminal at eleven, a drug addict homosexual at twelve, a seducer and a sexual exhibitionist as well as a successful purveyor of pornography by thirteen. I could picture the look on any adult's face as I narrated these events—or rather, I didn't dare.

Still, life was neither hopeless nor uninteresting. Our New York State map project won second prize at the school's Science and Art Fair, beaten out by an elaborate model of an auto factory assembly line from 9 SP 1 complete with toy cars and hydraulic lifts. I had finally persuaded Mr. Thirrel that I did actually know the essentials of Geometry, and was no longer at the bottom of that course. My short story was retyped and entered into the citywide contest.

My social life also improved. My short, tempestuous affair with Franny had suddenly "placed" me among the female students, my unwillingness to talk about why we had stopped seeing each other suggested the truth: that I had dropped her. So I took on the reputation of a lady-killer. I was once more invited, and now began to attend, some of Michael and Barry's parties stag, where I met several girls to flirt with, to dance with, to kiss and even sometimes neck with. I never tried to "go further," knowing I had been spoiled and probably also fearing the consequences.

At this time music entered my life to complete the triumvirate—along with art and literature—that would sustain me years afterward. Until then, music was a mysterious aural communication that made little sense to me. Our "music class" in elementary school had consisted of an elderly teacher playing "The Storm," "The Stream," "The Armies On the March," and other such picturesque folderol on a poorly tuned auditorium upright. At home, we had the radio songs of the early '50s: "Shrimp Boats are Coming," "Doggy in the Window" "Hernando's Hideaway"—music so banal, if tuneful, that we used to look forward to and then laugh at each new presentation the producers had thought up for Dorothy Collins and Snooky Lanson to "act out" each Saturday night on television's Hit Parade.

One evening, my idea of what a song could be changed forever. I had just managed to convince my sister to iron a white shirt I had to wear to school the next day for assembly. She had clothing of her own to press, and insisted I remain while she worked. To pass the time she made me get her small black plastic RCA radio. I'm not sure what the station was, but it played Rock and Roll: Fats Domino and other black groups. I paid little real attention to it, although she hummed and sang along, working faster as a result.

I was sitting there, waiting for my sister to finish ironing her blouses and get to my shirt, when it happened. For the first time I heard tones, chords. I wasn't sure on what kind of instruments, but I made out a guitar, maybe two guitars, perhaps a piano and drums. (The rhythm was more that of a lullaby—although very dark, even somber—than surging and fast, like a Fats Domino song). An odd man-woman voice began to sing. Not only sing, but also to tell a story, one which engaged my attention, even though it couldn't be construed as a ballad. The voice was shattering, filled with pain, anger, and bitterly forlorn, and I found within it all the emotions I'd withheld or repressed for months, perhaps years. When the song was over, I was so embarrassed I grabbed my shirt off the ironing board and rushed trembling up to my bedroom.

    I didn't know what to do with myself. I sat at my window desk and opened my homework. I immediately closed it. Night was falling, the sun had already set. The houses and trees across the way were silhouetted almost ebony by an electrically blue sky that appeared to shiver with anticipation of the cobalt darkness that surrounded its momentary eerie brightness. Before this moment, before that song, I'd possessed the child's love of the day and fear of the night. But I had just heard the night encapsulated in a song, in a voice. Not familiar evening, but long after midnight, luridly lighted by amber and scarlet neon, reflected in streaked puddles of filthy water, flanked by empty liquor bottles, crushed cigarette ends, a lipstick scarred handkerchief, a dropped wallet. Somehow I knew this kind of nighttime would become my time, my life's deepest sympathy; I knew that from now on I would become conspirator with the night.

    Some days later, I casually asked my sister about the song. She had an unerring memory for popular songs, and if I gave her a lyric or two, she always knew what song I meant. She did this time too. It was called "Heartbreak Hotel," and the singer had the extremely strange name of Elvis

Presley. "Heartbreak Hotel" was the first forty-five r.p.m. record, the first record I ever bought: a red vinyl disc with a large spindle hole in the middle, quite different from the black, heavy wax seventy-eights my parents owned and listened to. I had to buy a spindle adapter to fit the disc onto our phonograph. I played my Presley record whenever I thought I was alone in the house. I liked the flip side, "Hound Dog," less, although whenever I brought my record to dance parties that side was played more often, as we danced the fast, gyrating Lindy.

I was already a good dancer, it turned out. My sister and I sometimes practiced at home to music from her radio tuned to Alan Freed's Rock and Roll show, often beamed live from the Brooklyn Paramount Theater. We listened to and danced to Jerry Lee Lewis' "At the Hop," Chuck Berry's "Maybelline" and "Johnny B. Goode," and other hits by Frankie Avalon and the Hollies. I preferred the slower, more bluesy songs; the ones played at parties when they were beginning to wind down, the lights dimmed, only three or four couples still out on the floor dancing the Fish so closely that an hour later I could see indentations the girls' hard brassieres made on my chest. This dance was so slow it was really necking while standing up. Long deep kisses, body rubs, an occasional unintended orgasm when the rubbing got too serious. My favorite partner for dancing the Fish was blonde, pert Dina Auslander, who wore skirts wide enough to hide the stiffest erection, and she seldom knew I had one.

Even Dina's obvious attractions couldn't hold me down. I had become fickle, uncaring. I'd wait until a girl became obviously interested in me after a party or two, then I'd drop her, ignore her the next time I saw her, spend my time with my male friends, or make time with a new girl brought to the party by or for someone else. Once or twice, I pushed my luck with one of my best friends' girls—Ellen or

Lolly—who were always willing to do something to annoy Barry or Michael. All as a reaction to Franny's betrayal. But I didn't know it. Barry ought to have shoved me against the wall for the way that I pawed (and she let me!) Ellen one night when we were all a little drunk on beer one boy had pilfered from his father's store. That might have stopped me.

I erred by offering them excitement: scenes, spats, break-ups, reconciliations. I was the fox in the chicken coop playing by no rules at all; I was the invisible man pinching people in a crowded elevator; someone else was always blamed.

Girls weren't my only victims. I screwed up boys' lives too. Item: Bobby Fields. Bright, charming, with close-cropped ink-black hair and a sincere face; serious, all too pervious to a bad influence. One evening at a party in the most exclusive section of the county, where we fifteen adolescents had been left to our own devices, I found Bobby and said, "Let's go outside. I have cigarettes."

It was a nippy night. I pointed to the Lincoln Continental Dina's father had left in the driveway and suggested we sit inside to smoke. We sat in the front seat and I could see Bobby's eyes glaze over. "You know how to drive, don't you?" I said casually to hide the challenge it enclosed.

"Sure," he said, equally casually.

"Well, there are the keys in the ignition. Let's go."

He stared at the keys, then looked goofily at me. I reached over and switched the ignition on, then released the hand brake so the car gently began to roll down the driveway. After a half minute of hesitation and his first panic over, Bobby grabbed the wheel, steered the car clear of the parked side cars into the middle of the street. We drove one curving long road after another, then back up again. We finally stopped beneath the walls of Jamaica High to smoke another cigarette, feeling very debonair, making loud appreciative comments at the seventeen- and eighteen-year-old girls leaving night classes.

We'd been missed at the party. So had the Continental. Mr. Auslander met us at the front of his property when we drove back. He reached into the car for his keys, asked us to get out; and drove it into the garage, which he locked. All without another word.

Inside, the party was breaking up—our doing, I found out—and everyone was scandalized and some pleased by our act. Stealing someone's Continental was considered a "rash act," even if we did return it unharmed.

"You're really something, you know?" Barry said a few days later. We had walked into Cunningham Park and were sunning on the grass. It was still winter, but warm in direct sunlight. We unzipped our jackets. No one else was in sight.

"What do you mean?" I asked.

"Your stunts lately, you know," he tried. "Edging in on me with Ellen, and the way you led on Angie Carlton. What's with you lately?"

"It couldn't have been such a hot romance between you and Ellen or you couldn't have been pried apart so easily. She was looking for an excuse."

"You're right. You're right," he said, decisively admitting it. "Boys are better friends than girls. Everyone knows that. My father said to me, 'What are you moping about? A girl? Forget her! Go out and have fun with your friends. Soon enough, you'll have to have a girl. You'll have enough trouble then. Why anticipate?'"

"Your father's great," I said. Everyone liked Moe Schoenwald. But his son had given me the opening I was looking for to make more trouble. "What about David? You see him any more?" This, I very well knew, was opening an old wound.

Barry shook his head. It was clear Barry still hadn't fully accepted David's loss. "I thought I'd see him at the

County High track meet yesterday. He always used to go to track and field events. He never showed up."

"Anyone see you there?"

"Sure. Everyone."

"Then he'll find out you went looking for him."

"I didn't go looking for him," Barry protested.

"Sure you did."

Barry turned over and put his hands over his head.

"You know what he told Thom Meserole?"

"I don't want to know," Barry said. "What?"

"You don't want to know," I said.

He sat up, grabbing my lapel. "What!"

"I mean Thom didn't believe him. No one will."

"What!"

"He said you were a faggot. He said you were going out with Ellen just to show that you weren't a faggot."

Barry's eyes widened. "He really said that?"

David had said it. And Alan, from 7 SP 1, had repeated it to me to show what a louse David had become. But I didn't have to tell Barry.

I wouldn't answer.

"He did say it," Barry answered himself. "And we were best friends for ten years. Ten years. Since we were three years old." I thought Barry was going to cry.

All he did was ask, "Did he tell Thom why I was a faggot? Did he?"

"No. But Thom didn't believe him. No one will. Unless you keep looking around and going to places where you think he'll be," I said. "Especially when you know he doesn't want to see you."

"Since we were three years old," Barry repeated. "Our mothers were friends and they used to put us in a playpen together while they played mah-jongg. That's how long."

"Well then, I guess you've lost your best friend," I said, leaving Barry in despair.

Cleverer boys than Barry and Bobby Fields began to stay away from me. In class, I could be depended upon to make smart aleck comments under my breath. Most teachers grow accustomed to this barely audible classroom murmur, knowing it's idle to search out the perpetrator; she or he is only momentary and it will start up again with someone else in the room. Unlucky Mrs. King, our sandy-skinned black Social Studies substitute was the exception. This was her first job in an all-white school, and she was both insecure and defensive, demanding total attention and absolute quiet, which we weren't use to in Mrs. Roth's course as a rule. Thus the day she caught me commenting *sotto voce* upon something she'd just said, she made the mistake of asking me to stand up and tell the entire class what I'd just confided to my neighbor.

Annoyed with her smugness, I did. "Gladly," I said. "I was criticizing the superficial textbook explanation of the causes of the Civil War. The same explanation you and Mrs. Roth have attempted to foist on this class."

Stunned, she asked, "Superficial?"

"And shallow and condescending and probably hypocritical too."

"Do you mean to tell me I'm teaching this subject the wrong way?"

"You and every teacher in the school. I know it isn't your fault. You have a teacher's plan. But to tell us that an entire nation of fifty million people fought a devastating five-year war merely to free the slaves is shallow and superficial."

She became almost crimson with anger. Barely controlling her voice, she said, "Well, why don't you tell us the real reason for the war?"

"It was economic, of course. The South held one economic system, a feudal, agricultural system, based on chattel labor and on extensive foreign trade to Europe. The

North, on the other hand, had a growing industrial economy based on the ambition of its new working class and the greed of a few entrepreneurs."

She was surprised enough to say, "According to you, no one seems to come out sounding very good."

"Both systems were rotten, according to Fourier and Karl Marx. In fact, the Marxist position on the American Civil War bolds that, technically speaking, while destroying the entire South in its victory, it should have also destroyed its chattel labor force too. Instead of absorbing it, which we know was a costly and troublesome—"

"That's enough," she suddenly said. "You may sit down. I don't think this class is ready for what Karl Marx had to say."

"Well, somebody better teach them fast. Or we'll all end up a bunch of nitwits, believing some fool textbook."

"I said, that's enough." She returned to the blackboard attempting to pick up the thread of what she'd been saying. But it was lost in her anger and annoyance with me, and she floundered around for the next five minutes, very self-conscious that she was doing so, until the period bell rang.

I wasn't too surprised to be called out of gym, down to Mr. Wolff's office later that afternoon.

"What's all this about?" the Dean demanded. He wasn't at all amused. "I understand you've been baiting Mrs. King."

"I haven't been baiting her," I said, and began to explain as clearly as possible what I'd said in class, and how she wouldn't let me talk.

"Where did you get all that?" Mr. Wolff asked.

"All what?"

"Marx and Fourier. All that."

"From reading. I was in the library looking up the causes of the Civil War and the cumulative index of books led me to them."

"Very enterprising," he said ironically.

"Well, I didn't bait her," I said, not even sure what be meant by the word. "You can ask anyone in the class. I have twenty-three witnesses. In fact, I demand that you call witnesses."

"Calm down. This isn't a trial. Mrs. King may have misunderstood you. She felt you were being racist. Suggesting the extermination of black people is, you know, quite racist."

"I wasn't proposing that. I was simply repeating what Marx and Fourier said. Both white and black laborers are pawns of the capitalist system. They might as well be dead."

"We'll see if you feel that way when you become a pawn of the capitalist system yourself. Or," he quickly added, "do you intend to become one of the exploiters?"

"We all know that power corrupts," I answered back as slyly as he. "But I'm willing to see how much it corrupts."

"I'll bet you are. No more about Marx in class. If you want to write about it, go ahead."

"I will," I said, "In my term paper."

Mrs. King had our Social Studies class twice more that semester and never again called on me. But the following year, at a parent-teachers-students meeting, she swept across the cafeteria toward me and brought with her a tall, bearded, bespectacled black man whom she introduced as Mr. King, her husband. "This is my little Marxist," she told him. "You two ought to have a great deal to discuss."

In fact, Osborne King told me right off that my reading of Marx bad been correct, and then warned me to keep that reading to myself in school, at least until college level. It was only a few years since the Senate/McCarthy Hearings, and the slightest whiff of Marx sent people into paroxysms of anger and "Commie" shouting. He confessed that as a professor of history, he considered himself a "Radical Marxist," which he insisted was quite different than the

Leninist/Stalinist variety of Communism, and we talked for the rest of the meeting about history and politics. It was the first time a grown-up had talked to me as an equal, and I was very proud of the fact. When we parted, he called me "my man," and I felt even prouder.

While all this attitudinizing and trouble-making was going on, I still wondered about my short story in the citywide contest. It was already past Easter. The results should be posted soon. I still hadn't spoken to Franny Solomon, and her father had never called again. As far as I or anyone else knew, Franny wasn't seeing any boy in our school. I wondered what Mr. Solomon was doing for excitement. In retrospect, the incident was more sinister than anything I'd yet encountered in my life—Franny the victim, her father the exploiter—and it made me so sad and angry I tried not to think about it, especially because I felt so powerless in the situation, certain no one would believe me if I told them about it.

I wasn't ready one afternoon in the middle of May when Mr. Collins called me up to his desk at the end of English block to hand me my story, beautifully typed.

"What's this?" I asked.

Collins continued looking at some papers on his desk. "What does it look like?"

"My story. But . . . Is the contest over?"

"No. At least they haven't announced the winners yet."

"Then why am I getting this back?"

"It's been rejected by the committee," he said, still refusing to look at me.

"Rejected? Why?"

"I don't know why. You'll have to ask Mr. Wolff."

"You mean they wouldn't even accept it into the contest?" I was flabbergasted.

"I said it's been rejected."

"But you said it was a good story. Why was it rejected?"

"I told you I don't know. You have to speak to Mr. Wolff."

I held the short story in my hand and thought I would cry. Before I could say another word, I realized that students were filing into the room and sitting down for Collin's next class. I had to leave.

I cut the next class and went directly to Mr. Wolff's office. He was ushering two girls into the room and was surprised to see me waiting.

"Are you on a free period?" he asked.

"No."

"Go to class and come back when you're free."

"I have to talk to you now!"

"Later. Go to your class."

"It wouldn't do any good," I said. "I'm too upset to learn anything. If you won't see me now, I'm going home sick."

He shook his head, "Wait here, then."

Mr. Wolff was closeted with the two girls for what seemed a very long time. The late period bell rang, and suddenly all the classroom doors were closed, the hallway empty, quiet. Occasionally in the next fifteen or twenty minutes that I waited outside his office, a student would step out to go to the bathroom, or to carry a message between teachers. Several teachers walked by—the faculty lounge was nearby—and one stared at me, but I gave her such a look she didn't stop or say anything.

I was working up my anger, and also trying to control it. I would listen to what Mr. Wolff told me, and if that wasn't satisfactory, I would let him know it in no uncertain terms. I wondered how this could have happened to me, to my story. What possible reason could they have for rejecting it? I couldn't think of any.

The two girls came out, properly chastened.

"Now what's so terribly important that you have to

miss . . ." Mr. Wolff looked at my program card, "Spanish for it?"

As an answer, I tossed my short story onto his desk. "Mr. Collins said it was rejected by the contest committee. He said you knew why."

"Sit down," he said. "You're angry about this, and you have every right to be angry."

That was a surprise. No teacher had ever told me I was right about anything. I sat facing him, while Mr. Wolff went through a pile of papers looking for something. He finally pulled out a letter typed on Board of Education stationery. "This was the covering letter from the contest committee head, Mrs. Dichter. Would you like to hear what it says?"

Before I could respond, he went on, "I wanted to spare you this. But you have a right to know. Neither Mr. Collins nor Dichter nor the committee thought that, I want you to know." He paused, "Well?"

"Yes. Read it."

The letter was long and made several points. All but one on the committee objected to my story. Two members on moral grounds: they felt that it was unfit literature for a junior high school student to read, never mind write, because of its subject matter, and because of the "obviously manipulative role it paints of the girl's parent." They thought it went against the grain of obedience and respect that adults should be accorded at all times. Two other members of the committee found the story, "extremely well-rendered in its atmosphere, characterization, and plotting," but felt the story's subject far too "mature" to be of interest to readers in its category. One thought the story was plagiarized, although she couldn't tell where from. Mrs. Dichter wrote that my story was so far beyond any other they had received in its depiction of "the darker and more unsavory aspects of human nature" that it must have been written by someone far older, not by a seventh grader. Mr.

Wolff concluded reading with the committee's final words: "Even if the story is not by another hand than the purported author—and we are none of us certain this is true—it is unacceptable due to its subject matter, its harsh and cynical view of life, and for the way it shows older people exploiting children. We would not allow it to be published and read by any student in the school system."

When I'd caught my breath from this walloping, I said, "I wrote it all right. Ask Mr. Collins. He had to correct two grammatical errors and one spelling mistake."

"You could have copied it wrong," Mr. Wolff said. "Or purposely made those errors to disguise the fact that you plagiarized it."

"I can't believe this," I said, horrified. "I wrote it. Don't you see? It happened to me! All of it. Every word in the story is true. Only it was worse than that. Much worse."

"It's your word against the opinion of the committee."

"Do you think I copied it?"

"I don't know."

"It happened to me. It's my story. Only worse. I couldn't possibly put down on paper how much worse. But it's true. It happened to me. It's my life. And it's an unfair lie to say I copied it. I'd swear on a Bible that it's true."

He waited until I was done. Then handed back the story. "I'm sorry."

"Sorry? It's unfair. You know it is. So does Mr. Collins. Isn't anyone going to stand up for me?"

"Even if we did stand up for you, write a letter to the committee, show them your original manuscript, it still would never win. They're already prejudiced against your story."

He looked at me sympathetically; it was out of his hands.

I could hardly see him through the gloom that descended over my life. I was also angry. "If that's the case," I said, "and if the school system really is this corrupt, then I want no part of it. I'll leave school. Become a juvenile delinquent, like Smitty."

I stood up to leave.

"Take this," he said. "It's a pass back to your room. And take this too," he handed me the story.

"Everyone says you're a good guy, that you're the only Dean in the school who cares about kids. I know better than that now. You're just like all the rest of them." I grabbed the story, ripped it in half, tossed the pieces into his garbage pail and left the office.

I wandered through the hallways for most of the period, going into the boy's room for a while, and just managed to get to Mr. Sensale's class, hand over the pass, and sit down before the period bell rang, the last class of the day. But I was still so obviously upset, and the pass from Mr. Wolff was so compelling, that the normally unfriendly Spanish teacher stopped me as I was going out and asked if there was trouble at home. I didn't answer him and he didn't press me.

The rejection of my short story caused me intense grief for weeks, and threw me into a period of total introversion. At home I moved into a silence so complete my siblings went around making circles with their index fingers behind my back to show that I'd gone crazy. My younger brother was the only one who dared approach me—with a broken toy, or his second grade homework—and even he stared at me as I silently mended his dump truck or corrected his spelling. One time he burst into tears over my coldness, but I just walked away. From then on he too kept away from me.

Even though she wasn't in the best mood herself, my mother noticed my silence and isolation. Thinking I could still be reached by her maternal care as I'd been a scant two years before, my mother sat me down one Saturday afternoon to talk.

She: What's wrong, hon?

Me: Nothing.

She: Something must be wrong. You're going around this house like your best friend just died.

Me: (Silence).

She: Tell me. You know we're friends. You can tell me. Is it school?

Me: No.

She: Then what? Tell me, honey, Junior Pie. You're still my Junior Pie, big as you've grown.

Me: Nothing's wrong.

She: Then why arc you alone all the time?

Me: Because I want to be.

She: But you're alone all the time these days. You don't go out. You don't sec your friends. You won't play with your brother. You never talk to anyone, or watch television or ride your bike. Why not?

Me: I'm busy thinking.

She: Thinking? (As though this would be the last thing I would be doing). Thinking about what?

Me: Nothing.

She: You must be thinking about something all that time. Tell me what you think about. (Said in the tone of voice that convinced me she was half afraid of my answer. That forced my hand).

Me: I've been thinking about how rotten life is. All of it.

That took her by surprise. I knew she'd been thinking much the same for the past few months since my baby sister died. My mother had no response but surprise. I saw fear in her eyes—the true fear that she had lost me too in that moment. I felt sorry for her but unwilling to do anything to help her. I excused myself and went back to my room.

The school term finally ended. We were to go away for the rest of the summer to share a house with my Aunt Lucy and Uncle Billy and their two children on the shore of Eastern Rhode Island. I wasn't really looking forward to it, but at least it would be a change, and that was all that mattered.

I was coming home from Cunningham Park where I had gone to read and brood alone all day in a secluded place. I was walking along Hillside Avenue when I heard a car horn honk, then my name called out. I turned to sec Mr. Wolff. Traffic moved, and he pulled up to the curb.

"Where are you going?" he asked.

"Home."

"Get in. I'll drop you off."

"It's not far."

"Get in."

Reluctantly—he was still the Dean, and I still hadn't apologized for insulting him that day in his office—I got into the front seat of his Packard. I had just become interested in automobiles, mostly through looking at them and drawing them. I wouldn't be able to get a driver's permit until I was fifteen. I had been forced by my father to join him and my older brother at the annual automobile show held at the Coliseum in Manhattan, and to my surprise I had loved it. I'd wandered around alone looking at all the new models, at the foreign sports cars with their sleek lines and unbelievably high prices, checking out motorcycles and custom cars and antique autos. I'd been most impressed by the "Cars of the Future" that each major American auto manufacturer designed especially for the show each year, and since then I had bought a new sketch pad and had begun to design my own futuristic models.

It was 1957, and cars were already beginning to look futuristic. My favorite road models for styling were of course the racy Corvette and sleek Thunderbird two-seaters; and among the larger cars, Raymond Loewy's odd turbo-jet Studebaker and the most elegantly lined of all American autos, the Packard Mediterranean convertible. The sumptuous model that Mr. Wolff drove, in white and aqua with a fawn canvas roof and plush ecru leather interior, was so wonderful that although I really didn't want to talk with him, I couldn't resist getting inside. The Dean usually drove a dove gray Pontiac sedan to school, so I assumed this was his wife's car. Student rumor had it that Mr. Wolff, by virtue of his charm and good looks, had married a rich and beautiful woman, and didn't have to work if he didn't want to—a sign, no doubt, of his purported love of school and children that he did bother to come to our little junior high.

He certainly was dressed appropriately natty for driving the Packard, in a russet cotton v-neck shirt and pale yellow slacks with white wingtip shoes. I could hear his golf clubs rumbling in the back seat, and once, when we suddenly stopped at a light, he rearranged them so they were more tightly wedged in.

Mr. Wolff began with small talk, asking about my vacation plans, but he soon saw I no longer trusted him, so he asked if I would like a malted or hamburger. When I said no—we were approaching our local drive-in White Tower—he said he was hungry. He'd be dining out late. Would I mind stopping so he could get something to eat?

The smell of the hamburger inside the car was quite a temptation but I held my ground and refused when he renewed his offer to buy me one. When he got out of the car to throw away the plastic cutlery and paper dish I felt that I had passed a test.

We had parked in a deserted section of the parking lot behind the White Tower. Mr. Wolff lit a cigarette and asked how things were going. I said fine. He said he understood that I had been promoted into 9 SP 2, and he wondered if I were looking forward to next year at school.

"I told you before. I'm dropping out of school as soon as I'm sixteen. I'm going to enlist in the Army."

"At sixteen?"

"I'll lie. Plenty of guys lie to get in."

"That will be a real waste," he said. When I wouldn't respond, he added, "Your grades keep going up. All your teachers were very satisfied with your work in class. If not by your attitude. Most felt that it had changed for the worse in the last month or so of school. In fact, several came to talk to me about your sudden pervasive gloomy spirits. One, who shall remain nameless, even suggested I recommend you see the Board of Education psychiatrist." He said all this in a different tone of voice than I was used to, not as Dean to student, if not quite as one adult to another.

"They can all go to hell," I said, without emotion.

"Idiots!" He threw the cigarette out the window. "I was afraid that incident would embitter you. However, I thought you were strong enough to deal with a simple quirk of destiny like that."

"You thought wrong," I said.

"I see that now. I don't suppose it would do much good to tell you that Mr. Collins and I drafted and sent a strong letter of protest to the contest committee?"

"Thanks for nothing."

"Well, we thought it was something. After all, in doing it, we stuck our heads out. When we didn't even know if the story was—"

"You knew it was true," I interrupted.

He lit another cigarette. I admired his perseverance, at least. "So this is it?" Mr. Wolff said. "You're going to let one little incident spoil a promising career?"

"What career?"

"Whatever career you choose."

"You mean as a writer?"

"That wasn't necessary," he said curtly, "And it was rude." He faced forward, puffing on the cigarette. This couldn't be easy for him; even so, I wasn't about to help him. He hadn't been able to help me when I needed him, and now I didn't want anything to do with him. The smoke rose in a cloud, some slipped rapidly out his side vent, some rose to the Packard's tufted leather ceiling and slid down and around the back mirror and sun guards before seeping outside.

He began again, "In my office, you said it was true, but worse."

"If I had written what really happened, I probably would have been thrown out of school."

"So what you wrote wasn't exactly true?"

"It was true. It was softened up to protect the innocent."

"Meaning me? And Mr. Collins?"

"Meaning all of you," I said. "Yes."

"What really did happen? You're making such a fuss about it being the truth, why are you so afraid to tell it?"

"I'm not afraid," I said and I began to tell him. I didn't give names, of course, but I told him everything else, step by step, finding myself embarrassed at times, but figuring what the hell, I had nothing left to lose. It took about fifteen minutes and he went through two more cigarettes and avoided looking at me, staring out the side window, sometimes sipping his drink through a plastic straw.

"You mean he actually wanted you to find another boy?"

"Some nerve, huh?" I said. "He will. If not this term then next term. And as she grows older, it will be even easier to find boys to do what he wants. I'm sure he's found some way to arrange the mirrors so that no one will ever suspect like I did. It will go on and on, I guess, until . . ." I didn't know until when.

"Jee-sus!" Mr. Wolff said. He threw his head back into the thick leather headrest. "Jee-sus! And that's it, then? The truth?"

"The whole truth and nothing but."

"It's the most subtle and perfidious kind of child abuse. And we can't do anything about it."

"I'll never tell who it is," I said.

"Oh, we could find out, if we had to. But we still couldn't do anything about it."

"Will you drive me home now?" I asked. "I'm late."

He turned on the ignition.

As I was getting out at my front door, I told him how much I liked his car, then added, "Do you see why I feel the way I do about the story? No one would believe the half of it."

Unexpectedly, for he had to lean across the wide front seat to do it, he grabbed one of my hands. "Listen. Don't be bitter. Promise me. There's nothing worse than being bitter when you're still young. It's like an open wound inside, filled with poison. Everything good flows into it and becomes nothing at all. Please. Promise me."

"Thanks for your concern," I said. "But I can't promise you anything. I won't."

"Then promise something else: promise you'll go on telling the truth, no matter how much trouble it brings you, no matter how bad the results may be."

"Maybe."

I pulled my hand away and slammed the Packard door; it shut with a solid sounding thud, just like in the television commercials.

"The truth!" he shouted as I ran for the kitchen door.

The story "Mirrors" is lost somewhere in some bottom drawer of a dresser or under all sorts of other paraphernalia in a trunk in some basement or garage; perhaps thrown out long ago, destroyed in a bonfire when I left my parents' home never to return.

I did learn to get over the incident; learned to get over other, even more unjust incidents after it. I forgot that conversation with Mr. Wolff in his convertible, although it would be years before I forgot what had happened with the Solomons. Yet it was he, rather than they, who prevailed. I always tried to keep to and tell the truth, to point it out, to defend it as I had experienced it, knew it, even when all around me didn't want to acknowledge it, denied it for reasons of policy or business. New incidents, new tests would come along for me, and in all of their beginnings, I could taste that first complete defeat, and thus be able to arm myself in advance against the possibility of the worst occurring.

My life would double in years, grow a hundred-fold in experience, before I again consciously sat down to write a story in which some truth I'd learned, felt, earned, was central, embedded, often disguised.

Another equal length of time had to pass, during which I became a published author, before one day on a late August beach, I would be overwhelmed by memory, feel all that had happened years before as though I were thirteen years old again, be saddened and angry again. Later on that week, I picked up my trusty Mont Blanc fountain pen and began to write of Franny and Mr. Solomon, of Mr. Wolff and Mr. Collins and the story writing contest; of Gregory and Martin O'Connor and James Kallas and the field mice holocaust; of Homer and Ricky Hersch and our bicycle race under the Hillside Mall; of the two dentists; of Mr. Hargrave and the Flaherty sisters, blond, brunette, and especially the seductive, red-haired Susan: the people who, more than my parents or my family, made me the person, the writer, that I have become. Uncertain from beginning to end whether the truth would be malleable, workable in my hands, and whether I could remember it fully enough, transform its details when necessary so that I retained its intensity, its integrity, its ambience intact; so it would become not only my life but your truth.

About the Author

Felice Picano's stories, novels and non-fiction are translated into seventeen languages, and include national and international bestsellers. Four plays were produced. He's received awards for poetry, drama, short stories, novels and memoirs. His duology, *Pursuit: A Victorian Entertainment* and *Pursued: Lillian's Story* are new, also Volumes 2 and 3 of his Sci-Fi *City on a Star* Trilogy: *The Betrothal at Usk,* and *A Bard on Hercular.* In 2024, ReQueered Tales will reprint Picano's earliest novels, *Smart as the Devil, Eyes, The Mesmerist,* and *To the Seventh Power*, as well as a commemorative edition of *Like People in History.* Beautiful Dreamer Press also published Picano's critically acclaimed novel, *Justify My Sins: A Hollywood Novel in Three Acts.* Picano lectures on Vintage Hollywood, screenwriting, and other types of writing. More information at *www.felice.picano.net*

Printed in the USA
CPSIA information can be obtained
at www.ICGtesting.com
LVHW091531260424
778547LV00001B/65